Black or
Right

Black or Right

ANTI/
RACIST
CAMPUS
RHETORICS

Louis M. Maraj

Utah State University Press
Logan

© 2020 by University Press of Colorado

Published by Utah State University Press
An imprint of University Press of Colorado
245 Century Circle, Suite 202
Louisville, Colorado 80027

 The University Press of Colorado is a proud member of
Association of University Presses.

The University Press of Colorado is a cooperative publishing enterprise supported, in part, by Adams State University, Colorado State University, Fort Lewis College, Metropolitan State University of Denver, Regis University, University of Colorado, University of Northern Colorado, University of Wyoming, Utah State University, and Western Colorado University.

∞ This paper meets the requirements of the ANSI/NISO Z39.48-1992 (Permanence of Paper).

ISBN: 978-1-64642-146-6 (paperback)
ISBN: 978-1-64642-147-3 (ebook)
https://doi.org/10.7330/9781646421473

Library of Congress Cataloging-in-Publication Data

Names: Maraj, Louis Maurice, author.
Title: Black or Right : Anti/Racist Campus Rhetorics / Louis M. Maraj.
Description: Logan : Utah State University Press, [2020] | Includes bibliographical references and index.
Identifiers: LCCN 2020033429 (print) | LCCN 2020033430 (ebook) | ISBN 9781646421466 (paperback) | ISBN 9781646421473 (ebook)
Subjects: LCSH: Blacks—Race identity—United States. | Rhetoric—Study and teaching. | Cultural pluralism. | Hashtags (Metadata) | Anti-racism. | Black lives matter movement. | United States—Race relations—21st century.
Classification: LCC E185.625 .M328 2020 (print) | LCC E185.625 (ebook) | DDC 305.800973—dc23
LC record available at https://lccn.loc.gov/2020033429
LC ebook record available at https://lccn.loc.gov/2020033430

The University Press of Colorado gratefully acknowledges the support of the University of Pittsburgh toward the publication of this book.

Front cover: sculptures by Michelle Cohen; photograph by the author.

FOR MY MUMMY

CAROLIN GEMMA MARAJ

AH LOVE YUH

Contents

Acknowledgments

For life, lens, and literacy, a million thanks to my dear mother, Carolin Maraj, who done arready know I have a plan and always believe in it, without a word said— forever my strength and my faith. To my father, fireman (Alfred) "Freddie" Maraj, thanks for de support and presence, eh. Leiselle Donald, my sister, my ride or die from small, an', of course, Reanaldo Donald, eternally grateful to both ah allyuh, for laughter, Atlanta holidays, memes, the official "AT&T" thread, etc. etc. etc. Shoutout to my sweet lil Goddaughter, Lara Khaleesi Donald—I hope someday yuh will read this, baby girl. Lermie (Lemuel Maraj), thanks eh bredda. He could tell a story forever! Big up to "Stories from Staubles" for showing me autoethnography. Sara (Ramroop), I hope yuh doin' ahright and keeping your pumkin safe. Luanna (Budden), bravin' de cold in de land of Eng, ah thinkin' about allyuh, you and Shelby. Laverne (Maraj), keep good, yuh hear? To my nephews, Joey, Josh, Isaiah, please get educated: we need a next generation! It still have time. *Please*! Dayo, you too. Thank you to Granny (Rita Senhouse)—rest in peace— and de aunts who help raise me, Tanty Mer (Merlyn Taitt), Tanty Ros (Roslyn De Labastide), and Mama (Jacqueline De Labastide)—gone too soon—and can't forget yuh, Uncle Calvin (De Labastide). *Family is Family is Family*!!! Cousins, de whole crew, allyuh done know: Jade and Joselle (De Labastide); The Fulchans: Anissa, Joey, and the chirren; Andre, Anson, Nadia (Taitt); Clint (De Labastide); Steve and Aneisha (Lashley); large up. Daddy family, representin' too.

To my life partner, Alexis McGee, the light in my sky, the gold in my deep blue: I love you, sunshine! Every day together is a blessing.

Miss Sandy, my beautiful kitty, Cootz, you have taught me emotional maturity and how to take care of myself. To my grad school crew, you knew this book in infancy: Sean Kamperman, you my dude. To my Crispy Boy, Caitlyn "Gam" McLoughlin, much love. Pritha Prasad, keep prithing. To the rest of my A Team,

Colleen Morrissey, Zach Harvat, and Drew Sweet, yuh large! Michelle Cohen, your art stays with me. Special mention to Indya Jackson, you're an inspiration.

Friends that have kept me on, thank you! You know I mean Norman Rasmussen III, definitely you, love you, brother. Thanks to your whole family, Krista, and the kids, for their years and years of hospitality. Dellison Charles and Jean Marc Tardieu, the original coatie crew, big up yourself. Can't forget Antonio Reyes and family—glad allyuh could make de weddin'—and I must give all my (QRC) boys in blue and blue a bligh.

To the teachers, I say: *you have shaped me!* Teacher Noreen, Mr. Murray, will never forget you. Rhona Bissram, Mr. Carter, Mrs. Bowen Forbes, Mr. Warner, Ms. Wendy McKenzie (who taught us what Haiti means!), Hinkie, Sio, Mr. Prince, and the educational space of Queen's Royal College, I'm grateful. Kathy Sunshine, you saved my life. Jackie Skrzynski, I learned so much from you about myself at our advisement center. To the poets who believed I had it, James Hoch in particular, thank you! The poems still coming knocking. Lara and Tim Crowley, I appreciate you both and your kindness is beyond words. Kathleen Griffin—could not have gotten through grad school without you! I'm beholden to Wendy S. Hesford for the guidance, Beverly J. Moss for being a rock, Margaret Price for letting me be vulnerable, and all three of you for thoughts on raising this project. Cristina García, I won't ever forget when you introduced me as one of your "favorite poets" out in the desert at that retreat. You are so kindhearted, generous, and caring. Juan Felipe Herrera, "the voice" keeps speaking. Carmen Kynard, bless up! Grateful to all others who have mentored me along this path in some way or shape, like Ersula Ore and Tamika Carey—there are certainly more—and to my students, past and present; I continually learn from you.

My Pitt people, my gratitude to you. Talkin' bout Peter Odell Campbell (for feedback, questions, solidarity), Khirsten L. Scott, Shaundra Myers, Yona Harvey, and yea, Imani Owens and Lauren Russell, y'all still in this party. Was' de scene, R. A. Judy?! Thank you for being you and for the direction on this project. To the Black grad students at Pitt—you know who you are—you were a key part of my support system while getting this ting done. Also appreciative of colleagues like Ben Miller, Elizabeth Pitts, Jean Ferguson Carr, Stephen and Cassie Quigley, Annette Vee, and Corey Holding.

Special thanks to others whose comments, conversations, and kindness helped this monograph in some form, including (but not limited to) Andreá N. Williams, Bob Baker at the *Village Voice*, Sara-Maria Sorentino, David Marshall, Christa Teston, Adela C. Licona, Tara Cyphers, Karma Chávez, and especially Rachael Levay, University Press of Colorado and Utah State University Press staff, and their anonymous readers of this manuscript. Shoutout to the whole DBLAC family network too!

I acknowledge the support of the Richard D. and Mary Jane Edwards Endowed Publication Fund, the University of Pittsburgh Department of English, Kristin Hopkins, Gayle Rogers, and Don Bialostosky for this publication.

An earlier version of chapter 1 was first published with the same title as Louis M. Maraj, 2018, "Are You Black Though: Black Autoethnography and Racing the Graduate Student/Instructor," in *Precarious Rhetorics*, ed. Wendy S. Hesford, Adel Licona, and Christa Teston, 212–33 (Columbus: The Ohio State University Press). The poem "Monkey on Down" featured in that chapter initially appeared on the American Academy of Poets' website, poets.org. I'm thankful to the *Village Voice* for permission to use the opening stanza to Audre Lorde's "Power," originally printed there in 1974. For use of his photo in chapter 4, I'm appreciative to Mike Bierschenk.

Blessings to de spaces, places, and phases I lived, labored, and loved: Pittsburgh, Mahwah, Sloatsburg, Lubbock (yea we still have beef, but yuh make meh think), Columbus, India—you are beautiful—and of course, my home and heart, Trinidad and Tobago, where I wrote and revised major parts of *Black or Right. Trinidad! I love yuh too bad!!!*

For de sounds dat help me to listen, I'm especially indebted—to soca and dancehall for teaching love poetry, calypso for social critique, extempo kaiso for teaching me to think on my feet, Papa Bois and Anansi tales for what is power in story, "that is bamboo bussing or gunshot ah hearin'?" Amen.

Preface
Mash Up De Place
NOTES ON APPROACH / APPROACHES TO NOTE

Aye Readers,

Where I from, to "mash up de place" signals a desire to revel while also denoting destruction, though sometimes the phrase might conjure one in the other. "Jump and mash up de place," while a popular refrain in Trini music, could be heard in my childhood and youth in admonition as in "allyuh chirren like to mash up everything eh." *Black or Right: Anti/Racist Campus Rhetorics* attempts in most senses to mash up de place. It disrupts given ideas about the academic monograph, space, place, objects, subjects, meanings, semantics in order to read/ write Blackness with/in its varied terms. Meanings fragment, tings evolve, sometimes you may feel connection and not know what it signals.

Dear Readers,

I write to provide some orientation to material in *Black or Right: Anti/Racist Campus Rhetorics*. This move becomes necessary because its styles do more than inflect its contents—they entangle to shape arguments offered here. Style is content, content style, with Blackness between, in, across, and outside. Expressive form and resultant meanings augur mimesis and/or also escape it, continuing to evolve with (re)telling. We might understand these dynamics as mining gaps between narrative and analysis, as seeking possibilities for academic writing to undiscipline knowledge from tightly packed siloing containers.

Yea Readers,

Blackness as content, as subject, like creole languages, tends to consistently shift. As Martiniquais philosopher Édouard Glissant explains, "in Relation every subject is an object and every object a subject" (Glissant 1997, xx). This monograph harvests the rich potential in such, between diasporas of Blackness. But fixing an analysis of Blackness to the page becomes a problematic task. So, I use slashes (/) to enjoin terms throughout, not to suggest that both sides of the slash mean de same ting or are interchangeable but as semantic noting of the spaces in which meanings fracture with/in and between terms involved in such an equation. The spaces between is in/side, along, and out.

Woi Readers,

'cuz dem spaces operate dis way, annotations make way for what can't be contained in Blackness' excess. Footnotes radiate as more than ancillary: dey's ah key part ah de action. I invite you to approach notes in noting this approach to *Black or Right* where there's always some ting more to the story. Dig deeper.

'scene Readers,

Wha goin on? Yuh ketchin meh drift? This project shifts between registers, dialects, poetics, analyses, performances, and aesthetics of Blackness to interrogate space and the relation/ships between bodies, environments, and where their excess rifts. To read *with*/it might involve understanding exhibition as critical, criticism as exhibit and the spaces in between and across those ideas. *Black or Right: Anti/Racist Campus Rhetorics* provokes dialogue, affective, discursive, or otherwise. It wants to trouble place and space as a/temporal, to think through (with you) what happens when Blackness comes up against white spaces—those entrenched in domination, domination usually producing violence. What shapes do Black processes take in everyday antiBlackness?

Word Readers,

You might be confused. Embrace it. Or don't. Blackness often obfuscates, often disorients, often shatters/scatters fungibility but offers much by way of meaning. *Take care.* That is to say, like poetry, the artful craft of de ting lies in being okay with not knowing in order to know.

So leh we mash up de place together, nah?
    Later,
    Louis M. Maraj

Black or Right

Introduction

"It ain't that deep"

DEEP RHETORICAL ECOLOGIES AND PARA/ONTOLOGICAL BLACKNESS

Ontology—once it is finally admitted as leaving existence by the wayside—does not permit us to understand the being of the black [being]. For not only must the black [being] be black; [they] must be black in relation to the white man ... The black [being] has no ontological resistance in the eyes of the white man.

FRANZ FANON ([1952] 2008), *BLACK SKIN, WHITE MASKS* (82–83)

Every research project has a story, which is the story of an arrival.

SARA AHMED (2012), *ON BEING INCLUDED* (2)

"Fresh off the boat," as they say, just arrived in the United States, I join the student newspaper at the small northeastern liberal arts college I attend.[1] I was up in de cold to major in journalism—a service industry in my homeland, Trinidad and Tobago, then lacking the professional ethos that this bachelor's degree would afford me. I want to use writing—something I feel is my only real "skill"—to serve my communities: telling public stories, exchanging information, mediating the world to engage it. My own "story of an arrival,"[2] then, truly was a "dream" in the stereotypical "American dream" sense: my parents had high-school educations; my mother did clerical work; my father was a firefighter, later a fire officer, for most of my upbringing; my siblings and I grew up in a mostly stable but modest home in a somewhat "sketch" neighborhood; we rocked handmade cloth backpacks to school, waited for the $1TTD (about 15 US cents) from Tanty Mer every Friday not knowing what an "allowance" was in our childhood; and received clothes, books, and toys handed down from each other. In an early 2005 email, my mother describes my attitude in bagging a full-ride scholarship to a US university: "I realize that you have dreams and that you are determined to fulfill them. I also recognize that you will do what you have to do to get there." So, she let me leave the islands to try chase them.

DOI: 10.7330/9781646421473.c000b

3

My first newspaper assignment, a joint one with another freshman—a white woman, Laura[3]—requires us to sit in on a board meeting and note-take. Getting off the bus, I see her waiting outside the building with another figure. Laura brings a white male not assigned to the story—and not involved in the paper— with her. It's strange. Is this what Americans call a "date"? They seem fidgety. She pulls on her straight brown hair, looks continually anew at mostly bare walls once we get to the meeting room. Laura and this white boy don't make physical contact. "They not even talkin' to each other," I think. I immediately feel a rupture, a sense about my *self* mapped from their presences and non/interaction with each other and with me. Why, in the fall early-evening, would her friend care about a dreary budget meeting? After leaving the meeting room, I watch as they get into separate cars, still puzzled by their exchanges with each other, by neither of them really talking to me.

In the freshman English classroom, I learn about the (white US) middle (?) class "struggle" as we read Arthur Miller's *Death of a Salesman*. My white woman instructor dresses like the kids on *Freaks and Geeks*—a TV show a subsequent white roommate exposes me to. Her clothes resemble several canvas bags stitched together to make some kind of functional sense. I'd later associate that aesthetic with hippies—though her philosophies, teaching or otherwise, were by no means progressive. Shakespeare's *Othello* features the only character of color on the syllabus— one mediated through the author's sixteenth/seventeenth-century imagination through discourses of antiBlackness. I receive a C– on my first paper—after three pages, a slash across every one after with the message that the instructor stopped reading there. The lavish prose I was brought up on in the British Caribbean education system wouldn't work here. *Americans want a thesis*. Panicked by the high grade point average I need to continue holding my scholarship, to stay in the country, I adjust quickly and finish the course with a low A. Assimilative conversion, then, becomes my recourse. Similar to the historical colonial paradigm of my upbringing: "Education would be the condition under which [Blacks] could be perceived and recognized as fellow human beings" (Mbembe 2017, 87).

Through these encounters, I start learning what my Black(ened),[4] im/migrant male presence and literacies in the US Northeast mean and try to "fix" to suit. But I don't do that learning alone. I live with three other Black men who fill in the picture through their experiences. Two of them—Ronald and Sean—are first-generation Jamericans who immigrated to New York City with their parents; the other roommate, Andre, is a classmate from my secondary school in Trinidad, whose mother works as a live-in nurse for a rich white family in Jersey. Ronald and Sean dip in and out of Jamaican and US registers and dialects. I notice in particular how Sean's very "articulate" standard American English on display in public spaces falls into patois when we argue about race. As Martiniquais political philosopher Frantz Fanon ([1952] 2008) explains, proximity to whiteness, demands a whitening of the pidgin. The reverse applies in our discussions. Sean warns me not to "get take" for "no boombaclat eediat" when I naïvely contend that jokes he and Ronny make about white people play into US racial divides. But more than first lessons on code-switching, Sean clues me in through these disagreements to the fears we, as Black Caribbean im/migrant men, prompt from white peers—from Laura, from her companion. That discomfort between Laura, her companion, and me arises from a series of spatial and temporal relations: the strange, white institutional space of a budget meeting, our new roles as public mediators of information, long-standing and continuing histories of white women and Black men's "tense" relationships, white men's anxieties and (often violent) reactions in relation to those histories, and revisited public fears about Black and brown im/migrants after 9/11. While I'm surprised about the C–, Sean and Ronny explain that our Caribbean literacies are out of place—I gotta do what the white man wants me to do. I must shunt Blackness.

In the midst of my first ever winter, "what the white man wants" according to Sean and Ronny manifests itself in extremity through a series of online images posted by a white male alumnus of our historically white institution. In a Facebook photo album titled "Worthless," the former student posts an image of a handcuffed Black toddler with the text "arrest them now before they turn into criminals," another image of Lego blocks constructed to illustrate a scene from slavery, another with a cereal box tagged "Negro-ooos," and another depicting a Black university staff member with a photoshopped noose around his neck. The white seniors running the show at the newspaper assign me to cover this incident as my first major story—but, of course, I'm not trusted to do it alone. I'm particularly (though not explicitly) tasked with getting the scoop from Black folk on campus and go to the ones I know best: my roommates. In the news report, I navigate my Black male im/migrant-ness to open vistas into Blackness for the white institutions' publics—to conjure Black being in response to whiteness, as Fanon (1952, 82–83) above suggests.

The story is front-page news: "President, campus, outraged at racist images on Web." But in the article's organization, the editors orient the story and headline around the white university president's outrage; they foreground quotations from white university officials—the usual "racism will not be tolerated" mantra; they completely sidestep using the word "Black" in describing campus responses, leaving that signification up to a description of Andre (quoted) as "an international student from Trinidad and Tobago"; and they relegate me to second fiddle in the byline. I juggle the racial stress caused by the hyperracist images, the newspaper's student staff's uncredited tokenization/exploitation of me as the "race" reporter, my increasingly complicated relationship with my roommates who use the article's publicness to speak their truth to power about antiBlack racism, and the institution's attempt to "prevent" racism from recurring—via email, a school official issues a plea with students to get off of Facebook (then, in nascence): it could ruin our careers.

These series of relations converging to fluidly re/create and negotiate my racial identity exemplify the ecological, relational, and dialectical workings of race in the historically white educational spaces of my alma mater. Affective,[5] and *para/ontological*, fractures between the roles I attempt to play in the above rhetorical situations reveal much about race, racialization, and categories of identity. Here, "para/ontological" simultaneously describes concepts conjured in ontological "being," the "paraontological" (beside, adjacent to, subsidiary to, and beyond being), and, importantly, what flows and moves in between and across those two ideas.[6] White spaces, characterized by dominance and resultant violence, forces (human) being, as Fanon argues, on to the Black body on whiteness' terms (1952). I'm interested in attempted resistances to such exertion and how they interrelate with philosopher Nahum Chandler's concept of paraontology—where Blackness "is the anoriginal displacement of ontology" (cited in Moten 2013, 739). For Chandler, Blackness shatters racial purity (and all its manifestations) in order to make space for nonexclusionary forms of collectivity (Black Study Group 2015), with paraontology inviting "the possibility and the necessity for theoretical work to cultivate an order of critical theoretical fiction as a fundamental dimension of its practice" (Chandler 2017). Between and along Chandler's conception, on one hand, and oppressive being in relation to dominance, on the other, para/ontology mines the fluid, fracturing, reiterative escape from Blackness mapped in "human being" on to it in white spaces.

In investigating expressed conceptions of Blackness attempting to make moving—potentially antiracist—meaning with/in para/ontology, I follow Black feminist interdisciplinarian Zakiyyah Iman Jackson's notion of ontological plasticity (Jackson 2020). Jackson explains plasticity as "a mode of transmogrification whereby the fleshly being of blackness is experimented with as if it were infinitely malleable lexical and biological matter, such that blackness is produced as sub/super/human at once, a form where form shall not hold: potentially 'everything and nothing' at the register of ontology" (2020, 3).[7] I focus on *rhetorical fluidities of Blackness as being* across, about, in, and outside of this "everything and nothing" in antiBlack spaces—moments where racial stress reveals fractures, pullings, tuggings, breakings—in what Black being might mean. Notice how the white university through administration and mediated messages uses Blackness as putty for antiracist ethos, while dodging articulations of Blackness altogether. With/in these fractures, I navigate meaning-making between/across *attempts at being* a new Black im/migrant in US white institutional spaces, as a reporter for publics, cultured white, while the public voice for a marginalized community of Black students proper and Black im/migrant males specifically above. Simultaneously, I endeavor to fulfill the promise of an im/migrant "dream" in relation to histories, ideologies, and realities criminalizing and authorizing violent racist fears of Blacks in the United States.

But, what if—as I'm routinely accused of via the ableist metric of "overthinking"—it just "ain't that deep"? Well, in this regard, I follow cultural studies scholar Sara Ahmed's paradoxical logic that "if you say something does not matter, it usually implies that it does" (2010, 94). Let's dig deeper then. *Black or Right: Anti/Racist Campus Rhetorics* articulates and demonstrates a lens for reading what I call *deep rhetorical ecologies* or, sometimes simply, *deep ecologies*.[8] These ecological networks of interconnected relationships consist of evolving series of rhetorical situations in which communication occurs, which are interrelated through bodies, spaces, cultures, and contexts with *specific* regard to power dynamics and race relations.[9] Why power? Why race? Why now? Because in late-stage capitalism, we cannot eschew reminders of the intricate historical relationships between power, race, environments, and economics. The events of 9/11 and its sociopolitical consequences, my undergraduate historically white institution, or even my freshman writing class at that university might be considered deep ecologies, as each represents overlapping sites of rhetorical encounters where bodies produce/negotiate meaning through exchanging power dynamics.[10]

My analytic framing of these ecologies pays particular attention to how artifacts, archives, and interactions draw on, live, and propel histories of cultural identity. Through an approach that *shows and tells the stories* of those artifacts, archives, and interactions, *Black or Right* attempts to mobilize them as literacy events,[11] with evolving possibilities for meaning-making. Through this monograph, expressive/narrative style entangles with content to suggest that mimetic media/modalities of Blackness offer potentials to resist objecthood through a kind of object-being. Stylistically, this book itself conjures a deep ecology: through its object-being performance, through its shifting movements between academic monograph and "critical theoretical fiction" (Chandler 2017), through its seemingly "scattered" style that actively builds ecological knowledge, through para/ontology. Reading between and across related discursive encounters within ecologies in these ways, rhetorical and media theorists might more fully realize the machinations of power dynamics in rhetorical networks and how these dynamics help to produce/negotiate fluid identities, categories of identity, and spatial culturing.

I take up Blackness as primary focus because, as political theorist Achille Mbembe explains, "the noun 'Black' is . . . the name given to the product of a process that transforms people of African origin into living *ore* from which *metal* is extracted . . . The progression from *man-of-ore* to *man-of-metal* to *man of money* was a structuring dimension of the early phase of capitalism" (2017, 40). While neoliberalism repackages the ways in which the capitalist state engages with this structuring, the Black Lives Matter movement has recently made more visible the disregard for Black subjects in the contemporary United States and the use of Black bodies as kindling for the antiBlack state, while the resurgence of the white supremacy's philosophical and physical threat means we cannot look away.

I'm particularly concerned with instances of fracture with/in deep rhetorical ecologies. At these affective, para/ontological junctures, deep ecologies and their subjects/objects offer possibilities for producing racial meaning. Occasions narrated above when I receive a C–, when I notice Laura's white male companion, when antiBlack images appear on Facebook—moments, thus, constituted by high racial stress—present opportunities for digging into Fanonian epidermalization. Looking at these racializing instances allows us to (re)discover how such meaning might be made or negotiated ecologically—that is, in a subject's non/being that operates para/ontologically. Black feminist and surveillance scholar Simone Browne pinpoints this epidermalization: "[I]t is the moment of contact with the white gaze ... that produces these moments of fracture for the racial Other, indeed making and marking one as racial Other, experiencing 'being for others'" (2015, 98). I follow Browne in insisting that "this making of [B]lackness as out of place must be read as also productive" (98). These junctures of possibility offer what fellow Black feminist Christina Sharpe calls "knowledge of the wake"—that is, operation "in a past that is not the past, a past that is with us still" in the afterlives of slavery (2016, 62). I join with Sharpe in "wake work," in "plotting, mapping, and collecting the archives of everyday Black immanent and imminent death, and in tracking the ways we resist, rupture, and disrupt that immanence and imminence aesthetically and materially" (13). In doing so, I suggest technologies/rhetorics of these fractures in order to move toward Black rhetorical agency—thinking about how it arises, how bodies and spaces attain it or fail to attain it.

I use the term "agency" throughout this project to describe potentials for social action and power.[12] While this summoning of agency might pose questions about energy, it also concurrently grapples with expressive form in relation to that energy—in polysemic Aristotelian ideas of ἐνέγεια (*enérgeia*), where energy tussles constantly between act and expression.[13] Such potential power is co-constituted through individual bodies *along with* relations to their discourses, environments, and narrative re/tellings by/about those bodies. I choose to purposely sidestep the humanist (Bawarshi 2003; Vieregge et. al 2012; Canagarajah 1999; Cooper 2011; France 2000) / posthumanist (Herndl and Licona 2007; Lundberg and Gunn 2005; Ewald and Wallace 1994) dichotomy that tends to underscore discussions of agency within rhetoric/communication and writing studies research, looking instead toward African indigenous relational models of agency. The concept of *botho* or *Ubuntu* "requires respect and the recognition of all things living and non-living. Reality is all our connections and all our marginalized efforts to protect and preserve those that are essential to the continued existence of all relations. Relatedness is at the core and permeates all research activities" (Chilisa 2012, 820). This theory of relatedness and how it shapes humanness, nonhumanness, and the spaces in which these concepts occur pervade *Black or Right* in its examination of deep ecologies.

Fifteen years after my "story of arrival," this project exemplifies my ongoing effort to understand racialization in the United States: how it feels, how it works, how it moves, how it manifests, performs, and churns every day. I continue to learn and live race, im/migrant-ness, and Blackness inside, outside, and in-between the classroom, as my US experience remains centered in and around educational institutions. I now also *teach* race, im/migrant-ness, and Blackness inside, outside, and in-between the classroom. I confront institutional whiteness on the daily. In some ways, I represent Ahmed's "melancholic migrant": "a rather ghostly figure, haunting contemporary culture as a kind of unnecessary and hurtful reminder of racism" (2010, 148). It won't go away. I won't go away. Yet still, I want better institutions and classrooms for marginalized folk through telling the many stories like mine. But these desires extend beyond me or my stories. I strive for spaces for Black people and our literacies as means to possible anti-racist agency, though on some days and in some ways, I'll admit, I embody the wretchedness of social death. In style/content, race work exhausts. Because to study Blackness involves living Blackness and vice versa, I hope that this project, through its Black feminist relational and African indigenous approaches, demonstrates the fluid, polysemic multiplicities in Blackness in its everyday struggles with/in white spaces.

With this theoretical background at hand, *Black or Right: Anti/Racist Campus Rhetorics* ultimately grapples with notions of Blackness in white institutional spaces to theorize how Black identity operates with/against neoliberal ideas of difference in the age of #BlackLivesMatter. The book asks: Despite diversity's theoretical "non-performativity" (Ahmed 2012), how do those racially signifying "diversity" in US higher education (and beyond) make meaning in the everyday? My move to respond critically inhabits those fractures in deep ecologies where Blackness operates para/ontologically to think through what Black antiracist rhetorics emerge and how they do so. I thus offer Black autoethnography, Black hashtagging, Black inter(con)textual reading, and reconceptualized Black disruption as possibilities.

"Yuh want to what now?": Methodology and Intervention

This study adds to a growing body of work in rhetoric/communication, writing, and literacy studies, that centers Black and brown rhetorics, literacies, and compositional practices.[14] Alongside these studies, more recent scholarship engaging specifically in antiracist critique/pedagogies in such disciplinary areas have also taken up understanding race through an interrogation of whiteness to destabilize hegemonic classroom and institutional cultures/discourses.[15] Peggy McIntosh's 1989 "White Privilege: Unpacking the Invisible Knapsack" lays a foundation for what has emerged as the burgeoning impact of whiteness studies in rhetoric/communication and writing studies.[16] Krista Ratcliffe, for example, offers "rhetorical listening" as means to interrogate "gender and whiteness in the public sphere, in rhetorical scholarship, and in composition pedagogy" (2005, 1). Inoue's *Antiracist Writing Assessment Ecologies* applies antiracist motives in assessment practices, critiquing what he calls the "white racial habitus" as a default for composition assessment practices (2015, 17). Both these monographs received critical acclaim and broad visibility in rhetoric/communication and writing studies, especially as winners of the Conference on College Composition and Communication's Outstanding Book Award—Ratcliffe in 2007, Inoue ten years on in 2017. Likewise, the edited collection *Rhetorics of Whiteness* edited by Tammie M. Kennedy, Joyce Irene Middleton, and Krista Ratcliffe was recognized with the same award just recently in 2018. With the fields' recent visible attentiveness to whiteness studies in antiracist efforts to combat the re/emergence of public white supremacist energy—which has dangerous consequences for our classroom and institutional spaces—scholars' push to sustain such lines of inquiry remains crucial.

Black or Right adds to that growing corpus of antiracist research in centering Black folk and their traditions, languages, literacies, and rhetorics in white institutional spaces. A focus on the traditions and theories of people of color responds to Adam Banks's (2010) and Lisa Corrigan's (2016) calls to these fields for attention to be paid to them. Continuing such work remains vitally necessary as scholarship and classrooms in the United States continue to marginalize people of color, particularly Black folk, and their cultures/literacies. So, while excellent work has been done to acknowledge and openly critique whiteness in recent antiracist scholarship—*work publicly celebrated*—I examine marginalized antiracist endeavors by reading relationships between meanings of Blackness in the United States vis-à-vis antiBlack institutional power. In spotlighting Black people and their antiracist energies, this study offers means by which these fields might destabilize institutional oppression that do not paradoxically center whiteness (in investigating its manifestations primarily).

I approach this task from intensely cross-disciplinary angles, bridging Black studies and critical race theory with rhetoric/communication, writing, and literacy studies. The project thus entwines scholarship in, and related to, those five areas from critical theory; sociology; social science; history; political science; women's, gender, and sexuality studies; digital media studies; criminal justice; media theory; postcolonial studies; and historiography, among others, striving to dynamically and intersectionally analyze Blackness' multiplicity in white institutional spaces. Echoing Sharpe, *Black or Right* seeks to "undiscipline" the study of Blackness (2016, 13) from what Black feminist Sylvia Wynter calls "our narratively condemned status" (1994b, 70). Such departure necessitates "a turn away from existing *disciplinary* solutions to blackness's ongoing abjection . . . It requires theorizing the multiple meanings of that abjection through inhabitation, that is, through living them in and as consciousness" (Sharpe 2016, 33; emphasis in original).

In so doing, *Black or Right* takes up a transdisciplinary Black feminist approach in order to highlight relational lived experiences. At the core of such a relational methodology I use Black feminist thought (Lorde, Hill Collins, Cohen, hooks, Wynter, Sharpe, Browne etc.), buttressed by historical/theoretical work in Black studies (Fanon, Du Bois, Weheliye, Mbembe, Judy, etc.), via an African indigenous methodological approach, Ubuntu. The Black feminist philosophy of literacy as the practice of freedom underscores my work here. I pick up the concept from (Black feminist thinker) bell hooks (1994) to mobilize the processes of literacy—reading, writing, identity performance, body language, orality, and so forth—in a move to open spaces for Black peoples, cultures, and rhetorics. That endgame, however, does not bracket other uses for this project's arguments, as it seeks, more than anything, to open up *possibilities* for understanding Blackness. As the concluding chapter shows, my findings might operate in the service of Black humanism, Black posthumanism, Afropessimism, Black antihumanism, racial realism, or a combination of any such epistemological approaches.

To center Blackness and Black feminism not only means being conscious about the content of our Black study but also involves political citation practices as well as cognizance of the schools of thought we resort to for theorizing. Black people and Black women accordingly primarily populate this study's references. In terms of philosophy, I stretch diasporically across philosophies of Blackness from Caribbean, African, and Black US authors in order to signal/experience/ read/write Blackness with/in its constant spatial, temporal, and deep rhetorical movements. I join folks such as Vivette Milson-Whyte (2015) and Kevin Browne (2013) (and others) in bringing discussions of diasporic Blackness to rhetoric/communication and writing studies. It would be in disservice of my own Blackness (and my theories thereof) to ignore how scholars from outside the US shape/read Blackness involved inside it. This project eschews borders— geographic, philosophic, and otherwise.

In analyzing deep ecologies and their fractures, I employ a Black feminist lens that highlights interrelations between human bodies and their environments in rhetorically analyzing how meaning is co-constituted by those relations. While "new" materialist theoretical frameworks have recently garnered much attention in rhetorical theory, this project offers as a major intervention an application of

Black feminist and African indigenous philosophies of being that stress interconnectedness and co-constitutive meaning-making that predate this "new materialist" turn. Bringing attention to these theories and methodological frameworks not only pays respect to peoples routinely absent from citation lists and syllabi in rhetoric/communication and writing studies, but also stresses their social justice roots that strive toward more just futures in their applications of relationality.

As Lorde explains, "the quality of light by which we scrutinize our lives has direct bearing upon the product which we live, and upon the changes which we hope to bring about through those lives. It is within this light that we form those ideas by which we pursue our magic and make it realized" (1984, 36). Lorde thus demonstrates the impact of our environs on shaping our subjectivities and vice versa. Patricia Hill Collins, relatedly, emphasizes the importance of alternative forms of communal relationships, stressing "connections, caring, and personal accountability" in confronting interlocking systems of oppression's objectification/commodification of Black women ([1990] 2000, 222). As Black studies scholar Alexander Weheliye stresses, Sylvia Wynter's project to "[highlight] the complex relationality between different forms of oppression," along with Hortense Spillers's criticism, speak to the foundational Black feminist positions of the Combahee River Collective ([1977] 2017, 23–24). Black feminist relationality therefore considers the exchanges between individuals, identities, bodies, cultures, and spaces and how they dynamically shape each other to produce/negotiate meaning in striving toward societal impact. This (intersectional) relationality arguably aligns with new materialists' recognition that "phenomena are caught in a multitude of interlocking systems and forces" and attempts "to consider anew the location and nature of capacities for agency" (Coole and Frost 2010, 9) in investigations of matter. However, while I gesture to these new materialist interests in spatial constitution to consider particularly the material-discursive—how, for example, words/phrases like "nigga," "plantation days," and "aight" operate in educational spaces in chapter 1—I foreground Black feminist thinkers who prioritize relationality long before recent scholarship's "new materialist turn" to spotlight racialized precarities and rhetorics of Black agency in a Black feminist tradition.[17]

Likewise, Botswanan social scientist and methodologist Bagele Chilisa's work emphasizes that African indigenous relational methodologies that stress connectedness, and multiple relationships between humans, their environments, and discourses, deserve attention in anti-imperial transdisciplinary research (Chilisa 2012, 2017; Chilisa, Major, and Khudu-Petersen 2017). Identity narratives can form an important basis for demonstrating such decolonizing frameworks (Drahm-Butler 2016) and thus feature prominently via my Black feminist autoethnographic orientation in this project's first chapter, which filters throughout ongoing ones. Such narratives "provide information about one's physical space, cultural locations, ecological connections and relationships to others"; "through African ontologies of connectedness and relatedness to the living and non-living, research participants come to develop awareness of oneself and of belongingness and of their responsibilities to one another and to their environment" (Chilisa, Major, and Khudu-Petersen 2017, 333).[18] As I move to the composition classroom's digital extensions to analyze my students' hashtag use in chapter 2, to broaden the scope of my analysis in reading the #BlackLivesMatter movement's inter(con)textual meanings in chapter 3, and to interrogate anti/racist policy practice at a historically white institution in chapter 4, I sustain this focus on interconnections, relationality, and ecological meaning. In the conclusion, I use this relationality to consider potential bridges between other strains of Black philosophy so that we might walk away understanding the possibilities rooted in the *processes* of Blackness rather than oriented primarily in their future horizons.[19]

Scholarship using ecological frameworks, conceptually, are familiar territory for rhetoricians and writing studies scholars. In the 1980s, Marilyn Cooper's work, for example, theorized the ecological systems in which writers operate through their compositions: "The systems reflect the various ways writers connect with one another through writing: through systems of ideas, of purposes, of interpersonal interactions, of cultural norms, of textual forms" (1986, 369). Yet, for Cooper, these systems are "concrete," as all elements could be readily "investigated, described, and altered" (369). More recent work sees ecologies as much more fluid. In Edbauer's (2005) "Unframing Models of Public Distribution: From Rhetorical Situation to Rhetorical Ecologies," the rhetorician builds on previous theories of the rhetorical situation (Bitzer 1968; Biesecker 1989) to reconsider rhetorical situations as "rhetorical ecologies" made up of fluctuating lived encounters and affects between actors, bodies, and so on, within evolving rhetorical publics. Edbauer argues that in this ecological, affective framing, rhetoric becomes a "process of distributed emergence" and is "an ongoing circulation process" (2005, 13), which can be read via "testifying"; "such testimonies would invent new concepts and deploy them in order to theorize how publics are also created through affective channels" (21). In this project, I look to literacy events as means to define and explain these testimonies, aiming to take up more fully the inter(con)textual environment of them, while highlighting the power dynamics—specifically racial power dynamics—occurring in and across these events and their racializing fractures that co-constitute deep rhetorical ecologies. I push us toward understanding Blackness as something ontological, paraontological, and para/ontological, as the ecological context for racial meaning cannot be divorced from the Blackness of a Black body qua Black body in its excess.

While Inoue also deploys the ecology in antiracist work, and does so specifically with regard to racial power, his monograph theorizes writing assessment practices rather than public rhetorical interactions through this model (2015, 9). He proceeds by explaining the hegemonic "white racial habitus": dominant discourse cultured in the US as white and middle class that underlies classroom interaction (17). Departing from a contained focus on the classroom, from starting with whiteness and its undoing as the basis for antiracist agency, and from Eurocentric masculinist theoretical backgrounds, I take up a Black feminist intersectional and African indigenous relational model of the rhetorical ecology that prioritizes Blackness. Bringing such an approach to rhetoric/communication, writing, and literacy studies, I move toward *proactive* antiracist approaches rather than reactive ones. The project thus does not primarily strive to repair whiteness or white cultures but instead looks to transformative possibilities and questions that a focus on Blackness might offer.

"Wha'is de scene?": Scope

In Trini dialect, the familiar greeting "Wha'is de scene?" collapses a what and a when. It asks "how are you?" through an inquiry about one's place/position: it "scopes out de scene." Although this project's analysis inherently extends beyond one site of reading because of its ecological framework, my main focus is Midwestern State University (MwSU),[20] a large historically white land-grant university in the midwestern United States. The main page of the university's website does not explicitly define the institution, though it provides its locations visually through a map of its home state, along with user-solicited photographs through the use of "#My[Midwestern]State" ([Midwestern State] University 2018a). By asking users to visually pinpoint their own versions of the institution, the university's website places its identity within an individual/institution dynamic. Although the prompt to "Upload your pics" suggests that students have a role in defining what Midwestern State looks like, surely the institution uses some behind-the-scenes selection process for what images it features. When the website does work toward more traditional definition, through its "Discover [Midwestern] State" page, it emphasizes the university's "physical presence throughout the state" ([Midwestern] State University 2018b). Its influence might therefore be understood as not simply bound by the geographies of the physical campus—no doubt conjuring the reflexivity of its name. These snapshots articulate the university's identity as one of physical expansiveness, made up, however, of (curated) individual contributions and posturings. In terms of its human presence, as of the autumn 2018 semester, MwSU's main campus (the primary site of investigation here) comprised 61,170 students. Its website designates 21 percent (12,873) of that campus's population as "total minorities," of which 6.1 percent (3,713) are termed "African American" ([Midwestern State] University 2019).

Black or Right reads Midwestern State and its contexts within the sociopolitical context of the Black Lives Matter movement. I describe this temporality as "post-Ferguson," emphasizing the heightened tensions and public visibility of race relations after the events of the Ferguson Uprising in the summer of 2014. These race relations specifically (re)call attention to tense historical and cultural conversations and protests surrounding Black life and state violence against it. After the acquittal of George Zimmerman for the murder of unarmed Black teenager Trayvon Martin in 2013, #BlackLivesMatter came into the US public spotlight and that focus heightened exponentially with the police shooting death of Michael Brown in Ferguson, Missouri, in August the following year. While I use the preposition "post" to signify its literal meaning "after," the phrase "post-Ferguson" does signify a different understanding of racialization in the United States than understandings prior to the Uprising. With the reanimation in the age of social media of the idea that the US legal system remains inept at validating Black folk as human via rights-based discourses, coupled with the notion that video evidence of injustice routinely fails to prove such injustice in both the courts of public opinion and the courts of law, the movement sparked widespread (pro-Black and allied) digital and in-person resistance in the United States and worldwide. That resistance is importantly led by Black queer women and their antiracist philosophies. Chapter 3 also demonstrates how previous race-related events (like 9/11 and the election of President Barack Obama) set the table for racial dynamics of the post-Ferguson cultural moment by feeding into heightened state and public suspicion of Black and brown bodies in reaction to the dangerous ideology of racial "colorblindness." By placing my analysis within that sociopolitical context, I think through how larger-scale (sometimes national) events inform the spatial and cultural relations in historically white educational spaces—particularly Midwestern State's.

"How yuh going?": Objectives

Another typical Trini salutation, "How yuh goin'?," and its usual response, "I there, X,"[21] signal a how and a where. The greeting queries one's current condition on the basis of movement, with an assumption that a subject ontologically is both temporally and spatially present and moving; in a way, the call and response gestures to the para/ontological. *Black or Right* foregrounds its Black feminist rhetorical analysis with an eye toward this kind of fracturing multiplicity, building from Ahmed's work in *On Being Included*. I expand Ahmed's focus on diversity practitioners, while also zooming in on one particular institution in fluid relation to related cultural artifacts and events. Ahmed dynamically follows diversity documents and the people who use them around in her study. She asks questions about what diversity does and fails to do, about where it goes and fails to go, and in what and whom it is deposited and not deposited to "not only talk to diversity practitioners, but also to inhabit the world of diversity, to offer an ethnography of this world" (2012, 11). Engaging in "Black British feminism" (13), Ahmed draws on her own position and experiences as a diversity practitioner, apposite meetings, conferences, workshops, "fleeting encounters," and events to flesh out this ethnography. Inspired by the complexity of Ahmed's monograph—and, indeed, its mobilization of interconnected relations between people, documents, and events related to diversity in analysis—this project builds on her pronouncement that such an approach requires a kind of "multi-sited"-ness due to the "mobile subjects and objects . . . networks and connections that are necessary for things to move around" (11–12). I therefore emphasize differing positions/locations within the historically white institution as I move through chapters, while adopting differing vantage points or roles from which material is analyzed.

These shifts work to enact and reflexively validate the project's African indigenous and Black feminist relational methodology, highlighting how identity and reading might shift in fluid spatial, temporal, and even intellectual field orientations. I therefore move through the roles of autoethnographer and archivist with a concentration on graduate student / instructor positionality in chapter 1; the roles of digital media critic and critical pedagogue in investigating undergraduate student digital composition in my antiracist writing classroom in the following chapter; the role of cultural rhetorician / media theorist to interrogate the sociopolitical context of historical, populist, and pedagogic meanings of #BlackLivesMatter in the third chapter; and a combination of all three previous roles through critical discourse analysis as I read the praxis of institutional policy at Midwestern State in the fourth. *Black or Right* works—through each chapter's particular argument—and in assuming multiple relationships to those arguments—to highlight the complexity of relations between the Black body, Black resistance, and Black meaning-making at a historically white university and beyond. Position, style, content, and analysis wrap up in each other throughout.

I call the field's attention to Black struggles and potentialities with/in those spaces to finally draw together the Black rhetorics of this monograph in theorizing (in chapter 4) what I call *rhetorical reclamations*. These rhetorical acts (gestures, performances, language use, embodiment) do "wake work" (Sharpe 2016); they draw on cultural histories, contexts, and traditions to suggest agency through re/asserting racialized identity in instances of fracture when white institutions stigmatize Blackness. Such reclamations respond to *white institutional defensiveness*, policies, and practices that posture tentatively (often in racially colorblind ways) so as to avoid causing racial stress for white individuals in institutional spaces.[22] In arriving at these theories, I ask the following key questions through various chapters:

1. What are the multiple meanings of Blackness playing out in the United States—in particular, in white educational spaces of Midwestern State University—in relation to institutional power during the post-Ferguson cultural moment?

2. How would/could we define that "cultural moment" as it relates to institutional power?

3. What roles do the #BlackLivesMatter movement play into fashioning those multiple meanings of Blackness in historically white educational spaces and in defining the post-Ferguson cultural moment?

4. How do those multiple meanings of Blackness play out as they relate to (a) graduate students/instructors at the historically white institution; (b) undergraduate students in composition classrooms; (c) antiracist policies at the university; and (d) racist, and particularly antiBlack, practices resulting from, or encouraged by, policies at the institution?

4. What are ways in which students can find potentials to resist oppressive meanings of Blackness at Midwestern State?

5. How does the style of our Black study mimetically conjure, while entangling, possibilities for resistant Black energy?

"We does remember verse and not chapter"

Home again in summer 2019, listening to my brother's car radio, I hear Trini media personality and comedienne Rachel Price make the above declaration. It strikes me as critique of impulse-driven thinking sometimes demanded of Black survival—of living for a now without the context of now. Let's resist such a politics of temporality as we move through *Black or Right*, routinely drawing on relations, to im/mediate (re)turning to our above questions. Verse, in ways, is chapter, is world, if we open ourselves to such possibilities. I invite you into the coming chapters in a fractured state of here and there, as I embody differing roles in each.

Chapter 1: "'Are you black though?': Black Autoethnography and Racing the Graduate Student/Instructor," offers a Black autoethnographic approach—an application of African indigenous methodological "self-knowledge"—as potential antiracist rhetoric to mobilize my positionality as a Black im/migrant instructor at historically white institutions. That mobilization aims at presently reading my precariousness as a Black graduate student / instructor in the past, nuanced through my reflexivity/reflectivity as an able-bodied Black im/migrant male. I take this Black feminist autoethnographic approach to operationalize my ecological lens in rhetorical analysis based in a methodological tradition of Black *griots-as-scholars* in US academia. Griots-as-scholars intertwine Black personal narratives to fuel their critical analysis. I chart an ancestry of such work in rhetoric/communication, writing studies, and literacy studies from June Jordan (1985) to Carmen Kynard (2015).

Mobilizing the history to which this chapter belongs, I propel it onward in three sections: visualized, (em)bodying, and (per)forming difference. In grounding my narrativized analysis in historicity, I contemplate how a historically white liberal arts college uses my Blackness to publicly visualize their diversity. In considering my (affective) (em)bodiment of difference in relation to historically white universities, I relate an account of being profiled and jumped by a white vigilante in the Midwest. I historicize that account with an anecdote of similar profiling and brutalization by Texas police while a graduate teaching associate in a "colorblind" first-year writing program. I end by (per)forming Blackness and its racialization in white educational spaces. This chapter seeks to reflectively/performatively analyze the racing of the Black graduate student/instructor through a method that prioritizes African indigenous agency, acknowledging the politics of one's own interconnectedness to the deep rhetorical ecology's meaning-making potentials. "Are You Black Though?" argues that Black autoethnography generatively disrupts the Black object-being's rhetorical bind of representing the "problem" of difference for historically white institutions.

"Composing Black Matter/s: Hashtagging as Marginalized Literacy," chapter 2, develops means by which undergraduate students at Midwestern State University might engage with conversations on race and Blackness through Black annotation (Sharpe 2016) to contribute to viral Blackness (Greene Wade 2017). We engage hashtag composition in the neoliberal space of the classroom as a means of resistance, as a Black rhetoric—not as a fetishized "extra" assignment/requirement but as the backbone for decentering traditional ways of reading/writing in that space. The site of intervention is my second-year writing class, which fulfills Midwestern State's general education social diversity requirement. I introduce the "Tumblr Commonplace Book" assignment, which asks students to interact in racial ecologies through conceptualizing and composing hashtags as counter/public commonplaces on social media to analyze texts on Black resistance. "Composing Black Matter/s" marks hashtagging as a *marginalized literacy* based on social-media-user demographics and recent social movements mobilized by hashtagging—as picked up by the next chapter with #BlackLivesMatter. I specifically use the term "marginalized literacy" to describe how hashtagging as a literacy practice has been encultured through use by oppressed populations to invert the tags' potential hegemonic purposes as commonplaces and/or to strive for social justice for such peoples.[23]

Hashtagging also represents an "out-of-school" composing process used mainly for the purposes of social media communication. By deploying an agential nonacademic composition process in academic spaces, I blur the nonacademic/academic binary as a call to looking beyond the academy for agentialized literacy. In doing so, "Composing Black Matter/s" argues for hashtagging as a creative, analytic composition process with potentials to build, curate, archive, protest, and continue histories that interact with, and themselves co-constitute, social acts. Hashtags as both rhetorical objects and performances in the service of Black rhetoric augur a kind of epistemic rupture, here in relation to "diversity" requirements at historically white institutions. I examine students' use of hashtags to demonstrate the creation/negotiation of fluid racial meaning as students participate in a process of arguably culturally nonappropriative counter/public Black activism. The chapter analyzes participation in Black protest in attempts to foster classroom culture that mobilizes generative Black agency to counteract notions of antiracist work as punitive to "destructive" whiteness.

Chapter 3: "'All my life I had to fight': Shaping #BlackLivesMatter through Literacy Events" considers the broader question of what Blackness means during the post-Ferguson cultural moment in the United States as it relates to institutional power, through an inter(con)textual Black feminist relational reading of three artifacts related to the #BlackLivesMatter movement. It argues for inter(con)textual reading as rhetorical means to Black antiracist agency particularly congruent with #BlackLivesMatter's dynamics. This kind of reading points to and provides conditions for interconnections not readily noticeable between bodies, identities, movements, and it finds meanings within deep ecologies that produce/negotiate ways to question co-constitutive meaning. In the role of cultural rhetorician/media theorist, I more fully explicate my critical lens for such reading: deep rhetorical ecologies, made up of fracturing literacy events (Heath [1982] 2001) that (re)make racial meaning through rhetorical encounters. I contend that notions of inter(con)textual meaning-making implicitly forwarded by the #BlackLivesMatter movement through its activist discourses demand such a lens that can reflexively read Blackness in the movement's cultural moment (post-Ferguson). Institutional confusion in conceptualizing race and Blackness provides exigence for it, and I demonstrate how antecedent cultural moments play into white institutional defensiveness that results in #BlackLivesMatter's overtly Black feminist intersectional stances.

The chapter then employs that lens in reading three cultural artifacts or literacy events that demonstrate the movement's historical, populist, and pedagogical institutionalization. These "events" illustrate resistant Black meaning-making in the post-Ferguson United States in each respective category: Alicia Garza's "Herstory of the #BlackLivesMatter Movement" (2014); Kendrick Lamar's "Alright" (2015a); and Frank Leon Roberts's blacklivesmattersyllabus.com (2016). Throughout my inter(con)textual analysis, I implore that we maintain cognizance of the archival production/negotiation at work in reading across those artifacts in such contexts. Reflexively, this chapter argues for remaining attuned to, and reflective of, the generative role of historiography in the re/making of racial meaning, central to resistant methodologies.

The fourth chapter, "The Politics of Belonging . . . When 'Becoming a victim of any crime is no one's fault,'" uses the previous chapter's lens to interrogate discourses that make racial meaning with specific regard to the practice of policy—regarding diversity and security—at Midwestern State. It asks what happens when we reconceptualize Black disruption/deviance in relation to diversity policy's nonperformativity and white security as generative Black rhetoric. To do so I rhetorically analyze three literacy events: the April 2016 *Black Lives Matter in Classrooms* events; public safety alerts from a six-month period in 2016 and related public safety efforts at MwSU; and a YouTube video, "[MwSU] Administration Threatens Expulsion against Students" (Keep[MwSU]Public 2016).

I spotlight *Black Lives Matter in Classrooms* ([MwSU]BLMIC.org 2016) to consider the university's attempts at antiracist work, paying close attention to its visual rhetoric, keynote presentation, and interrelations with pedagogy. That visualization and its keynote work in ways to demonstrate what Black agency might look like framed as coming from or situated within the institution. I concurrently investigate a series of public safety email announcements, highlighting how they not only criminalize Black bodies within the historically white institution but also how through these messages Blackness operates as a specter of cultural criminality. Related public safety publicity artifacts highlight the *white institutional defensiveness* that couches such cultural criminality. I also read the YouTube video to consider a critical incident where Black bodies encounter policy-makers in protest, analyzing racial meaning at play between notions of difference and security. In that video, the specter of criminalized Blackness materializes as white authorities use policy as justification for threatening expulsion of Black bodies from the institution. Analyzing these events, I characterize the work that policy explicitly and implicitly performs in producing/negotiating racial meaning at the historically white institution, looking to fractures in deep ecologies to tease out ideas of para/ontological Blackness in relation to disruption and prospects for inverting those relations through *rhetorical reclamation*.

The concluding chapter, "De Ting about Blackness (A Meditation)," thinks through Blackness in relation to "new" materialisms. It spends some time with rhetorical reclamation, acts of turning stigmatizing racialized attention mapped onto Black identities back onto the gaze of historically white institutions to publicly question/critique their power in moments of fracture. Rhetorical reclamations tie together the arguments of each respective chapter of *Black or Right*, demonstrating how rhetorics of Blackness—in Black autoethnography (chapter 1), hashtagging (chapter 2), inter(con)textual reading (chapter 3), and reconceptualized Black disruption (chapter 4)—offer potentials for resistant Black antiracist agency in historically white spaces to counter white institutional defensiveness.

In further unpacking rhetorical reclamations, I show how the object-being of para/ontological Blackness allows for possibilities of mobilizing objectness that speak across a spectrum of Blackness (and Black theoretical frameworks) from rhetorical silence to technologies of cancelling. Since this project focuses on multitude, I end by rhetorically asking of Blackness:

How do we write its story if we become objects acting in it while being acted upon?

How do we write its story if we do or don't claim humanity?

How do we write its story if we refuse to write its story?

1

"Are you Black, though?"

BLACK AUTOETHNOGRAPHY AND RACING THE GRADUATE STUDENT / INSTRUCTOR

The difference between poetry and rhetoric
is being ready to kill
yourself
instead of your children.

AUDRE LORDE (1974), "POWER" (71)[1]

As usual, as I ease into a fresh semester at the Midwestern State University, I can count the Black-identified students in my second-year writing class on the one hand: two men, one woman. The Black woman, Shaina, is vocal, speaks to her biraciality, to one of her parents' experiences as a Black Caribbean immigrant, and calls out white privilege when she sees it. One of the men is typical of the Black male students I encounter at Midwestern State: shy, withdrawn, but willing to speak sometimes, though not always in debates directly related to Blackness. The other Black man, T, outspoken, consistently challenges me in overt, often excoriating ways. For the first time, he puts my Blackness as an instructor at a historically white institution routinely up for open debate.

Unlike most Black men I encounter in other white spaces here, T performs "stereotypical" Blackness: through his clothing, speech, and in ways through his writing. I remember gold chains with large pendants and felt pride knowing that T could dress like this in a classroom here—my classroom. He drops "nigga" frequently, nonchalantly, throughout discussions from the jump. That he says it so freely in front of all the white students in my class engenders a kind of selfish confidence for me.

The first time T asks "Are you Black?" in some discussion of a Black authored-text, I'm shook. At the front of the classroom, I feel coerced into disclosing my identities. Having worked through a positioning activity during the first week of class, asking students to consider their intersectional identities, T and my own pedagogies

DOI: 10.7330/9781646421473.C001

compel me to respond. I want to empathize—though this response requires public disclosure. I explain my background. I identify as Black, though ethnically both Afro- and Indo-Trinidadian (hence my light skin tone). He doesn't push further.

~~~~~~

My aunt and twin cousins visit from Trinidad. I invite them to see me teach. My immediate family never see me in this role and don't know my academic life, and my aunt is a retired schoolteacher I look up to. They sit as I review paragraph structure. My histories crisscross my present, living, as though its own body, with its own voice, in the classroom space—with my "Yankee-d" accent and flailing gesticulation—finally revealing another Lou, not the quiet, introverted child they know, here in "the States" at a major university, teaching (mostly) white kids how to write in a plaid button-up and jeans. Their videos and pictures document my teaching for the first time, letting me look at myself as an English instructor while a Black Caribbean im/migrant working in a privileged role. I proudly introduce my students to my relatives at the beginning of class and listen eagerly to their reaction to my teaching.

~~~~~~

"#schoolboyLou" shows up on the margins of student assignments throughout the semester. T develops this nickname for me, which begins to appear on his and other students' handwritten work. I never directly ask. I infer that T is signiyin' on the name of LA rapper ScHoolboy Q. Although it seems subversive, I feel honored that a Black male student thought it his business to give me a new name, a Black name. I want to find something generative in what might be typically deemed disruption. Because it riffs on the name of a rapper associated with "wokeness,"[2] I think honor into what seems like his identification of me via urban Black masculinity. But such identification makes its way into the classroom as interrogation again, where, in a white space, we engage in some kind of antagonistic, verbal throw-down for Blackness.

During group project presentations, I sit at the back of the room. T's group is up next, and as he shuffles to the front of the class, he turns and asks in the lag between projects: "Are you Black, though?"

I sigh exasperatedly "Uh *yea*." But before I can even vocalize that, Shaina, seated in between us, responds immediately: something along the lines of "He *already* told you he was Black. Why do you keep asking?" T ignores her, again engages with me, as I continue what must be a critical, staring-at-the-sun look at him. T's next question has me even more shook: "So, like . . . if this was plantation days, would you be in the house while I was in the field?"

~~~~~~

I begin this story to give an intimate sense of how my experiences as a Black im/migrant able-bodied male graduate student/instructor frames my analysis of deep rhetorical ecologies at white institutions. In its fractures, my Blackness, perceived by others or articulated by me, cannot be separated from these spaces and communities with/in which I operate. When I use the word "space," I speak to the ecological and environmental conditions that surround, constitute, and embody social intra-action and interaction. Interdisciplinary feminist theorist Karen Barad conceptualizes spatial meanings as co-constituted by such "agential intra-actions" between spaces' components, a concept integrating Marxist, feminist, and antiracist approaches (2003, 815, 810–811). But although I nod to these (re)new(ed) materialist interests in spatial constitution, I foreground here an analysis of Blackness informed by Black feminist—and supported by African indigenous—approaches that prioritized relationality long before rhetorical scholarship's recent "new materialist turn." Sylvia Wynter, for instance, through the sociogenic principle, explains how the physiological processes of the body cannot foreclose "being human," as Western Man's governing codes mean that human life forms enact "a third level of hybridly *bios* and *logos* existence" (1994a, 6). In other words, selfhood *and* its social environments, and vice versa, always already mediate the body (Wynter 2001). Meanwhile, Denise Ferreira da Silva, argues that modern thought, in treating humans as objects in studying racialized others and their regions, formulated and spread prevailing ideas intertwining notions of globality and raciality. Western philosophy mobilizes what the Black feminist calls the hegemonic "transparent I" of rational self-determination in contrast to racialized minorities as "subjects of affectability" needing control by exterior reason (2007, 40). Conscious of these lenses, I re/present my Black im/migrant experiences through Black feminist autoethnography,[3] revealing the insidious ways that racialized precarity operates with and in US educational spaces vis-à-vis/with/in its long-standing in/justice systems.[4]

Focusing on "everyday, taken-for-granted knowledge" (Hill Collins [1990] 2000), I pick up and extend disability studies scholar Margaret Price's notion of "kairotic spaces"—"the less formal, often unnoticed, areas of academe where knowledge is produced and power is exchanged" (2011, 60)—to spaces not traditionally considered "academic."[5] The above narrative demonstrates not only my inability to separate my subjectivity from this project but also the inevitably of being read racially based on my spatiality and (literal/metaphorical/identity-based) positions within the institution. My para/ontological Blackness moves with/in my body's position in the frame of the classroom, where, for instance, being at the back of the room might invite T's attempted subversion. My relationship with T deeply puzzled me for a while: How could I at once be #schoolboy-Lou while also some kind of Black poser? Some house slave (contingent English instructor) for the white massa (MwSU)? How is it that Shaina sought to defend my Blackness in all of this?[6] What roles do the writing classroom—and, by extension, "white" campus spaces—our material identities, and our stories unfolding within them play in theorizing difference in rhetoric, writing, and literacy studies? And what histories within the fields do those roles speak with, push against, draw from, and add to? Let's dig deeper.

In this chapter, I offer Black autoethnography as a rhetoric to theorize Black, potentially antiracist, agency within rhetoric, writing, and literacy studies. Ratcliffe's *Rhetorical Listening* notably deploys autoethnography as the first of several steps in her titular antiracist concept. Though she views autoethnography as "valuable," for her theory, it remains "admittedly limited in its perspective" and separate from "academic research" in disrupting white supremacy in our fields (2005, 37).[7] In merging style and content, autoethnography as a *principal* methodological orientation—rather than a cursory or introductory one—holds greater possibilities for our fields, as scholars of color and particularly Black scholars in it have demonstrated. Forwarded through a Black feminist intersectional lens, this chapter presents my autoethnographic stories as a Black im/migrant male student/instructor while situating my narratives in a reflexive charted history of Black storytelling traditions within the frames of rhetoric, writing, and literacy studies. I mobilize and push forward that history, charting it from Jordan's "Nobody Mean More to Me than You and the Future Life of Willie Jordan" (1985) to Kynard's "Teaching While Black" (2015).

Within that tradition, my analysis considers how my Blackness and im/migrantness visualize/d, (em)body, and (per)form difference (and consequently institutional "diversity") for/against US historically white institutions. Through this approach, I fracture understandings of the precarious positions of the Black graduate student/instructor at these institutions, wrestling with how my meaning-making produces/negotiates with/in these white, capitalist, nationalist, heteropatriarchal spaces.[8] "Precarization means more than insecure jobs," as political theorist Isabell Lorey shows; "by way of insecurity and danger, it embraces the whole existence, the body, modes of subjectivation" (2015, 1). In embracing my racialized precarity, I explore how I am criminalized in spaces of social death, building on critical race scholar Lisa Marie Cacho's stance that in so doing, possibilities for agency that come from the decision to struggle matter more than its outcomes (2012, 32). Indeed, fractures within deep rhetorical ecologies allow us to recognize where social death is most visible. I thus present experiences to demonstrate how these educational spaces entangle my identities in a kind of self-defeating bind where Blackness becomes tangled in an object-beingness. Black autoethnography as antiracist rhetoric highlights the paradox of that bind by (per)forming resistance along with certain spaces and temporalities—a kind of para/ontological object-being. Through its presentation, this study calls on our disciplines to pay more attention to Blackness and Black gendering in ways that might involve our particularly theorizing/performing the latter to destabilize static cultural binaries and stereotypes that diversity policy often maps onto Black bodies in white institutional spaces.[9]

As cultural studies scholar Marie Louise Pratt demonstrates, autoethnographic texts "involve a selective collaboration with and appropriation of idioms of the metropolis or the conqueror . . . with indigenous idioms to create self-representations intended to intervene in metropolitan modes of understanding. Autoethnographic works are often addressed to both metropolitan audiences and the speaker's own community. Their reception is thus highly indeterminate" (1991, 35). Despite that potentially precarious reception, both white scholars[10] and scholars of color within our fields have embraced, and in some ways appropriated, women of color and Black feminism's application of autoethnography—theorized/practiced by Lorde, Gloria Anzaldúa, hooks, and so on—in their work in critiquing identity in educational spaces. Those scholars of color include Richard Rodriguez (*Hunger of Memory* 1983), Victor Villanueva (*Bootstraps* 1993), and Morris Young (*Minor Re/visions* 2004), among others.[11] But here, within that subsection, I particularly prioritize the tradition of Black academics whose work in rhetoric/communication, writing, and literacy studies take up autoethnography as their central methodological framework to extend this tradition through my own stories.

I highlight this long-standing, though unrecognized, foundation utilized by Black academics in our fields through the figure of the *griot-as-scholar*. Such a move follows on Banks's call to "build theories, pedagogies, and practices of multimedia writing that honor *the traditions and thus the people* who are still too often not present in our classrooms, our faculties, and in our scholarship" (2010, 13–14; emphasis mine). Autoethnographic orientations align with African indigenous relational paradigms that emphasize self-awareness, belonging, and ecological accountability, which should permeate community and thus research engagement (Chilisa, Major, and Khudu-Petersen 2017). Moreover, Black historian Carter Godwin Woodson describes the storyteller's importance to African/diasporic communities. They—often older women—tell stories to youth to maintain posterity of the tribe's traditions. These persons, venerated in the community, play crucial roles in social functions and through daily performance of stories (1928, ix–x). Storytelling, thus linked with both educational and the daily performance of communal being, holds a particularly esteemed value in customary Black knowledge-making.[12] I interrogate the functions of reflective stories that position Black rhetoricians and me within the griot-as-scholar tradition,[13] to advance this project's Black feminist analytic that "affirms, rearticulates, and provides a vehicle for expressing in public" an already extant Black consciousness (Hill Collins [1990] 2000, 32).

I think through racialization as relational because, as Alexander Weheliye explains via Black feminists Wynter and Spillers, relationality potentially "reveals the global and systemic dimensions of racialized, sexualized, and gendered subjugation, while not losing sight of the many ways political violence has given rise to ongoing practices of freedom within various traditions of the oppressed," a lens particularly important and productive in Black studies (2014, 13). Pursuing that analytic, I consider the conditions of particular environments and how they engage with bodies (and vice versa) through fracturing to produce/negotiate identity and meaning with/in them. Each of those bodies has stories to tell, and this chapter spotlights mine in particular. And more than simply acknowledging my subjectivity as significant in ongoing analysis, such a move calls attention to how Blackness engages/emerges in academic labor. Sharpe reminds us that despite our knowing better, the academy often drafts Black academics into servicing our own destruction by adhering to research methods that do "violence to our own capacities to read, think, and imagine otherwise . . . We must become undisciplined" (2016, 13). I join with Sharpe in this pursuit of what she describes via Dionne Brand as "a kind of blackened knowledge, an unscientific method, that comes from observing that where one stands is relative to the door of no return and the moment of historical and ongoing rupture" (2001, 13). To delve into that fracture, to undiscipline, I engage in a process of Black storytelling, of Black autoethnography.

"If This Was Plantation Days" (Continued)

As I calmly articulate why we shouldn't frame ourselves in relation to slavery, T makes his way to the front of the class. I can't help but think about our bodies' positionings in the space—his resistance arising as he takes to the front of the room and I sit in the back row that he usually occupies. Where is the house in this classroom? Where is the field? And though I readily dismiss the planation metaphor—because I don't want T to perceive himself as white chattel or to think myself some white overseer's lackey, lingering aloof over T on massa's behalf—deep down it holds weight. Both Black bodies exist in relation to white authority, bound in different ways by, and up in, oppressive matrixes of domination: our exaggerated truths. We are in the fracture; we are "in the wake": "as the meanings of words fall apart"—in my explanations that I do not buy for moving away from the plantation—"we encounter again and again the difficulty of sticking the signification" (Sharpe 2016, 77). And while slavery's political, racialized power relations meant that slaves were denied the opportunity to gaze (hooks 1992, 115), T, in our classroom ecology, usurps that denial by racializing me as dominant "house slave" through the mechanisms of the academy. In the hierarchy of commodified objects that the wake signals, T resists by putting my governing role on blast.

~~~~~~

By the last day of the semester, I grow quite attached to this group. Having had particularly difficult, lengthy, delicate, and complex discussions about Blackness, resistance, and their relationships to whiteness/institutional power, one day— prompted by Shaina's emotional response to a video on the Ferguson Uprising—I tell my story of being a victim of police brutality in Texas. I'm so comfortable that I want to give this class a takeaway: on that final day, we watch parts of a documentary on racism. The clips address the "n-word," as well as the question "Are all white people racist?" Following our viewing of the former, T asks, "Do *you* say 'nigga'?" And before I can resp—"Are you Black though?"

At this juncture, I need to know why. What motivates the question? What pre-occupies T throughout the semester, so much so that it manifests itself openly through these interjections? "I am. Like I explained before. Why do you keep asking this question though?"

"Is it the color of my skin?"
"Is it the way I dress, or the way I speak?"
"Or is it that I'm standing in front of this classroom? What is it?"

"Because you're standing in front of a classroom," T explains. My position as an instructor at a historically white institution means that my Blackness is inauthentic, out of place, or at the very least questionable. But it's my Black masculinity. And my lack of urban Black male performatives. How could I be *a Black man* teaching this shit? That a Black male student would think that Black masculinity couldn't be found or performed in the position of instructor in an English class at MwSU somehow implies that I am, in some ways, a whitewashed, feminized version of Blackness—and it's true. But from his choice of my Black body's spatial location as the root of his questioning, rather than biological markers, or my material/linguistic racial/gender performance, T identifies an impossibility in the efficacy of my possible antiracist Black agency.

By evoking the word "nigga,"[14] in co-constitution with "#schoolboyLou" though, T also conjures a different kind of racial hierarchy typical to the white classroom in order to critique my space in it—one of a world in which Black authenticity relies on a hardcore-rap nexus of the hypercommodification of Blackness. We become two things in a space where Blackness must read as things. Yet, the white classroom can only exist on a hierarchy—hence T's earlier fracturing question of our respective positions as field versus house slaves. Black studies scholar R. A. T. Judy explains, "A nigga forgets feelings, recognizing, instead, that affects are communicable, particularly the hard-core ones of anger, rage, intense pleasure . . . The possibility of the nigga rests on the twofold of experience and affect, and the fact that experience is essentially infungible" (1994, 228).

T, therefore, highlights my position as an instructor in the white university (and its assumed experiential enculturation) in an attempt to destabilize my "nigga authenticity" (Judy 1994), but simultaneously fractures our understanding of the deeply ecological white space itself and how it co-constitutes our Blacknesses. For him, because of my place in surrounding whiteness—which my white fields substantiate and contribute to—and perhaps due to my lack of US Black hyper-masculine performatives, affects, or experiences—my centering of Blackness in teaching needs to be conspicuously critiqued. It is suspect.

Between Poetry and Rhetoric[15]

To dig deeply into these differences to which Lorde alludes in the epigraph to this chapter—and to use them creatively as Lorde implores as critical of Black feminist imaginaries (1984, 110–113)—I position my forthcoming stories in a tradition of Black autoethnographic work within rhetoric, writing, and literacy studies. Below I lay out aspects/aesthetics of studies in that tradition on which I continue to build. These elements include (but are not limited to) the affordances of Jordan's treatment of affect in relation to Black language in classroom spaces (1985), Keith Gilyard's ecological analysis detailing the developmental process of learning race/language (1991), Jacqueline Jones Royster's exploration of how Black voice operates as a "thing" almost outside of the Black body in institutional environments (1996), Vershawn Young's (2004, 2007) genre-bending study/performance of Black masculinity in relation to white educational spaces, and Carmen Kynard's (2013, 2015) overt exercising of various Black registers and positional awareness in telling stories that confront the traumas faced by Black students in educational settings. I mixtape these autoethnographic tenets in order to remix the method forward through my own stories.

In contending with T over Black language and our roles within institutional spaces, interrogating my affective responses as a Black instructor in relation to a Black student, and bringing autoethnographic reflexivity to bear on analysis through a Black feminist relational lens, my reading here follows on teacher/scholar/poet Jordan's. Her 1985 essay, "Nobody Mean More to Me than You and the Future Life of Willie Jordan" wrestles with the Black feminist's experience teaching Black English to a mostly Black class.[16] Jordan's (1985) pedagogical reflection takes a sharp affective turn when one of her students, Willie, loses his brother to a police shooting. Utilizing the highly politicized teaching/learning of Black vernacular, Jordan and her students grapple with responding with protest. The essay deploys storytelling as a means to center contemporaneous issues significant to Black life/learning. It demonstrates Black autoethnography's potentials to weave through "the eloquence, the sudden haltings of speech, the fierce struggle against tears, the furious throwaway, and useless explosions"

(135)—aspects of the methodological genre I engage directly. Though different from my encounters with T, Jordan's relationship with Willie demonstrates how Black pedagogical stories might help us think through Black identity, language, and their institutionalization—a critical aim of this project.

Prompting his suspicion to its climactic head, T's doubt about my use of "nigga," a term fraught not only by histories of racialized violence but also by Black reclamation, underscores language's role in racializing, classing, and gendering subjects. My relationship with T seemingly hinged on our individual/mutual relationship with the word—a use of which meant a co-constitution with/in it—here, within a historically white space. That use of Black English situates us in, and reminds us of, debates within rhetoric, literacy, and writing studies surrounding the publication of a landmark Black autoethnographic text—Gilyard's *Voices of the Self* (1991). Engaged in tensions on Black students' relationships with Black and standard English, Gilyard narrates his negotiations with literacy from "birth" to the end of high school in every other chapter of his monograph, carefully studying his sociolinguistic development in scholarly conversations in intervening ones. He justifies his methods by explaining the validity of autobiographical artifacts and a transactional analytical framework (12). In such a model, actively propelled by my own stories in this chapter, subjects like T and me "continually [negotiate] with an evolving environment" (13). Though Gilyard frames his orientation as autobiographic, the study's scholarly analysis of his schooling in conversation with major, concurrent intellectual discussions characterizes *Voices* as a full-scale autoethnographic investigation into those discourses. Gilyard's book and Jordan's (1985) essay exemplify "critical autoethnographies" that "foreground a writer's standpoint and makes this standpoint accessible, transparent, and vulnerable to judgment and evaluation" (Adams, Holman Jones, and Ellis 2015, 89).

The vulnerability in reflecting on my exchange with T allows analysis of various "voices" I embody as an able-bodied Black im/migrant male student/instructor in white educational contexts. In the narrative, these include my "voices of the self," my own accentuated identity as a foreigner employed in a nonnative space—aurally identifiable through speech—as a race-radical Black instructor, as a contingent laborer for the white institution, and as a male, privileged in a middle-class space through instructional authority. I wrestle with a similar desire as Gilyard's to embody the "hip schoolboy" in T's nickname "#schoolboy-Lou"—a persona "impossible to achieve" (1991, 160).

On the selfsame notion of "voice," Royster's "When the First Voice You Hear Is Not Your Own" capitalizes on metalevel prospects for autoethnographic storytelling to investigate "voice" as a "manifestation of subjectivity" not only tied to the spoken/written but also acting "as a *thing* heard, perceived, and reconstructed" (1996, 30; emphasis in original). Here, we might navigate how "voice" constructed in ways beyond the Black body works para/ontologically (in a non/being in but outside itself) to make/negotiate Blackness. Working in the very mode she sees belittled by the white academy ("stories"), Royster multi-dimensionally critiques how academic spaces misconstrue voice—specifically hers—cleverly pushing against that distortion to fund her thesis. Likewise, "If This Was Plantation Days" shows how the classroom space in an ecology at MwSU works with/against my voiced identities, racializing my body in transactional contexts with notions of dominance and subordination. Royster's article operates alongside Black feminist theorist hooks's contemporaneous *Teaching to Transgress*, which, through storytelling, extends sometimes beyond narrated personal responses to teaching/learning situations to active, reciprocal encounters with scholarship, countering various "systems of dominion" (1994, 10). hooks's call for instructors to "practice being vulnerable in the classroom, being wholly present in mind, body, and spirit" (14) parallels Royster's (1996) emphasis on the varied, intersecting ways voice can be embodied (or move beyond biocentric notions of bodies) for Black feminist griots-as-scholars. In utilizing multiple angles of Black storytelling, both thinkers press Black autoethnography forward, demonstrating how subjectivity might be complicated through layers of analysis to resist institutional oppression.

Like Vershawn Young, in his article "Your Average Nigga" (2004) and subsequent monograph by the same name (2007), I stereotyped T based on his clothes, demeanor, and language. And while my initial reaction to T was optimistic, as opposed to Young's reaction to his "ghetto" student Cam (Young 2004, 699), that impression does not make my profiling any less harmful. Having grown up in a neighborhood unlike Cam's or Young's[17]—mind you, not a "ghetto" in local parlance but one boasting a "drug zone," "pipers," and my mother's routine question, "That is gunshot ah hearin'?"—my relationship with US Black masculinity differs from Young's, Cam's, and T's. Deploying autoethnographic techniques, Young's article contends that proponents of code-switching essentialize race construction, resulting in damaging consequences, particularly for Black urban males. The monograph pushes his use of this methodological orientation to other spaces in his personal (the ghetto, his living room, his brother's house) and professional (the classroom, a teachers' meeting, and a university teaching job interview) life (Young 2007, 8). His arguments stage and study scenes from them, performing a "merger of what's often considered academic (and white) with what's considered creative (and raced)" (10). Such emphasis on performativity and spaces in which performativity occurs marks *Your Average Nigga* as an amalgamation of critical autoethnography and "narratives of space and place" (Adams, Holman Jones, and Ellis 2015, 86).

Growing up, my situation differed from Young's in that school and bookishness were not necessarily socialized as feminine. In postcolonial Trinidad and Tobago, parents, teachers, and even culture beat learning into us as a clear alternative to drugs, poverty, and violence. I distinctly remember calypsonian Gypsy's refrain, "Little Black boy, go to school and learn, little Black boy, show some concern, little Black boy, education is the key, to get you off the street and out poverty." But I was an inside child from quite young and, because of mixed heritage, did not identify with the song when it was popular. My relatives' presence in "If This Was Plantation Days" also seemed, to me, to legitimize my Blackness, particularly my im/migrant Blackness and ethos in an antiracist classroom. They were other Black bodies attesting to my racial and ethnic "authenticity." However, in T's struggle with me over Black masculinity, my im/migrant blackness undermined my (US) Black masculinity—and perhaps contributed to T's doubt about my use of "nigga." The word's enculturation and commodification in hip-hop and rap discourses and those discourses' operation as "an authentic African American cultural form against its appropriation as transnational popular culture" (Judy 1994, 229) contribute to tension that leads to fracture—where the deep ecology of the white classroom cultures us on different planes in relation to racialized hegemony. Caribbean Blackness thus reads illegible when gradated by US Blackness via a low-key nationalization of the ecologically white space. The junctions of Blackness, in particular temporalities/spatialities in both Young's and my analyses, illustrate the dynamic capabilities of autoethnography within the griot-as-scholar lineage.

Methodologically, Young (2007) locates his text with *Voices*, explaining it as a predecessor, though he attempts to merge seamlessly autobiography and criticism, as opposed to Gilyard's chapter separations (1991, 11). Young (2007) also explicitly draws from W.E.B. Du Bois's *The Souls of Black Folk*, calling it a model for blending genres. Notably, Du Bois recalls first coming to the question prompting his formative theory of double-consciousness, which haunts this very project—"How does it feel to be a problem?"—in a "wooden schoolhouse" (1903, 1–2). Du Bois's socialization within an educational institution teaches him, through reflective/reflexive interrogation, how to embody, affectively and materially, his Blackness.[18] Although Young (2007) frames *Your Average Nigga* as autocritography,[19] it might usefully also be considered Black autoethnography, working from that latter form through self-aware attunement to subjectivity, identity formation, and genre manipulation. This chapter explicitly builds on Young's performativity, reflexivity/reflectivity, attentiveness to space, and use of poetry,[20] revealing a conscious propulsion of autoethnography and how it could be fruitfully employed in studying diasporic Black identity.

Following on Young's conspicuous and metalevel use of storytelling as a means to analysis, Carmen Kynard's (2013, 2015) scholarship exhibits Black autoethnographic methodologies in its prioritization of personal narrative in reflexive relation to academic conversation. It embodies critical self-awareness of her positionality as a Black feminist race-radical griot-as-scholar and how that awareness shapes and furthers research. Kynard's *Vernacular Insurrections* intertwines several vignettes with revisionist histories of writing studies in relation to the Black Freedom movement. Calling her work "Intellectual Autobiography" (2013, 1), Kynard also foregrounds her language usage (like Young), claiming a "cross amalgamation of many styles and registers" from "high academese" to "high urbanese" (13). My above story in two vignettes and the critical reflections in proceeding sections similarly slip in/out of academic, colloquial Black US, and Trini dialect. Kynard explains the self-involvement required in Black autoethnography when she pronounces, "You are always right there in the mix, no matter how much you have been written out, spanning much wider than the token representation you have been allowed" (12), harkening back to Royster, and pushing outward from the commodification of Blackness in white spaces.

While *Vernacular Insurrections'* organization reminds us of Gilyard's (1991) *Voices* in separating chapters featuring personal accounts from explicitly critical conversations, Kynard's (2013) shifting deployment of language to story her work operationalizes and forwards the all-encompassing autoethnographic analytic offered in Young's scholarship. In her article "Teaching While Black," Kynard remains "conscious" in using "stories to understand and present the lives and literacies of students of color where [her] own cultural role as a *black female storyteller* enacts its own critical inquiry" (2015, 4; emphasis mine). Kynard's scholarship not only overtly brings the Black feminist griot-as-scholar role to conversation, but also emphasizes positionality, reflexively marshalling the inherent political Black agency and traditions from which it comes as a mechanism for scholarly analysis.

Employing that mechanism, I re/mix autoethnographic frameworks from an amalgam of predecessors, pushing onward, while doubling back, from V. Young (2004, 2007), Kynard (2013, 2015), and others in the heritage. My stories thus stand on their own as criticism and entertain academic conversation, fluidly navigating dialects, and eventually leave only the creative (yet analytical) text. In further mulling why my "standing in front of a classroom" at MwSU caused intraracial tension, I offer more stories to uncover and ecologize how my Blackness functions, or fails to do so, on US college campuses. These stories, like "If This Was Plantation Days," ask: How might my histories, identities, and experiences cut across spaces/temporalities to fracture notions of Blackness in antiBlack environments? How does engaging moments of racial stress evoke para/ontological rhetorical possibilities where objectified Blackness might emerge/sojourn? How does autoethnography merge style and content to suggest a means for antiracism? My analysis's Black feminist lens follows purposefully on Royster's claim that individual stories placed against each other construct credible evidence, a basis from which "transformation in theory and practice might rightfully begin" (1996, 30). Building from the outlined griot-as-scholar tradition, I present them

to critique the institutionalization of Blackness and de/constructions of my precarious identities, continuing to also pose Du Bois's question: "How does it feel
to be a problem?" (1903) while navigating agency through that push.

Visualized Difference: On Becoming Token

On the glossy cover of the summer 2009 issue of Liberal Arts College's (2009)
Liberal Arts College Magazine,[21] a publication by its Division of *Institutional
Advancement* (emphasis mine), my image stands out like a Black thumb. Of
the six individuals pictured in graduation regalia, I am the only one not a
white woman. But it's also my hair: while my scraggly beard signals gendered
difference from the rest of the group, my dreadlocks—that ironically cannot
fit under the graduation cap—place an inordinate amount of visual attention on my role in the photograph. The caked black tentacles that defined
my identity back then overshadow the decorative ropes and medals that signify institutional achievement. Embracing the two of the five white women
I know personally, I smile with the group, proudly above the first of two text
boxes that reads: "Cover Story: Tomorrow's Stellar Alumni: Stories From This
Year's Honors Convocation Celebration." We stand under the maroon arch, an
icon for the university on official documents, with the title of the magazine,
named after the university, flanked atop the page. Liberal Arts College lifts its
name from a nearby range in the Appalachian Mountains that runs through
the Northeast. The mountain range's name has some relation to an indigenous tribe of about 5,000 persons, who, according to the *New York Times*, "are
economically strapped and very rural, which sets them apart from most of
the residents of [their] wealthy [county]" (Kelley 2006). Here: in one of the
wealthiest counties in the United States, in one of its wealthiest states in terms
of median income, the name of an indigenous tribe signifies not its cultural
underpinnings, not the histories of the genocide, poverty, or socioeconomic
degradation inflicted upon its bearers by white settlers, but the public liberal
arts college located within it. Its *Magazine* sets my Black im/migrant male face
in service of that unjust history.

This section recalls the use of my image by this historically white institution
I attended prior to MwSU to orient the autoethnographic reading of my position as a Black graduate student/instructor. It tells the story of a pair of photographs used by my undergraduate alma mater, analyzing how my identity as a
Black male im/migrant does diversity work for the institution. I deploy literary
and Black studies scholar Houston A. Baker's idea of "critical memory" (1995): a
"continuous arrival at turning points," that evaluates the Black "past that it never
denies as well passed." We might well understand Baker's concept as a technology of Sharpe's (2016) "wake work" in its "cumulative, collective maintenance

of a record that draws into relationship significant instants of time past and the always uprooted homelessness of now" (Baker 1995, 3). These photographs recall fractures made present when my Black imaged self was/is/will be used by white institutions that conjure conforming Black stereotypes.

I am commodified as palatable Blackness. Among a group of white women in the cover image, I smile, the happy slave: my affect signaling that I do not represent a threat to white male hierarchies. As Frantz Fanon explains on relations between Black men and white women, "the Negro is a savage, whereas the student is civilized" ([1952] 2008, 50). In a country where media often casts and recasts Black men as dangerous threats in specific relation to white women (and their sexualities), justifying notions of white supremacy though such essentialization (James 1996, 28; Kozol 1995, 658), the photographer and/or the magazine and/or the institution seem to communicate that I am just "one of the gang"—nah, not the Black kind. Note that the photograph chosen for the cover does not center or bookend my presence (as the one male and tallest body in the image) but attempts to create an M shape, fitting neatly within the arch and metaphorically within the college community. The picture positions my body as integrated within the shape of daily life here.

The *Magazine*'s second use of my image, situated (before all of the other notable alumni) along with the introduction to the cover story article "Tomorrow's Stellar Alumni," displays my body seated with both hands in clear view—again nonthreatening. My oversized shirt and tie are thrift store purchases.[22] While smiling, as requested, my left hand clutches my knee, indicating my discomfort with being put on display—a quiet act of Black refusal (Campt 2017). The caption for the photograph reads "Louis Maraj / Poetry." Yet, the college does not offer "Poetry" as a primary course of study. It erases the three majors I completed. Effectively, whether because of space constraints or otherwise—not because of ignorance—the caption essentializes my work as "Poetry." I am both the exceptional Negro and the stereotypical poet/entertainer, an ontological all or nothing. Through the racialized minimization of my work, it becomes "the random droppings of birds" (Lorde 1990, xi), where the white academy diminishes Black scholarship, discounting it as "simply stories" (Royster 1996, 35). And while the article's prose alongside does mark my credited majors, among other accomplishments, it describes these achievements with "his academic load would not tolerate delay" ([Staff] 2009, 8); the load itself becomes subject, the actor. The deep ecological fracture (in the wake) means—in relation to slaveness, to the concept *"work for life"*—"the body, as such, is not endowed with intrinsic meaning" (Mbembe 2017, 143): "his" carries only the possessive description of the load. The pristine greenery of the college campus together with the mirrored building in the background belie the complex realities of what engenders my Black im/migrant survival.

The accompanying article, however, with its chance to alleviate these omissions, does little to make up for them. I remember the journalist excited when their initial questions led them to learn details of my health problems while attending Liberal Arts. The success/progress narrative they craft from the interview characterizes the institution as the white savior that steps in to rescue, to give meaning, to the model minority. It begins by casting me as a fish outta water: "Louis Maraj had never stepped foot outside Trinidad and Tobago before venturing to the United States in 2005" ([Staff] 2009, 8). The article discusses the particulars of my health condition, giving intimate details of the help offered by a professor who assisted with the process that led to the removal of a life-threatening brain tumor. The account ends with a quote from me about the impact of a white male professor on my poetry writing, noting that with his "encouragement" I plan to attend graduate school (8). With a group of six interviewees, only one of whom identified as male, it is telling that the magazine chooses to present my image and narrative first. That choice, along with my tokenization as exceptional and exotic, and positioning with/in the histories of the institution's name, demonstrates the deep ecological rhetorics of white capitalist heteropatriarchal educational institutions.

What's more, the next narrative features the only other international student, beginning with a similar first line: She had "no cell phone, and no computer" ([Staff] 2009, 9). The exclusion of racial and gender dynamics—explicitly not pointed to in relation to the playing up of our pathetic nowhereness ("he doesn't know where he is"; "she doesn't have technology")—contributes to a depiction of diversity and difference as "universal"; "each cultural group [here represented by individuated images and accounts] is deemed to be the *same* and *equal* precisely because they are all equally *different*" (Halualani 2011, 248; emphasis in original). The institution plays its "diversity cards" before all others, illustrating how "women (and people of color) need not expose their autobiography; the institution already projects its autobiographical scripts onto their visual selves" (Hesford 1999, 105). In such scripts, my image delivers to alumni, parents, and fellow students a notion of inclusivity via race and citizenship status; the attached caption provides a notion of the "unlearned" engaging in a "creative" racialized simplicity; and the account of my "success" pats the white institution, its appendages, and contributors on the back. The *institution*, indeed, *advances*.

Such re/presentation solidifies the idea that institutional diversity now "overwhelmingly [means] the inclusion of people who 'look different'" (Puwar 2004, 1), demonstrating "how it can keep whiteness in place" (Ahmed 2012, 33). Further, the narrative in the article—"a form of affective conversion," to use Ahmed's term—and apposite photos attempt to discipline bad feelings and the unhappy objects associated with them into good feelings and happy objects (Ahmed 2010, 45) in the affective economy of the white institution. I remember another fracturing moment under the white gaze: being first confronted with a copy of the magazine by the mother of a white friend at a summer graduation party as she gushed, "look it's you on the cover." Her white daughter adds, "with your dreads and all."

(Em)bodying Difference

**TO THE BLEEDING WHITE MAN WHO JUMPED ME
FOR SEEMING THE BLACK KID WHO MUGGED HIM**

—FOR TRAYVON MARTIN

Tell me my headstone reads 'warhorse,' I'm worth
its very concrete, my body before
it's emptied in latenight rainshower's burst
better unnoticed, in water, in war.
Tell me you've already heard my namesong's
encore: it means nothing, just like any
other. My mother, just another—wrong
for raising a thug like me—like every
one, mourns my name gone. No armor, no gun,
no well-tailored suit, no master's degree,
no eloquent president, no nation
post-race, no, see, not even a hoodie
protects me from *sob* stories my skin tells
in deep night, my heart, its own, loud, Black knell.

I think about Trayvon Martin a lot—maybe too much. I think about what he means to whom and why. Perhaps it is because a child, because of his clothes, his skin color, and environment, because of his racializing assemblage, represented to a man some deviant problem. Weheliye contends that "the idea of racializing assemblages construes race not as a biological or cultural classification but as a set of sociopolitical processes that discipline humanity into full humans, not-quite-humans, and nonhumans" (2014, 4). I have sought, through poetry mostly, to consider, repeatedly, Du Bois's thesis question "How does it feel to be a problem?" (1903) in relation to Martin. In Weheliye's conception, this means "How does it feel to be not-quite-human or nonhuman?" (2014). Delving into that feeling, that fracture, "is to live in the no's, to live in the no-space that the law is not bound to respect, to live in no citizenship" (Sharpe 2016, 16). In this section, I continue to probe those "no-spaces," to ask these questions, that make racial difference within college campus environments. While reacting to the alleged "colorblindness" of US society during Obama's presidency, the above poem arises from two particular incidents in 2015 and 2011. Both occurred in "off-campus" areas,[23] in the Midwest and Texas, respectively, and demonstrate how I (em)body and affect certain notions of Blackness in particular environments.

The man to whom I dedicate this poem jumped me while walking home one night several summers ago. Through the poem, I follow Lorde's call to "claim anger and to hear in anger a certain claim" (Ahmed 2012, 171). Like the Black feminist thinker, "my response to racism is anger. I have lived with that anger, ignoring it, feeding it, learning to use it" (Lorde 1984, 127). I return from a white male friend's home after playing video games. As I continue up the street where I live, three Black youth run by me. They wear an assortment of shorts, T-shirts, and sneakers. In a college town, such scenes are commonplace late Saturday night, with bars buzzing, alcoholic energy quickly peaking. I distinctly know, from my own experiences, that responses "to Black males in common spaces, in public spaces, [send] powerful messages to [them] about how their presence is unwanted" (Brooms 2017, 100). I continue until I notice a white woman lying on the opposite curb, clutching her foot. I cross the street, wanting to be an ally, offering help. She groans. I prod, asking, "Are you okay?" I understand why a white woman, injured, lying on a curb at midnight, wants nothing to do with a strange Black man. Somewhat fortunately, another man—a white man—approaches and asks similar questions. I don't possess language or reason without him. We begin to find out she twisted her ankle.

With my back to the street, I'm shoved forward. I spin to a bloodied, skinny, short white dude, who shouts, "Gimme my shit! You took my fucking shit!" I calmly explain that I don't know what he's talking about, but furiously he again pushes his stained hands, now, into my chest, still shouting about his "shit." I am almost twice his size (not a big man, not a fighter, I don't want to hurl able-bodied anger against a vulnerable, injured person). As he continues to aggravate me, the white man who stopped to help explains to the aggressor that I'm not who he wants: "I think they went that way." The vigilante stares at me blankly, recognizing in those few seconds that he profiled, picked a fight with, and assaulted me, before crossing the street, screaming into oncoming Saturday-nighters, "They took my shit!"—his "they" still categorically criminalizing the Black men he encounters that night. As author/editorial writer Brent Staples explains, there's "no solace against the kind of alienation that comes from ever being the suspect, against being set apart" ([1986] 2001, 565). I walk a couple blocks home, remove my sneakers, shorts, and T-shirt, now bloody.

Within the campus environment, such vigilante action might be expected with the prevalence of the MwSU Public Safety Department's alerts via text messages, emails, and its website. These racialized "safety notices" give vague descriptions of Black men suspected of violent crimes, contributing to a vigilante culture that perpetuates antiBlackness. The spoken word piece in this chapter's final section contains excerpts from one such alert.[24] These announcements represent mechanisms by which white institutions criminalize Blackness and particularly Black males, placing us "under increased surveillance and control by community policing tactics on and off campus," rendering us "'out of place' . . . 'fitting the description' of illegitimate members of the campus community" (W. A. Smith, Allen, and Danley 2007, 562). In the temporal fracture in these deep ecologies, they conjure "the surveillance technology of the runaway slave advertisement," which "through their detailing of physical descriptions," "make the already hypervisible racial subject legible" as indeed "out of place" (S. Browne 2015, 54). The historically white institution's policies, which reflect the systemically in-built ideologies of most all US institutions, prompt affective responses from both Black males (paranoia, alienation, anger) and other members of on-/off-campus college communities about them. As sociologist Derrick Brooms highlights, fear of Black males in college environments aligns with how they are historically scripted (2017, 100). This narrative illustrates how embodying Blackness with/in these deep ecologies means wrestling with temporal/spatial affects produced by oppressive institutional forces, as well as through gender performance.

The following night, another eye-opening, fracturing incident speaks directly to individual behaviors that oppressive institutional environments birth (and vice versa), which undoubtedly feed into personal prejudices, a "most insidious danger" (Brooms 2017, 100). I go to a bar with the same white colleague from the night before to recuperate from my previous experience. At 2 a.m., while he smokes and chats up a white woman, a bottle breaks amidst a small crowd across the street near another bar's patio. I step away briefly to use the bathroom and return to him on the phone. "White, Black, or Hispanic?" the other end asks—I could hear. "Black," he says. "Why would you *call the cops*? Why would you say *they are Black*?" He looks at me as most white folk do when confronted with ghosts of slavery and Jim Crow. Here lies a limit of Black-white "friendship," "directly influenced by concerns about ethics and law" (Mbembe 2017, 74). Within sixty seconds, cops roll up. From the other side of the street, flanked by the man responsible for their presence, I see a white officer yell at, grab, and frisk a Black man walking by the nearby CVS. I see myself there, walking by that CVS as I hop off the bus daily. I recognize the disconnect that academia doesn't want me to. These particular acts of *seeing*—in eye contact with this colleague, with the previous night's vigilante, in living the distance between one side of the street and another—alert me to Du Bois's (1903) "Veil" mentioned throughout *Souls*. These fractures make visible the color line that institutional white supremacy and colorblind policies and ideology invite us to ignore. They reveal the shaping of racialized, gendered, nationalized, dis/abled notions of material identities inherent in US institutions that play into the re/active (per)forming of these identities.

I specifically choose off-campus interactions that push institutionalization up against identity to foreground how the Black graduate scholar engages with kairotic spaces not seen in classrooms, conference presentations, or pro-fessionalization workshops. As sociologists indicate, Black male students in "campus-academic," "campus-social," and "campus-public" spaces routinely face microaggressions causing "racial battle fatigue (e.g., frustration, shock, anger, disappointment, resentment, anxiety, helplessness, hopelessness, and fear)" (W. A. Smith, Allen, and Danley. 2007, 551). But, as public health scholars David R. Williams, Harold W. Neighbors, and James S. Jackson illustrate, we also expe-rience macrostressors or racial macroaggressions (2008). These traumas elicit the above range of affective responses that pile together, fashioning Blackness with/in and out/side of being.

MONKEY ON DOWN[25]
I'm a monkey to you: joke, juggler, clown,
three races as they walk into a bar.
"Has anyone told you that you look, sound,
like Barack Obama?" Yes. My ears are
large. My skin's brown. Yes. I articulate
the slight academic jargon you like.
D'you like me to dance, twerk, dougie my skit
on out your white community? My bright
gold teeth skinned, jeweled dental treasure chest?
We sit. The Black asks *ayo what's goin' down?*
The brown thinks *how do I best word this mess,*
an always already terrorist? Found
gut warns *bite down tongue.* Anger's insistence
tastes good. Chew the cud of most resistance.

Imagine a physical classroom where, as a student, you never meet five of the six assessors of your writing. They will evaluate through an online mechanism to which you submit your work, only knowing you through electronic documents. They do not know your name, what you look or sound like, when they open sub-missions. Unlike a strictly online course, your material identities matter within the classroom space to your instructor but play little role in how meanings you produce might be "valued" (through grading) by the neoliberal university. While a graduate student/instructor in Texas, I teach for this program that removes stu-dent identifiers from submitted assignments. When not teaching a syllabus, texts, assignments, and rubrics standardized across all sections of this first-year writing course, I "document instruct": I grade online from a pile of work, unmarked.[26] Identical guidelines and material across all course sections ensure that my lived identities as an instructor, like my students', matter minimally in assessing the information I deliver. In this colorblind institutional backdrop, I fall victim to racial profiling and police brutality, demonstrating how I am both "misrecog-nized as someone who committed a crime" while also "criminalized" through my Black im/migrant identities in being "prevented from being law-abiding" in social death (Cacho 2012, 4).

On the first day of Spring Break 2011, I return with two white coworkers from a music festival to my home at 9 p.m. I left the house at 2 p.m., with my roommate (a white woman from Dallas) away, so the porch lights remain off. I fumble my keys in the dark. I use my phone's backlight to identify the right one and get inside. Sitting in the living room, loudly watching television, a bang interrupts casual conversation.

(Pause.)

Another bang. "Police!"

We exchange frantic glances.

Another bang. "Open this door!"

My colleague Ben shouts, "No!"

I'm taken aback, but Ben knows that they need a warrant for intrusion.

I don't.

Another bang. "Open this fucking door right now!"

When Ben shouts, "No! What's the problem?!," the cop "explains," "I will kick in this door if I have to!" Reece relents. He opens to a hand, shoved, that yanks him out beyond eye-shot. Ben, closest to the door, gets ripped out next. I walk to it, and, by the hand, am raffed,[27] cuffed, face-slammed onto the concrete porch.

They check IDs. "I live here!" The white male cop takes my passport out my back pocket. I cut my dreads when I went for my new visa photo. My regrown dreads couch my face from the ground. The passport, I suppose, seems sketch. In the barrage of questions, Ben asks, "Why is there a dog here?" "To bite your ass!" the white woman cop snaps. Still cuffed, I am dragged by the white male officer through my living room. He asks about my roommate. Her framed pictures stare back at me, an indictment. This is a nice white lady's home. The cop shoves me through each room, asks to see my mine, surveys my papers and poems: "You go by 'Lou'?"

He takes me back to the porch, sets me back on my face and stomach.

They chat.

I panic.

I don't understand what's happening. I rock back and forth screaming, "Help!" "Please!" "Why?!" The cops panic.

Ben asks, "Can we tell him to shut the fuck up?"

"Yes."

"Lou! Shut the fuck up!"

Eventually, they uncuff Reece. He again explains that all we did was go to a concert and come home. I live there. We ask for their names. They say only, "Next time, open the door when we fucking say to!" I eat my porch. I am humiliated. No record exists of the near-half-hour incident. All they offer at the station is a mostly blank sheet indicating a call was made: three men; one with a light, opening the door; my body, profiled, suspect. Blackness, im/migrantness, fracture/ mean violently. It means no home nowhere, not even in a body. The rationale given by the cop I complain to later on the phone: I would want the law to treat an intruder the way I was treated. They need to be brutal because the situation demands it. I, myself, ask to be brutalized.

(Per)forming Difference

In "asking" to be brutalized, in ecologically materializing "suspect," I succumb to what Ahmed calls "a life paradox: you have to become what you are judged as being" in representing difference (2012, 186). Like my clash with T over our material-discursive relationships with "nigga," (em)bodying and (per)forming racially precarious rhetorics (above, through dreadlocks, my im/migrant identity, etc.) means being rendered non-law-abiding, an object. In this section, I continue exhibiting this bind of object-being, which does diversity work for educational institutions that sustains dominant whiteness (33)—labor built into US socioeconomic infrastructures for Blackness. I break completely from formal critical conversation, concluding only with a spoken word dedication to T.

Such a conclusion aims to facilitate (autoethnographic) scholarship in rhetoric/communication, writing, and literacy studies that encourages, as Lorde consistently does, knowledge-producers to take into account how "even the form our creativity takes" operates within oppressive matrixes. We must welcome work "which requires the least physical labor, the least material" (1984, 116). In continuing the griot-as-scholar methodology, this study opens up what counts as valid knowledge-creation, situated within the complex systematic positions that Black folk occupy. I call on autoethnographers and nonautoethnographers "to consider the accessibility of their texts . . . asking what value or benefit our work might have for our participants and readers, as well as ourselves" (Adams, Holman Jones, and Ellis 2015, 44).

This creatively critical inquiry into my Blackness as an able-bodied Black im/migrant male graduate student/instructor adds to Kynard's demand via LaNita Jacobs-Huey (2002). I mobilize what the latter describes as "'gazing and talking back' in ways that explicitly interrogate *the daily operation of white supremacy in our field and on our campuses* rather than more performances of psychologically-internalized black pain for the white gaze" (Kynard 2015, 14; emphasis in original). It offers Black autoethnography as rhetorical means for potential antiracism. This chapter enacts that clap back in object-being, a fracture in multiple ecologies, building on a tradition of resistant storytelling struggling for potentials to liberate our work, language, and daily material realities.

SELFIE AS #SCHOOLBOYLOU

—FOR T

What yuh think this houseslave life bout?

Is not no skinning, grinning, or sipping tea. We work that kitchen, waiting: me, Uncle Langston, and Miss Audre. What you think we for, T? I pay my dues: I wear dis skin like the blues I sing, fill de white man's drink when low.

What you think you know? T, they comin for all ah we.

"Safety Awareness Message: We are sharing this news on behalf of the [City] Division of Police for a crime that occurred in the off-campus area"

See, one mid-morning, rainy, I walk to my office from the on-campus gym. Cross the street when I come up upon a guided tour. It's always tours. T, I watch from the other side. A white man leads white parents in North Face and New Balance. He got stories—rehearsed—his mom's concern for his "safety," she texts. At night, on campus, he assures his white parent, his audience, "I feel very safe." But to keep you and me in check, Midwestern State's Campus Alert is "an awesome feature that informs us on these issues." I think bout Trayvon Martin shot by a vigilante in the rain. I stop.

T, dey won't stop comin for all ah we. House or field, ain't matter the work we do for free.

"Suspect #1 is described as a black male in his 20's standing 5'6" and weighing 135 pounds. He was wearing white t-shirt and blue jeans."

Nah, you wouldn't wear a white tee. All black, de usual.

"Suspect #2 is described as a black male in his 20's standing 6'1" and weighing 180 pounds. He was wearing a black t-shirt, black baseball cap and blue jeans."

Maybe? You
taller than me. But you got that black beanie. Does it matter, T? What we wear, where we sleep, nigga, what we tryna be?

Schoolboy, houseslave, I'm just tryna be, aight?
"He aight," T writes on an eval, for de massa to see.

2

Composing Black Matter/s

HASHTAGGING AS MARGINALIZED LITERACY

Hashtags make and unmake. When my student T nicknamed me #schoolboy-Lou to produce/negotiate my and his Blackness, the handwritten tag spoke and speaks to a series of connections drawn together and spread offline, while highlighting its viral potential. The name, after all, circulated to other students in the class quickly. But the tag and its transmission also emphasize how Blackness in white spaces entangles with white supremacy, even in the "most Black" discourse of our exchanges—always already surveilled, we operate as rhetorical objects in such environments while making Black meaning. The tag itself represents qualities of contagion. T theorized my Blackness as co-constitutive with/in deep rhetorical ecologies of intellectualism (and potential whiteness) and associations to rap culture (and possibly wokeness), while producing/negotiating his own Blackness wrapped up with mine and said ecologies. Hashtags permeate. More than digital catchphrases that call out online trends, this tool for spreading information on social media today indeed takes form in these ways in in-person communication, becoming oral markers of the destabilized boundaries between material and virtual spaces. "The hashtag is now one of the most recognizable symbols of communication itself," contends communication theorist Nathan Rambukkana (2015, 30). Hashtags decode. As founding publisher and editor of *Hashtag Feminism* Tara L. Conley explains, hashtags can translate the textual to the verbal and vice versa. Conley posits that these tags, particularly "Black feminist tags," summon "thresholds between dehumanization that is lived and livable; they are sites of struggle over the politics of representation" (2017, 29).

Importantly, protests against governments and state violence shape the ways in which digital media users deploy these sociocultural linguistic units in online spaces. Researchers in several fields such as linguistics, sociology, and

DOI: 10.7330/9781646421473.c002

communication studies have found these tags—because of their burgeoning political influence—incredibly useful in analyzing language and society in dynamic ways; hashtags offer distinct affordances as field sites for scholarship (Bonilla and Rosa 2015). Consequently, recent scholarship works to consider issues of identity, specifically racial identity, for the prospect of understanding how categories historically and culturally tied to biological bodies operate in virtual spaces seemingly divorced from them. In this context, hyperfocus has been placed on online communities such as Black Twitter and the linguistic formations that develop in them (such as Blacktags[1]). Such focus often raises not only ethical questions for researchers in terms of objectifying/exploiting historically marginalized groups but also on the validity of their studies. How can we know that someone is *really* Black online? Digital-media-oriented critical race theorists such as Lisa Nakamura and Peter Chow-White (2012), Sanjay Sharma (2013), and Andre Brock (2012) demonstrate how "social networking relations, modes of online communication and digital identities have been revealed to be far from race-neutral," in response (Sharma 2013, 46). Sharma and Brock in particular show how Blackness unfolds through hashtags to theorize racialization in these spaces.

For all their cultural relevance and social agency, hashtags remain understudied in mainstream writing and literacy studies publications, though opportunities exist for such work in those fields.[2] Here I consider the classroom potentials for teaching race/Blackness and engaging students with Black resistance at a historically white institution through tags, while valuing them as culturally marked linguistic tools that can reshape how we read/write/think/note-take. Hashtags represent a kind of marginalized out-of-school literacy, and through a foundational assignment I use in my writing/composition classroom—the "Tumblr Commonplace Book Assignment"—I consider tags deployed in the service of "viral Blackness" (Greene Wade 2017) as a form of fluid digitalized counter/public commonplacing that engages in "Black annotation" (Sharpe 2016). This chapter offers hashtagging as a Black rhetoric with antiracist potentials.

Media studies scholar Ashleigh Greene Wade argues that virality destabilizes hegemony, cannot be contained, and offers transformative potentials (2017, 35). Viral Blackness functions "as a deterritorializing mode of subversion to white supremacist systems that seek to restrict Black bodies, silence Black voices, and quell Black thought" in a Black feminist thrust,[3] "to release blackness from essentialization" (Greene Wade 2017, 36, 41). I situate Black annotation as a technology to enact viral Blackness, with capacities to fracture deep rhetorical ecologies and to do "wake work" that Sharpe conceptualizes such annotation as doing. Sharpe explains Black annotation as "trans*verse and coextensive ways to imagine otherwise" (2016, 115): "Annotation appears like that asterisk, which is itself an annotation mark, that marks the trans*formation into ontological blackness. As photographs of Black people circulate as portraits in a variety of publics, they are often accompanied by some sort of note or other metadata . . . in order that the image might travel with supplemental information that marks injury and, then, more than injury." Because these Black images/texts are often co-opted to communicate hegemonic messages, such annotation becomes vitally necessary for Black being in the face of non-being (116).

We have countless digital and nondigital textual examples of Black death exemplifying such co-optation predating and through #BlackLivesMatter (the Rodney King and Eric Garner videos, etc.). Black hashtags thus become a matter/means of Black object-being. They can reveal potentials to radiate the meanings/moments of Fanonian epidermalization: the juncture of fracture in contact with the white world, of where inferiority marks Blackness (Fanon [1952] 2008, 5) "through an experience of sensitization" (Zardar 2008 xiii). #BlackLivesMatter, after all, re/calls how Black lives do not in fact matter under white oppression, and tagging that makes that sentiment visible and can place us in this fracture in/between non/mattering. As contagious digital objects (Sharma 2013), Black hashtags mobilized through viral Blackness for Black annotation might evoke epidermalization, revealing the potentials for meaning-making in para/ontological Blackness. Here/in lies pedagogical possibilities.

Located with/in this context and deep ecology of #BlackLivesMatter, students, through the process of the assignment, use hashtags to challenge and remediate historical understandings of commonplaces and commonplace headings as tools that reinforce strands of dominant ideologies. While holding potentials to reinforce the archaic sense of the commonplace (*koinòs topos*) as pedagogical device and as instruments in the constitution/transmission of a consensus knowledge, the culturing of hashtags offers otherwise avenues for actively countering that sense. Through students' hashtag compositions, I locate these tags as contemporary, digital, linguistic commonplaces that mobilize Black feminist ideologies of everyday relationality: the tags themselves might represent/mark/name deep rhetorical ecologies and their fractures with the capacities to do antiracist social justice work in college writing classrooms centered in Blackness. These tags might also *position* such classrooms and students within them in larger cultural spheres (and broad ranging deep ecologies)—particularly making them active in the possibilities of viral Blackness—possibilities so often closed off by more traditional essays that fail to matter as artifacts beyond classroom spaces. Because they do so, they provide opportunities for instructors interested in process-based composition activities and pedagogies with the promise of social engagement (and consequently possible antiracist social influence).

The first section of this chapter conceptualizes hashtags as digital counter/public commonplaces. The second situates cultural histories of commonplacing, commonplace books, and hashtags, and sketches the digital environment (Tumblr) for the assignment being analyzed, while arguing for hashtagging as a marginalized literacy due to their enculturation. The third section foregrounds the "Tumblr Commonplace Book" assignment and the classroom ecology in which that assignment is deployed and analyzes tags used by my writing students through their hashtag compositions that demonstrate how they open windows for resistant Black feminist relational and rhetorically ecological meaning. Through these interconnected explanations, I forward notions of hashtagging as a creative, analytic composition process with potentials to build, curate, archive, protest, and continue histories that interact with, and themselves constitute, social acts. I emphasize how—through practical composition assignments grounded in students' "self-sponsored" out-of-school writing practices—writing students and instructors might engage in (arguably culturally nonappropriative) digital Black annotation in historically white campus settings. I employ a "marginalized literacy" in the white capitalist heteropatriarchal space of the classroom as a means of resistance, as a move toward epistemic rupture—not as a fetishized "extra" assignment/requirement but as the backbone for decentering hegemonic ways of reading/writing in that space to mobilize the Black feminist philosophy of literacy as the practice of freedom (hooks 1994).

Hashtags as Digital Counter/Public Commonplaces

Compositionist David Bartholomae's oft-cited "Inventing the University" explains "a 'commonplace,' . . . is a culturally or institutionally authorized concept or statement that carries with it its own necessary elaboration. We all use commonplaces to orient ourselves in the world; they provide a point of reference and a set of 'prearticulated' explanations that are readily available to organize and interpret experience" (1986, 7–8). In a student's essay about an on-the-job experience, Bartholomae, for instance, points to phrases such as "lack of pride," "no incentive," and "lazy" as examples of commonplaces that each come with sociocultural associations (8). Students might employ them in writing as points at which they might try to identify with or enter discourse communities. In such attempts, however, such reliance on commonplaces might serve to reify presiding systems of thought that can translate in and beyond the classroom to sustain white heteropatriarchal systemic power. All three of the above examples might advocate for historically scripted and neoliberal understandings of racially marginalized, im/migrant, or disabled peoples' lack of "American" labor ethics, based on context. Indeed, Bartholomae goes on to explain that "commonplaces are the 'controlling ideas' of our composition textbooks, textbooks that not only insist upon a set form for expository writing but a set view of public life" (8). But if antiracist teachers and scholars look to hashtags, can we perhaps re/conceive these tags as commonplaces representing deep ecologies that might push against stasis and hegemonic ideologies in writing/composition classrooms today?

Hashtags, as discursive political networks, can offer entryways, vistas, and easily recognized ways of engaging the world in online communication spaces. According to digital media critics Axel Bruns and Jean Burgess, "as a concept, the hashtag has its genealogy in both [Internet Relay Chat] channels and the Web 2.0 phenomenon of user-generated tagging systems, or 'folksonomies,' common across various user-created content platforms by 2007" (Bruns and Burgess 2015, 16). Their sociopolitical exigence has been most studied and evident on the microblogging site Twitter, where they serve as an "indexing system in both the clerical and the semiotic sense" (Bonilla and Rosa 2015, 5). Brock highlights that though originally developed for curational purposes, hashtags have evolved as an expressive tool for contextualization of tweeted content (2012, 534). And while Bruns and Burgess argue that they not only create "ad hoc" but also "calculated" publics because of Twitter's control and internal filtering of content found via tags (2015, 25), their political and cultural impact via social media cannot be denied. Through their use to snowball social movements in the last decade such as #OccupyWallStreet, #BlackLivesMatter, and #MeToo, some politicized hashtags demonstrate capacities for undercutting their intended neoliberal functioning. Indeed, as Sarah J. Jackson, Moya Bailey, and Brooke Foucault Welles's *#HashtagActivism* shows, marginalized peoples use hashtags to promote counternarratives, building networks of dissent (S. Jackson, Bailey, and Foucault Welles 2020).

Moreover, hashtags' archival function on social media networks provide users access to both commonplace points of reference and to opportunities to build ecologically on those points of reference, creating relational meanings with/in that building. Hashtags are, I argue, a "remediated" form of commonplaces and/or commonplace headings. New media theorists Jay David Bolter and Richard Grusin explain remediation as the idea that "media are continually commenting on, reproducing, and replicating each other" (2000, 55). Commonplaces—and commonplace headings when used as an organizational tool in commonplace books—in their traditional sense represent indexing, controlling ideas that allow users to draw upon established notions of those ideas for ethos. Hashtags, however, not only reproduce that referential affordance/constraint but also allow users to build upon, resist, and create relational and rhetorically deep ecological relationships with other tags and thus other archives. They demonstrate how "remediation always operates under the current cultural assumptions about immediacy and hypermediacy" (21), as they point to themselves as text (immediacy) while also pointing to themselves as other texts (hypermediacy). Hashtags, therefore, operate as hybrids: "text and metatext, information and tag, pragmatic and metapragmatic speech . . . deictic, indexical . . . between textual and chronological" (Rambukkana 2015, 30). Situated within contemporary contexts of their cultural significance in social protest (explained more fully in the next section), hashtags offer avenues through which histories of sociopolitical/intellectual dominance might be undercut for marginalized peoples.

If students understand hashtags for their *encultured* potentials as these kinds of commonplaces (or commonplace "headings") in a reconceptualization of particular social media spaces as "remediated" commonplace books in the writing/composition classroom, these tags can afford such writers means to resist dominant ideologies through communal/collective, deep rhetorically ecological frameworks. Preexisting hashtags proffer with their deployment in-built histories of relations, communities of "strangers" made members of such networks via previous use, and cultural signifiers based on (and reflexively built by) the unfolding identities of those strangers. The way in which tags mobilize these series of evolving relations, providing them the prospect to shape public knowledge and the deep ecologies they denote, lies very much in the workings of Black feminist relational discourse.

Positioned with/in such relational frameworks (Hill Collins, Lorde, Wynter, hooks), these tags can propel an everyday critical consciousness that works toward social justice aims, as section 3 of this chapter shows. As Black feminist means of fostering alternative forms of connection, community, and relation to publicly affirm an already-extant awareness (Hill Collins [1990] 2000), the antiracist tag can para/ontologize such moves. These tags hold promises to embody/perform a talking back, a response to multiple oppressions in the face of multiple violences aimed at disrupting hegemonic orders of intellect, epistemologies, and cultures. Such possibilities align with educational philosopher Paolo Freire's problem-posing critical pedagogy where "through transforming action" new situations might be created for more just futures in the classroom space (1970, 12). By stressing relationality and moving ecological meaning, hashtag composition not only "denies that [beings are] abstract, isolated, independent, and unattached to the world" (12) but also (re)make worlds, inherently stressing opportunities for interconnectivity and collectiveness that align with the African indigenous framework of botho/Ubuntu (Chilisa 2017). As Conley specifically shows, Black feminist hashtags "burst to connect to other stories, events, encounters, and desires, and form new(er) articulations of lived experience" (2017, 30). Using this digital media technology in/outside the classroom might thus show students and publics the sociopolitical impacts inherent in their daily routines of composing in social media spaces.

This study thus responds with recent work in writing studies, such as Paula Rosinski's (2017), that calls attention to the influence of implementing students' modes of digital self-sponsored writing into academic writing opportunities in order to destabilize the gap between the writing/composition classroom and out-of-school literacies and contexts. As digital rhetorician Adam Banks highlights, "beyond the tools themselves, meaningful access requires users, individually and collectively, to be able to use, critique, resist, design, and change technologies in ways that are relevant to their lives and needs, rather than those of the corporations who hope to sell them" (2006, 41). Deploying hashtags as an antiracist technology—particularly centered in articulations of Blackness—can re/form the cultural commonplace from its historical underpinnings/applications to provide means to enact that kind of transformative access.

"Common sense ain't always common": Decoding Histories of Dominance

Media technologies function with/in their particular histories, cultures, and socialization when employed. Cynthia and Richard Selfe have drawn digital media and writing studies' attention to these dynamics in their work on the exclusionary consequences of interface design since the mid-90s (Selfe and Selfe 1994). These fields have been well aware that if instructors bring technologies to the writing/composition classroom, they should be cognizant of their politics because even if "technologies are not inherently political, the conditions in which they are created and which they circulate into society are political" (Banks 2006, 23). Black feminist Safiya Umoja Noble's (2018) *Algorithms of Oppression*, for instance, spotlights how search engines like Google (our popular, twenty-first-century tool for autodidacticism) fund discrimination, particularly against Black women, under a veil of neutral operation. To more fully contextualize the particular media technologies on which I focus in this chapter, this section works through brief histories of dominance and marginalization in the Western intellectual tradition inherent in the classroom deployment of commonplaces, commonplace books, and hashtags.[4] It "decodes" this history through Conley's Black feminist notion that "decoding as a stance is a practical method for disentangling encounters, identifying dominant modes of knowledge production, and contextualizing the roots of those systems" (2017, 29). Such work is vital if we choose to cut away at those roots. We must remain cognizant of how our sense of what is "common" might not always be universally common. Our understandings of "common sense," then, cannot be one size fits all.

~~~~~~

Commonplace books have a rich past as a teaching tool in Western philosophy and education. That background comprises commonplace/book usage that generally reinforced culturally dominant systems of thought. The compilation of "common" ideas for intellectual and social use within that tradition can be traced to Greek philosophy: through his *160 commentarii*, the elder Pliny dictated excerpts of critical value to his scribes, which the younger Pliny championed as central to the elder's *Natural History* (Pliny the Elder [77 AD] 1979). Aristotle explains them as a "stock of arguments to which [a speaker] may turn for a particular need" ([4 BCE] 1932, 154). Roman Stoic Seneca the Younger later frames ideal reading and writing (through borrowings from Horace) with the student as a bee flitting from one source to another, picking what pollen might be sweetest for the production of honey—the former act representing reading, the latter act writing (Seneca [65 AD] 2001). In the early modern period, at the dawn of print technologies, the use of maxims became central to rhetorical exercises in European Latin grammar schools with Erasmus's mandate based on classical precedent. The philosopher's *De Copia* explains that students should

> prepare for yourself a sufficient number of headings and arrange them as you please, subdivide them into the appropriate sections, and under each section add your commonplace and maxims; and then whatever you come across in any author, particularly if it is rather striking, you will be able to note down immediately in the proper place, be it an anecdote or a fable or an illustrative example or a strange incident or a metaphor or a simile. This has the double advantage of fixing what you have read more firmly in your mind, and getting you into the habit of using the riches supplied by your reading. (Erasmus [1512] 1978, 302)

The commonplace book embodied such a practice—not only as a tool that proved useful in written and oral composition in the classroom but also as one representative of the physical basis for an individual's "moral" foundation. That foundation might take effect through the book's categorized headings, its collected quoted material, and symbiotic relationships between and across quotations and headings. Other prominent early modern European philosophers and pedagogues, Juan Luis Vives and Michel de Montaigne, endorsed these methods as a basis for rhetorical composition and moral grounding. As historians of early modern Europe Lisa Jardine and Anthony Grafton argue, reading and note-taking in the Western Renaissance moved beyond the passive and cerebral to become the basis for agency (1990, 30). These annotative ideas—a representative basis for a "common" culture and derived primarily from classical and biblical texts—became central not only in the composition/reception of contemporaneous literature but also in legal, political, and economic institutions. The use of commonplaces as linguistic units and more broadly as a basis for and practice of ideology helped to strengthen and disseminate shared cultural values of those in power, regardless of their institutional context.

When commonplace books found themselves versioned in print in various generic forms, that standardization impacted "common" rhetoric/thought beyond the classroom, as classical reception scholar Moss (1996) illustrates in *Printed Commonplace Books and the Structuring of Renaissance Thought*. The rise of what we call the humanities saw the common enter educational spaces with the aim of fashioning mass numbers of students into "morally sound" citizens. For centuries, these students, writers, politicians, philosophers, playwrights, and so on, both in Europe and the United States, were almost exclusively white, able-bodied males. And while students were predominantly lower/middle-class white males, because of the nature of material being consumed/(re)produced by these educational processes, what constituted a sense of the common flowed through canonical literature, histories, legal proceedings, and the like, with reinforcing oppressive ideologies perpetuated by church and state. Susan Miller's (1998) analysis of "common" writing, which includes commonplace books,[5] illustrates how early-American white males used these composition spaces to centralize white maleness and gender (and less explicitly racial) hierarchies.[6] In European and US society and educational institutions, canons of thought filtered through these writing exercises (both in and outside of schools) to legitimize hegemonic ideologies. Commonplace/book use in curriculum studies and in teaching style remains alive in writing studies entering the twenty-first century, as Dennis Sumara (1996), Lynee Lewis Gaillet's (1996), and Laura Micciche's (2004) work shows. And while these canons of intellectual knowledge have begun to be eroded and more radically transformed in the last fifty years or so[7]—and while rhetoric/communication, writing, and literacy studies as fields have certainly shifted to more socially conscious work in the last thirty years or so[8]—centuries of ideological dominance and practices that buttress that dominance require extensive undoing in college classrooms.[9]

~~~~~~

In the latter half of the 2000-aughts and onward, hashtags developed distinct associations with social movements, activism, and racialized discourse communities in social media spaces. While social media has been analyzed and credited with benefiting oppressed peoples in non-Western countries (Howard and Parks 2012; Diamond 2010), the role that hashtags play in spreading awareness of the conditions that these peoples resist has been of particular scholarly interest in US contexts. Specifically, much analytical attention has been paid to the dynamics of hashtag use in resisting racial oppression, particularly in the #BlackLivesMatter movement. Black people, for a number of years, have been shown to make up a disproportional amount of social media's general and most frequent users. Statistical information from the Pew Research Center from 2011 highlights that

"25% of online Blacks used Twitter, compared to 9% of online Whites" (Brock 2012, 529). While more recent data from the same source (Pew Research Center 2018) suggests that more white folk now use Twitter than shown in the earlier study (24% white adults as compared to 26% Black), such information still reveals numbers incommensurate with general US population dynamics. In 2018, a larger percentage of surveyed Black internet-using adults used social media on most social media platforms (Facebook [70%]; Instagram [43%]; LinkedIn [28%]; Twitter [26%]) than survey participants identified with other racial groups.[10] Given such demographics, Black folk have established counter/public cultures on social media that demonstrate the effects of these disproportional statistics, most notably Black Twitter—sometimes referred to as "Young Black Twitter" based on the age of users. Black Twitter thus attracts not only widespread popular online and social media attention but also scholarly attention because of its part in viral and activist movements via tags.

Researchers in a range of fields (such as ethnic studies, cultural/linguistic anthropology, media theory, rhetoric/communication studies) have studied #Ferguson, #RaceFail, #AliveWhileBlack, #IfTheyGunnedMeDown, #YouOKSis and, of course, #BlackLivesMatter (Bonilla and Rosa 2015; Rambukkana 2015; Prasad 2016; Conley 2017; Freelon, McIlwain, and Clark 2016). Deen Freelon, Charlton D. McIlwain, and Meredith D. Clark in particular, through a 2016 big-data study of #BlackLivesMatter, highlight the explicit public educational capacities of the social movement via its hashtags. Their findings detail that "the primary goals of social media use among [their] interviewees were education, amplification of marginalized voices, and structural police reform" (Freelon, McIlwain, and Clark 2016, 5). Evidence of such "education" of "casual observers" on Twitter came through "expressions of awe and disbelief at the violent police reactions to the Ferguson protests, and conservative admissions of police brutality in the Eric Garner and Walter Scott cases" (5). The study consequently shows the cultural impact and rhetorical efficacy of #BlackLivesMatter in engaging in a kind of freestyle public education project while undertaking its social justice aims. So, while corporate interests might wield these tags and their viral capabilities to assess and exploit market trends, and though the tags and tag data could be used insidiously for surveillance, marginalized groups see/mobilize their prospective subversive possibilities. Links that hashtags offer between the spread of education and Black antiracist efforts align with the Black feminist principle of literacy as the practice of freedom (hooks 1994) as well as the movement's overtly Black feminist stance on its philosophies outlined in its "Herstory" (Garza 2014).[11]

Here, I suggest that based on demonstrated usages of racialized hashtags—specifically #BlackLivesMatter—for counter/public education and the above-outlined statistics of heavy social media use by Black folk, rhetoric/communication, writing, and literacy studies scholars might usefully understand hashtagging as a *marginalized* (out-of-school) *literacy*. Such a move might reclaim the hashtag commonplace for its subversive potentials—offering a kind of (para/ontological) being through/in the moving rhetorical object. Black cultural inventiveness pervades hashtagging as a literacy practice, underlining the sociopolitical importance of these tags to digital/viral Blackness and contemporary Black protest. In joining with Black social media users in deploying tags that have been encultured in Black protest, non-Black users become part of racialized assemblages co/constituting deep rhetorical ecologies with which they may or may not offer political solidarity—through tag use and beyond—in social media and lived material spaces. Putting tags to Black feminist use—along with and alongside the application of explicitly Black feminist tags—works to "shake loose dominant logics to reveal new(er) relations that sometimes form on the basis of solidarity, sometimes not," as Conley suggests (2017, 29). Because of potential rhetorical agency in these hashtags and their possible virality, they represent counter/public commonplaces that offer nexuses of exchange allowing for moving aggregations of identity—the distinct promise that engaging in deep ecologies offer.

As Nakamura and Chow-White highlight, "race itself has become a digital medium, a distinctive set of informatics codes, networked mediated narratives, maps, images, visualizations that index identity" (2012, 5). Culturally aware, social-justice-oriented social media users, however, should be mindful of possible appropriative leaps that remain possible with particular tags. We must underline/ acknowledge their cultural histories, be mindful of neoliberal engagement, and position ourselves as rhetorical listeners (Ratcliffe 2005) and learners. Hashtags and other online technologies (such as retweeting, reblogging etc.), still, offer distinct possibilities for relational building across inter- and intraracial markers for the prospect of antiracist agency. Despite highlighted constraints, instructors interested in engaging in discussions/practices of online composition, identity, or racialization might recognize benefits in deploying hashtag composition (and the framework of deep ecologies) in twenty-first-century classrooms and in confronting frank discussions of appropriation, oppression, and systemic antiBlackness that might arise in their use.[12]

To be clear, such discussions need not be always already put in the service of recovering some "humanity" for Black folk, though such avenues for that use certainly exist. Black hashtagging as antiracist rhetoric suggests a *process of making*, a politics of inventive possibility. While Black media historian Kim Gallon offers that the "'technology of recovery' undergirds black digital scholarship"—adding the racial signifier "black" to conceive "black digital humanities" as bringing about "the full humanity of marginalized peoples" through digital means (2016, 42, 44)—this study seeks to generate questions about processes rather than ends.

Since hashtags reveal specific potentials to world-make through a paraontology that irreversibly disturbs ontology's time and place (Moten 2013, 739) while still operating as ontologized rhetorical objects (thus opening spaces for para/ontology), they allow us to consider the very question of the human vis-à-vis Blackness. As intimated earlier, the spaces in which conditions arise for these tags and their consequent imaginaries co-constitute their meanings and therefore deserve critical attention.

Tumblr, like Twitter, is a microblogging site; however, it does not enforce character limits on the lengths of alphabetic posts.[13] Founded in 2007, as of June 2020 it boasts 501.4 million blogs, with 14.6 million daily posts. Forty-two percent of its traffic is based in the United States (*Tumblr.com* 2020). Users may share posts in a variety of formats: text, audio, video, and hyperlinks. The main hub of a user's Tumblr blog, called the "Dashboard," features a standardized design layout and a stream of content from blogs that specific user "follows." A blogger can choose from a variety of themes and settings to set up their blog space, however, where different types of posts might be arranged side by side, vertically, or in other spatial arrangements—not always chronologically. Users have the option of adding as many hashtags as they would like to individual posts.

In humanities professor Alan Jacobs's (2012) piece in the *Atlantic*, he draws a comparison between Tumblr blogs and commonplace books citing their scrapbook-like qualities as users cull material from numerous sources to constitute their pages.[14] Jacobs does not mention how hashtags might act as commonplace headings for their indexing capabilities in his comparison, though such explanation does further illustrate them. Feminist and textile historian Amanda Grace Sikarskie explains that though Tumblr can be isolating for new bloggers, hashtags serve as a "primary means" by which users "connect with other bloggers of like interests and begin to build a sense of community within the site," in her analysis of Tumblr quilting communities (2015, 170). Indeed, according to *New York Times* journalist Valeriya Safronova (2014), while users of Facebook or Twitter tend to primarily engage with people they know in-person, Tumblr users connect via interests and themes. The culture of Tumblr, consequently, emphasizes tag use as means to connect, making it a suitable environment for students to experiment with and learn the various dynamics of hashtag composition as commonplacing.

That sense of community that Sikarskie (2015) mentions remains pivotal in the "social-justice halls of Tumblr . . . dominated by users in their teens, 20s and early 30s" (Safronova 2014). While Twitter receives much scholarly and public attention for its activist communities, digital protest on Tumblr responds similarly to Twitter during events involving public racial injustice. As Liba Rubenstein, director of social impact and public policy at Tumblr, shares, the site experienced "'extreme peaks' in the use of the 'social justice' and 'black lives matter' tags" after the ruling on the Eric Garner case (Safronova 2014). Writing studies scholar Meghan McGuire likewise describes that "communities involved with issues of race and LGBT use Tumblr as a space for discussion" with less worry about trolling backlash (2017, 120).[15] Yet while Twitter activism has been heavily researched, scholarly work on Tumblr tends to engage with fan communities and their identity politics (see Sikarskie 2015; Zekany 2017). This chapter attempts to help fill that gap in research, showing prospects inherent in doing such work in and on Tumblr's discursive material and rhetorical spaces.

Hashtags, Anti/Racism, and "Tumblr as Commonplace Book"

The English department's second-year writing course at MwSU fulfills two general education requirements: one in "Writing and Communication" and the other in "Social Diversity in the United States."[16] The latter, importantly, asks students to "describe and evaluate the roles of such categories as race, gender and sexuality, disability, class, ethnicity, and religion in the pluralistic institutions and cultures of the United States" and that they "recognize the role of social diversity in shaping their own attitudes and values regarding appreciation, tolerance, and equality of others." Ahmed argues that diversity language in "statements of commitment are non-performative: they do not bring about the effects they name" for historically white institutions (2012, 17). I fully agree with this sentiment but want to push at such statements for purposes *not* for "appreciation, tolerance, and equality of others" but to highlight antiBlack racism, to engage in viral Blackness, and to employ Black annotation in an effort to center Blackness for subversion.

"Appreciation" of difference requires recognition of the worth of "others": a request by those in power to assign such value means an enfolding in the genres of Western Man—the kind of enfolding that Sylvia Wynter presses us to avoid (1994a, 10). Wynter's "A Black Studies Manifesto" articulates clearly that operating in terms of such an order, where difference measures in relation to Western bourgeois man, means "our continued complicity with its *truths of power*—whether in its mainstream form or in the now proposed 'multicultural' variants" (7). The Black feminist calls for epistemic rupture through Black studies. Such rupture means that we cannot continue to "define our liberation in terms of a canon or multiculturalization of knowledge," which "simply serves to continue our destruction as a population group" (9). Hashtags as Black rhetoric facilitate, mark, and open space for such epistemic rupture; they cull a place and a no place, a para/ontological thought and a no thought always evolving. Greene Wade (2017) also emphasizes how viral Blackness moves against such acquiescence. In its spread, worlds make possible alternative ways of non/being. Hashtags in this way may not just serve as objects of study but as forms of rhetorical performance that can make alternate realities through the entangled narratives that they permeate.

"Tolerance," the endurance, allowance, willingness to put up with difference will not stop antiBlackness. The mere existence of different beings alongside those who carry histories of commodifying, manipulating, and exploiting those different beings by creating the very controlling categories of difference offer Black folk only more of the same. "Equality" suggests even playing fields / conditions exist; they do not. Rights, status, and opportunities always already operate with/in disproportionate logics in the Western world and can serve to lionize oppressive respectability politics. The Civil Rights movement in the United States offers an easy example of how notions/goals of equality can serve such means. So even if such diversity language did, in fact, perform to bring about intended impacts, pursuing them sacrifices precious space, time, and energy to work/live otherwise.

In light of these institutional aims, the hashtagging assignment could perhaps be understood "as theft, a criminal act" (Harney and Moten 2013, 28), though a very public one. While it does not exemplify what interdisciplinary scholar Stefano Harney and Black studies philosopher Fred Moten call Black "fugitive study" in "the undercommons of the university," it sheepishly enacts some of their study's qualities. For Harney and Moten, fugitive study steals resources from the university to create subversive collectives/thought-spaces (undercommons) that harness unprofessionalization, that work against neoliberal/bourgeois individualism. The scholars explain that "to enter this space is to inhabit the ruptural and enraptured disclosure of the commons that fugitive enlightenment enacts, the criminal, matricidal, queer, in the cistern, on the stroll of the stolen life, the life stolen by enlightenment and stolen back, where the commons give refuge, where the refuge gives commons" (28). Entering the deep ecologies of Tumblr, of protest tags related to #BlackLivesMatter, of the historically white classroom, of the temporal/sociocultural turn pre- and postdating the election of Donald Trump, and of those in between means to enter a different kind of commons, yet one might still endeavor with/in them to *steal back* space/s from the white university. Paradoxically positioned by the institution to engage in diversity and race talk, I take these opportunities with the specialized theme of the course, centering Black antiracism through the topic "Modes of Resistance." Students read primary and secondary material authored predominantly by Black writers, scholars, poets, musical artists, activists, filmmakers, and podcasters. The final line of our course theme description reminds participants that "our readings will acknowledge that our contemporary understandings of American resistance narratives both pre- and post-Ferguson have come to be shaped by the #BlackLivesMatter movement." Through this sentiment, I hope to orient students via the movement, informed heavily by Black feminist politics, so that our analyses/reading/writing of texts interrogate inter/relations between those texts and the post-Ferguson cultural moment.[17]

The "Tumblr as Commonplace Book" assignment functions as a semester-long project that combines digital media remix composition, critical thinking, and analytical writing through the use of hashtags and "reblogging."[18] On the second day of class I do a short demo on setting up a Tumblr blog, working through the site's privacy policy before highlighting the following assignment guidelines:

1. Students are asked to set up a Tumblr blog (either set to public or private) at www.tumblr.com.[19] They then share their blog's URL on the Discussion Activity board on [MwSU's online learning management system] with fellow students. Students should "follow" their classmates' blogs and the instructor's blog.

2. For every text discussed in class (provided on MwSU's online learning management system), students should pick their favorite line, image, sentences, lyrics, and so forth, and post quoted material onto their Tumblr page before we read that text in class. For alphabetic material, they should quote directly. For images, they should screenshot.[20] For multimodal texts, they can choose either. In either case, they should name the source and the author in their posts.

3. Along with the quotations or screenshots posted, students should use a series of hashtags to describe and analyze each text.

4. On days when "Reblogs" are due, students should locate a peer's post that they find interesting and reblog it to their own blogs with two to three sentences of explanation as to why they found it interesting. Reblogged posts can use hashtags as well.

5. As indicated on the syllabus, the Tumblr blog will be examined twice during the semester for completion and adherence to post format (as opposed to content).

The central purposes of this project are

1. To get students to begin analyzing what they find most interesting in a text through hashtagging: with those details categorized/described as concise, digestible concepts, each demonstrating an interpretation of that text and allowing for further readings with conjunctional hashtags

2. To use hashtags for practical composition and research purposes: as the basis for in class discussion, for foreseeing and preparing for difficult and controver-

sial topics, for terms in library searches; in coming up with research proposals and identifying topics and artifacts of interest to each particular student, and as a repository of info for their final papers

3. To engage students with ongoing critical discussions of hashtags as activism, such as debates on the #BlackLivesMatter, #Ferguson, and #[X]SoWhite movements, reflected on the course syllabus in articles by Jones, Faithful, and Bonilla & Rosa

4. To create a digital classroom where students interact with their peers without instructor input

This project aims to conceptualize hashtags as a tool for analysis, research, and curation, as well as to involve participants in understanding how tags work as a form of activism, especially for marginalized communities. Students might grasp how the everyday utilization of popular social media websites involves reading/writing/thinking analytically that can create, spur, and effect material change, illustrating a student/writer's sociopolitical agency realized through composition and critical thinking. They could also begin to understand the classroom space—both in-person and online—as a communal one, in which all members might choose to play a role in Black activism, solidarity, and actively pursue social justice.

~~~~~~

I read a cross-section of student hashtags in two sections of this second-year writing course, which I taught in the autumn 2016 and spring 2017 semesters (from August 2016 to May 2017). The racial make-up of my classrooms across both semesters was as follows: 30 students identified as white; 6 students identified as non-Black students of color' 5 students identified as Black.[21] For the purposes of this analysis, I collected and combed through 41 Tumblr blogs (21 from the autumn semester, 20 from the spring semester), all set to "public," looking specifically for instances where students initiate the kinds of relational, ecological reading of racialized texts that the assignment encourages. Such instances might be consistent use of the same tag across one student blog; deployments of already existing popular hashtags (such as #Ferguson), along with inventive or unconventional tags on the same post; tags that riff on preexisting/well-known ones (such as #allblacklivesmatter); tags that cut across multiple student blogs; and tags employed with multiple different associated primary text material. While I focus on examples of deep ecological composition, my emphasis does not aim to center notions of "success" at fulfilling the assignment's goals; rather, I illustrate students' pursuing performance/making of alternate meanings of Blackness that make them counter/public pedagogues.

Creating/Negotiating Relational Meaning

#blacklivesmatter #ferguson #police #policebrutality #innocent #unnecessaryforce #racism

1 note Jan 12th, 2017

TCB37 OLSON POST

"When they work together, this collective is proving adept at bringing about a wide range of sociopolitical changes. It doesn't take much effort to get users to rally together behind causes that may have an impact on their lives."

JONES, "IS TWITTER THE UNDERGROUND RAILROAD OF ACTIVISM?" (2013)

#community #together #racism #change #revolution #socialmedia #equality #blacklivesmatter

Jan 20th, 2017

TCB37 JONES POST

Because hashtags build meaning-making connections between texts, while being texts themselves, understanding them as reading/writing in the writing/composition classroom reveals possibilities to create relational meaning. These relations can develop between texts in an individual student's blog, as well as with other students' posts in our online classroom community, along with communities that already exist on Tumblr who deploy the tags a particular poster might pick up. These connections (and fractures between them) provide evidence of the deep rhetorically ecological prospects that hashtags promote in producing and navigating meaning across people, cultures, contexts, histories, associations, and spaces. Take student blog tcb37, for example. The student uses #blacklivesmatter a number of times throughout the semester to demonstrate, create, and negotiate dynamic meanings of the phrase (and by extension the movement) within the context of their digital commonplace book.

With a highly publicized photograph taken by Scott Olson (2014) from the Ferguson Uprising depicting a Black dreadlocked person with hands up being approached by numerous police officers in military riot gear, the student uses #blacklivesmatter, #ferguson, #police, #policebrutality, #innocent, #unneces-saryforce, #racism. They also employ #blacklivesmatter to analyze a line from an online article by Feminista Jones (2013) on Twitter as a modern-day underground railroad for activism. With the movement's hashtag in the second instance, tcb37 uses #community, #together, #racism, #change, #revolution, #socialmedia, and #equality. Using #blacklivesmatter in each case, the student creates a multitude of active, fluid connections: between police brutality and community, between ideas about unnecessary force and social media, between Ferguson and ideas of revolution. These connections spur discursive relationships that allow for further meaning-making and promote class discussion for me as an instructor f/or fur-ther artifact analysis by students. Questions easily arise from these juxtapositions; for instance: What role does police brutality play in preexisting Black communi-ties or in forming new (versions of) community? How has the use of unnecessary force impacted the cultures of social media spaces? How might the events of the Ferguson Uprising be or not be considered a "revolution" in US racial politics? These fracturing questions highlight—through an image of social death and an article actively searching for metaphorical connections between slave escape and social media—possibilities for "imagining that the work of Black annotation" can uncover "a counter to abandonment, another effort to try to look, to try to really see" (Sharpe 2016, 117). Functioning in fractures between contextuality and chronology (Benovitz 2010, 124), these readings/meanings cut across temporal-ities/spatialities, operating as points of connectivity and disjuncture amidst tex-tual artifacts, their associations, and the commonplaces used to index them.

"I didn't notice the size nor nothing else
only the color. And
there are tapes to prove that, too."
"POWER," LORDE (1974)

#racism #policebrutality #evidence #injustice #blacklivesmatter #institutionalizedracism
Feb 14th, 2017
TCB37 LORDE "POWER" POST

In another example from tcb37, the student again deploys #blacklivesmatter, but on an excerpt from the Lorde poem "Power" (1974). With the lines "I didn't notice the size nor nothing else / only the color. And / there are tapes to prove that, too," they deploy #racism, #policebrutality, #evidence, #injustice, #institutionalizedracism. These tags form further deep rhetorically ecological connections between notions of what counts as evidence in legal cases that involve racialized instances of police killings of Black folks, while also highlighting and interrogating the function of institutions in such incidents. The hashtags also link a poem from 1974 about the 1973 killing of a ten-year-old Black child with the events of Ferguson in 2014 through the tags #racism and #policebrutality. That historical association pivotally opens space for the student (or other students or public visitors) to understand the genealogies of oppression that exist in chronologically disparate incidents of police brutality—a patterning kind of analysis that can inform future rhetorical engagements with these topics in this classroom and elsewhere. The connections also offer insight into anti/Blackness as a/temporal and legalized injustice through cross-contextual bonds. Even within the one blog, these relational meanings help to facilitate understandings of Black resistance not tied to *singular* historical events, but building through a multitude of individuals, spaces, events, and temporalities. The use of hashtag composition offers avenues for fostering such dynamic reading/writing/thinking.

"However, in contrast to this body of literature whose celebration of women's power is often accompanied by a lack of attention to the importance of power as domination, Black women's experiences as mothers, community other mothers, educators, church leaders, labor union center-women, and community leaders seem to suggest that power as energy can be fostered by creative acts of resistance."

PATRICIA HILL COLLINS, "BLACK FEMINIST THOUGHT
IN THE MATRIX OF DOMINATION" ([1990] 2000)

#afrocentricfeminism #knowledgeispower #oppression #empowered
#community #individualbiography #resistdomination #suppressed
1 note Feb 7th, 2017

TCB22 HILL COLLINS POST

Another blogger in this course section of second-year writing, on their page, tcb22, uses #community on one of their posts, creating a connection with tcb37 across blogs within the digital space of our Tumblr class. Tcb22 turns to the tag with a quotation from Patricia Hill Collins's ([1990] 2000) *Black Feminist Thought* on how Black women's various roles in labor unions, churches, and their communities demonstrate how creative/concatenated resistance can undercut a lack of focus on the ways that domination is related to power. The post uses #afrocentricfeminism, #knowledgeispower, #oppression, #empowered, #individualbiography, #resistdomination, and #suppressed, along with #community. In establishing relationships between an academic/theoretical text by a Black feminist thinker with a popular online article about the possibilities for coalition on Twitter through the common #community, the hashtag offers students and Tumblr's general publics windows to notice, analyze, or even question how academic philosophy relates to social media activism. It also ties scholarly Black feminist thought with digital content produced by a Black feminist activist working through different communities toward social justice through Black resistance. From tcb22, #knowledgeispower becomes linked with #socialmedia via #community, relaying connective meaning through these deep ecologically implicated ideas. #community also links #individualbiography with knowledge-making, agency, and resistance, culturing those ties with #afrocentricfeminism while connecting to tcb37's notions of coalition-building through #change and togetherness (through #together in tcb37's Jones Post). For students and Tumblr's publics, the associations between these concepts can stimulate even more meaning-making in further thinking through the bridges between how communal knowledge on social media relates to "power" (systemic or otherwise).

In Tumblr's digital spaces, hashtags additionally present students with venues to make meaning in relation to other blogs not associated with the second-year writing course and their classmates. That affordance means that their reading/writing/thinking enters and shapes counter/public deep rhetorical ecologies, inherently dissolving the typical insiderness of classroom writing / composition. Because of the broad activist use of Tumblr, tags like #community, #oppression, #policebrutality, and #racism provide occasions for public meaning-making. #equality for instance, at the time of my first writing of this chapter, references blogs such as feimineach's (2018), and its article on institutionalizing gender budgeting; a post by pro-Black user i-will-personally-eat-yourhand (2018) and their call for more Asian representation in Western media; and news about transgender representation at a recent award show by user reginad1984 (2018). Because of the ephemeral nature of social media spaces, such examples have surely already changed, but encultured in a writing/composition classroom that centers (viral) Blackness, Black annotation, Black artifacts, antiracist pedagogies, and conversations about racialized politics, the tags students produce will likely engender such results beyond any particular temporal/spatial moment.

In composing hashtags, students thus open up their classroom education to a host of digital, activist, relational possibilities beyond the artifacts they read/write/analyze. McGuire's study on her students' application of Tumblr in a professional writing course similarly argues that "having access to a space where students can observe a diverse group of voices talking about diverse issues in ways they may have not seen before can be critical to helping students understand . . . how the rhetorical situation of communication on social media can be much larger than their immediate surroundings and can contribute to much larger cultural conversations" (2017, 120). The deep rhetorically ecological meanings that tags create/negotiate in such spaces suggest that students can engage in a mode of meaning-making that enacts/mobilizes these broader possibilities of digital activism, viral Blackness, and Black annotation.

"Tag it and bag it": Conceptualizing Key Terms

"Subjugated knowledges, such as Black women's culture of resistance, develop in cultural contexts controlled by oppressed groups. Dominant groups aim to replace subjugated knowledge with their own specialized thought because they realize that gaining control over this dimension of subordinate groups' lives simplifies control."

PATRICIA HILL COLLINS, BLACK FEMINIST THOUGHT: KNOWLEDGE, CONSCIOUSNESS, AND THE POLITICS OF EMPOWERMENT ([1990] 2000)

#domination #racism #feminism #sexism

Sep 23rd, 2016

TCB20 HILL COLLINS POST

"Bitch I'm me, hundred on the wrist, I ski
Art on the wall, Basqui, fuck who see Look
at you fake dope dealers"

NICKI MINAJ, "LOOKIN' ASS"

#feminism #powerful #successfulwomen

Sep 21st, 2016

TCB20 MINAJ POST

"I did not come to play with you hoes,
haha I came to slay, bitch I like cornbreads
and collard greens, bitch Oh, yes, you
besta believe it"

MESSY MYA AND BIG FREEDIA FROM BEYONCÉ, "FORMATION"

#powerfulwomen #independent #feminism

1 note Sep 23rd, 2016

TCB20 BEYONCÉ POST

"The queen of rap, slayin with queen Bey If
you ain't on the team, you playin' for team
D 'Cause we A-listers, we paid sisters This
watch right here done faced blizzards"

BEYONCÉ FT. NICKI MINAJ

#feminism #powerfulwomen #equality

1 note Sep 21st, 2016

TCB20 BEYONCÉ FEATURING MINAJ POST

"but i've been watching from the
slaughterhouse. ever since you named me
edible. tossed in a cookie at the end. lucky
man. go & take what's yours. name
yourself archaeologist"

FRANNY CHOI, "TO THE MAN WHO SHOUTED"

#feminism #sexism #equality

1 note Oct 17th, 2016

TCB20 CHOI POST

Hashtag composition also provides means by which participants might understand broader evolving terms, philosophies, and concepts in antiracist work. While most students bring to the writing classroom ideas about what "racism," "equity," or even "neoliberalism" mean, hashtag use allows students to actively pursue the *practice* of and *engagement* in meaning-making. For instance, a general understanding at the beginning of the semester often held by students about "feminism" is that it translates to women and men having "equal" opportunities. As students deploy the tag throughout the course in hashtag compositions, a multiplicity of relations arises, which then broadens and concatenates interpretations of the term. These classroom activities echo the work of viral Black feminist tags like Mikki Kendall's #SolidarityIsForWhiteWomen, which continue fracturing work of activists like Lorde in challenging problematic theories/practices of "white feminism," while "actively redefining the function of the hashtag beyond means of tracking and archiving data" (Conley 2017, 26).

On tcb20, one student deploys #feminism across five texts they read during the spring 2017 semester. These include theory by Patricia Hill Collins ([1990] 2000), lyrics by Beyoncé and Nicki Minaj (2014), lyrics from another Beyoncé track (2016) and by Nicki Minaj (2014), and poetry by Korean American queer writer Franny Choi (2014). Along with lyrics focused on ostentatious displays of wealth, the student uses #powerful, #powerfulwomen, and #successfulwomen.

Although these tags play into neoliberal notions of economic gain as "success," other hashtags used in conjunction with #feminism undercut these ideas. #sexism links Choi's (2014) poem about being racially catcalled with a quote from Hill Collins (1990) about subjugated knowledges and their suppression by dominant groups. Connecting a poem that stands in defiance of sexual harassment with theorization about Black feminist thought systems suggests potentials to understand spaces between abstractions about feminisms as ideologies and everyday manifestations of woman of color resistance, all while they also engage public definition of the terms for resistant purposes.

> "Momma taught me good home training
> My Daddy taught me how to love my haters
> My sister taught me I should speak my mind
> My man made me feel so God damn fine"
>
> "FLAWLESS (REMIX)," BEYONCÉ AND NICKI MINAJ

In order for men and women to ever be equal, feminism cannot just be a movement only supported by women. Feminism and confidence are learned from a young age from the most important people in a women's [sic] life, meaning men and family members also need to recognize equality and never make any women [sic] feel like she isn't worthy. Feminism starts and ends with the daughters, mothers, sisters, girlfriends and wives in the world.

#wokeuplikethis #flawless #support #feminism
Sep 20th, 2016

TCB05 BEYONCÉ POST

Tcb05's blog uses #feminism alongside #wokeuplikethis, #support, and #flawless to read the following lines of lyrics from Beyoncé and Nicki Minaj's (2014) "Flawless (Remix)": "Momma taught me good home training / My Daddy taught me how to love my haters / My sister taught me I should speak my mind / My man made me feel so God damn fine." They notably cull two of their tags from other (not quoted) lyrics of the track (#wokeuplikethis and #flawless), which represent versions of already-existing popular hashtags—and thus related deep rhetorical ecologies—that social media users typically attach to body-positive selfies (sometimes as feminist resistance to oppressive/normative beauty standards). Those links spotlight the interconnected Black feminist message of such rhetorical ecologies. Whereas tcb20 negotiates the meanings of feminism with power through #sexism, #powerfulwomen, and #successfulwomen, tcb05 contextualizes feminism with practical application—with ideas about self-confidence and the function of communal support.

Tcb05 also blurbs their own prose response to emphasize the support of allies as crucial to the aims of feminism. The poster's supplemental response demonstrates their interpretation of the material while acting as their own pedagogical gesture—destabilizing student/teacher boundaries of normative classroom spaces. Additionally, putting the connections made via #feminism on tcb05 in conversation with tcb20's focus on resisting #sexism by bringing awareness to catcalling, these hashtags make visible the potential connective spaces between their respective interpretations; those links put forward understandings of feminist resistance as self-confidence and allied support. But these connective spaces continue to evolve with further iterations of any of these hashtags and future tags associated with them and so on. Indeed, "hashtags push the boundaries of specific discourses. They expand the space of discourse along the lines that they simultaneously name and mark out" (Rambukkana 2015, 30). Such capacities for expansion make hashtag composition a valuable antiracist tool for writing instructors; they represent distinct possibilities for learning/engaging in fluid, deep rhetorically ecological meaning-making already existing and widely applicable beyond the writing classroom.

> "Advocating the mere tolerance of difference between women is the grossest reformism. It is a total denial of the creative function of difference in our lives. Difference must be not merely tolerated, but seen as a fund of necessary polarities between which our creativity can spark like a dialectic."
>
> LORDE, "THE MASTER'S TOOLS WILL NEVER
> DISMANTLE THE MASTER'S HOUSE"

#blackfeminism #standupforourdifferences #lgbtq+rights #endracismandhomophobia #independence

Jan 28th, 2017

TCB22 LORDE POST

> "Now we hear that it is the task of women of Color to educate white women—in the face of tremendous resistance—as to our existence, our differences, our relative roles in our joint survival. This is a diversion of energies and a tragic repetition of racist patriarchal thought."
>
> "THE MASTER'S TOOLS WILL NEVER DISMANTLE
> THE MASTER'S HOUSE," AUDRE LORDE

#feminism #whitefeminism #blackfeminism #fightthepatriarchy #racism #societalnorms

Feb 14th, 2017

TCB37 LORDE POST

Other bloggers, such as tcb22 and tcb37, make active distinctions between #feminism, #blackfeminism, #afrocentricfeminism (appearing in their Hill Collins Post presented earlier), and #whitefeminism. Along with quotations from the same influential feminist text—Lorde's "The Master's Tools Will Never Dismantle the Master's House" (1984, 113)—each makes pivotal rhetorical choices with their hashtags that shape the meaning of these tags, Lorde's essay, and other texts they use with them. On one hand, tcb22 reads their excerpt from "The Master's Tools," about using difference creatively instead of papering it over with calls for "tolerance," with #blackfeminism, #standupforourdifferences, #lgbtq+rights, #endracismandhomophobia, and #independence. Tcb37, on the other hand, selects #feminism, #whitefeminism, #blackfeminism, #fightthepatriarchy, #racism, and #societalnorms to analyze Lorde's resistance to a continuing history of Black women and women of color being asked to educate white women on difference. Tcb22's tags root its calls for action in #blackfeminism, while tcb37's attempt to break down Lorde's message in considering its main points. Yet these meanings connect through #blackfeminism, which then further relates through the popular use of #feminism by tcb37 and other students to interpret activist material. The interconnected meanings created with these students' exercising of varied tags spotlight the dynamic possibilities hashtag composition presents as students' interpretations work to join together/dismantle meaning from different vantage points and further promote possibilities for viral Blackness through the evolving (re)conceptualization of terms like #feminism.

As students navigate terms like "feminism," "racism," or "stereotypes," they also gather a repository of information from both primary and secondary material with which they can build further analytical investigations. When we approach Research Proposal assignments, I steer participants to see the distinct possibilities that hashtags offer as field sites of investigation, which reading by cultural/linguistic anthropologists Yarimar Bonilla and Jonathan Rosa (2015) bolsters and helps to explain. Students then review that store of curated hashtags, browsing their archives to determine where their interests lie within the course theme. Because Tumblr hashtags clicked through from a students' main blog page unpack an existing archive from that particular page, students can easily access numerous connections that they make and continue to make through hashtag composition. They can also use relational tags to deepen their interests on a particular topic by employing these terms in library searches. #feminism's relationship to #support or #lgbtq+rights, for example, might then help to fund further interests for tcb22's research process. The hashtags' practical research purposes tied with outlined activist meanings and consequences present a multiplicity of possibilities for their utilization as digital compositions in antiracist writing classrooms.

Ma(r)king #BlackLivesMatter

"When America pulls open the curtain of white supremacy, the truth emerges much like the Wizard of Oz—not only do Black lives matter, their lives are the reason that white lives still exist."

"#BLACKLIVESMATTER KITCHEN TALK," RACHAEL FAITHFUL (2014)

#blackculture #blacklivesmatter #stereotype #corruption #violence #survival #civilrights #racialpolitics

Feb 20th, 2017

TCB22 FAITHFUL POST

#blacklivesmatter #policeforce #innocent #stereotype

Jan 11th, 2017

TCB22 OLSON POST[22]

Is Twitter the Underground Railroad of Activism?

"Black Twitter" can be described as a collective of active, primarily African-American Twitter users who have created a virtual community that participates in continuous real-time conversations. When they work together, this collective is proving adept at bringing about a wide range of sociopolitical changes. It doesn't take much effort to get users to rally together behind causes that may have an impact on their lives. "We don't need a whole bunch of background information to fight injustice—if you tell us about a problem, we can fact-check online within minutes to verify, and be down the road on tackling inequality," says Angela Rye, director of strategic partnerships at IMPACT.

—FEMINISTA JONES (2013)

#Unity #Protest #InjusticeinAmerica #BlacklivesMatter
#VirtualBlackCommunity #SocialChange #NoLongerSlaves
Sep 2nd, 2016

TCB11 JONES POST

#BlackLivesMatter remains an important touchstone throughout each iteration of this particular second-year writing course. The social movement's application and spread through tags undergird the politics of our using them for activist pedagogies. So how do students specifically deploy or manipulate the tag through their interpretative note-taking to become parts of that particular deep rhetorical ecology? Of course, they often used the tag with content that directly addresses the Ferguson Uprising or articles about the movement creating relations with logically germane ideas—such as tcb22's associated tags #blackculture, #stereotype, #corruption, #violence, #survival, #racialpolitics, #policeforce, and #innocent on their Faithful and Olson posts. But some students push beyond these readily available connections and contexts. Tcb11, for example, negotiates temporalities/ histories with their usage of #BlackLivesMatter. In one instance, to read Jones's article on Twitter activism, the blogger deploys it with #VirtualBlackCommunity and #NoLongerSlaves (Jones 2013). These tags actively position the movement between a violent history of bondage and the digitized possibility of collectivity; through the fracture, the hashtags conjure a kind of conscious multi-situated-ness in the meaning of #BlackLivesMatter: one in a present that looks (and is) forward while looking (and being) back in the past. This fracturing evidences the "wake work" of Black annotation, making "Black life visible, if only momentarily, through the optic of the door" (Sharpe 2016, 123). Hashtags can open these doors.

> But we refuse to believe that the bank of justice is bankrupt. We refuse to believe that there are insufficient funds in the great vaults of opportunity of this nation. So we've come to cash this check, a check that will give us upon demand the riches of freedom and the security of justice.
>
> We have also come to this hallowed spot to remind America of the fierce urgency of now. This is no time to engage in the luxury of cooling off or to take the tranquilizing drug of gradualism. Now is the time to make real the promises of democracy. Now is the time to rise from the dark and desolate valley of segregation to the sunlit path of racial justice. Now is the time to lift our nation from the quicksands of racial injustice to the solid rock of brotherhood.
>
> MARTIN LUTHER KING JR., "I HAVE A DREAM SPEECH" (1963)

#Justice #BlackRights #Urgency #TakeAction #BlackLivesStillMatter
#Freedom #UnityandBrotherhood

Aug 30th, 2016

TCB11 KING POST

#blacklivesstillmatter #MichaelBrown #SayHisName #PoliceBrutality
#Justice #HandsUpDontShoot

Aug 28th, 2016

TCB11 OLSON POST

The same blogger deploys #BlackLivesStillMatter, which also plays with the temporality of the movement's meanings. The supplemental "still" suggests the fight for Black liberation as ongoing but might trouble particular temporal meanings in the movement's titular tag. The revised tag begs the question: How does the ethos of this declaration function if the assertion that Black lives matter suggests that they don't or haven't in relation to white supremacy in the United States? Does "still" acting as an adjective or even a verb rather than an adverb posit further ways to think through a kind of object-being of Blackness within that oppressive framework? The fractures mean. Tcb11 tags Olson's Ferguson photograph with it, along with the tags #MichaelBrown, #SayHisName, #PoliceBrutality, #Justice, #HandsUpDontShoot. The tags #Justice and #BlackLivesStillMatter, however, recur with an excerpt from Dr. Martin Luther King Jr.'s (1963) "I Have a Dream" speech, along with #BlackRights, #Urgency, #TakeAction, #Freedom, and #UnityandBrotherhood. Across these instances, the blogger's insistence on

71

the Black Lives Matter movement (and the Civil Rights movement) continuing to have relevance—by adding "still" to its phraseology—has ripple effects on its relational meanings with surrounding tags and textual artifacts. Let's dig deeper.

Linking #BlackLivesStillMatter with a photograph from the Ferguson Uprising to King's refusal to believe that the United States cannot pay its debts to Black citizens through voting rights fractures histories of Black US activism and emphasizes the "still" in #BlackLivesStillMatter. Tcb22's annotation #civilrights on a post quoting multidisciplinary healing artist Rachel Faithful's (2014) dialogic analysis parallels Tcb11's tag. The markers emphasize how a hashtag works as a "node of continued context across media, conversations, and locales . . . [emerging] temporally, self-developing through time, pointing to itself as it points to the other texts it marks as within its ambit" (Rambukkana 2015, 30). Moreover, these tags suggest opportunities for classroom intervention to explain the philosophical discontinuities between the Civil Rights movement and the Black Lives Matter movement that activists have insisted be made clear. Hip-hop artist Tef Poe declared the latter's disjunctions from the former in protest to a speech by the then NAACP president during "Ferguson October" events in 2014 (Taylor 2016, 161). Black Lives Matter cofounder Garza's (2014) "Herstory" outlines how the current movement breaks away from the Civil Rights movement by centering Black queer women, Black feminist ideology, and countering narrow visions of Black identity and liberation. Upon recognizing the possibility for conflation between the movements, I adjusted future syllabi to further drive home these important differences through active comparison (a kind of Black feminist dialogue), including Black feminist political scientist/activist Cathy Cohen's (2015) lecture on the theoretical and temporal differences between them. These hashtag compositions present opportunities for (re)visioning Black/antiracist pedagogies.

Tcb11 offers more cross-contextual possibilities and problematics for viral Blackness along with transforming #BlackLivesMatter to a tag like #BlackLives StillMatter. The first instance, #BlackLivesStillMatter in tcb11's Olson post, draws on popular tags associated with the movement like #HandsUpDontShoot, while changing #SayHerName—importantly popularized on Twitter to spotlight the lack of attention placed on Black women victims of police violence (Freelon, McIlwain, and Clark 2016, 83)—to #SayHisName. While the change might endeavor to gender the victim in Olson's photograph male, it reinscribes the omissions that #SayHerName attempts to address. This instance illustrates that while hashtags do bring with them subversive potentials, such subversion might turn back in on themselves, even with possible activist rhetoric, ethos, and agency and the described classroom context. However, in this fracture, where we might understand the weight of white heteropatriarchal insistence intervening to regender a Black feminist tag, generative, pedagogical opportunities again arise. Here lies an opening for the space of the classroom to enter and, in particular, for the mobilization of the Black feminist epistemological tenet of the use of dialogue to assess knowledge claims. As Hill Collins stipulates, "Not to be confused with adversarial debate, the use of dialogue has deep roots in African-based oral traditions and in African-American culture" ([1990] 2000, 261). #SayHisName gives rise to possibilities for a (material) classroom discussion on that tag and its associated movement, its histories, and its origins and for re/orienting students toward #BlackLivesMatter's Black feminist ideologies and motives. Likewise, in the digital space, possible responses on social media to such a tag could reveal similar potentially educative moments. The fracture, digitized and/or material, rips open a space in the deep ecology between Blackness and its non/being for para/ontological Black resistance.

"#BlackLivesMatter is not #BlackCisMenMatter"

RACHAEL FAITHFUL, "#BLACKLIVESMATTER KITCHEN TALK" (2014)

#equalityforall #allblacklivesmatter #discussion #inclusion

Oct 5th, 2016

TCB05 FAITHFUL POST

Tbco5's transmutation of #BlackLivesMatter to #allblacklivesmatter also raises questions through its fractures in linguistic and textual associations. Garza's "Herstory" addresses the phrase and hashtag "All Lives Matter" as a racialized erasure. But Garza's point of contention lies not with the meanings of "all"; instead, she points out that "when we deploy 'All Lives Matter' as to correct an intervention specifically created to address anti[B]lackness, we lose the ways in which the state apparatus has built a program of genocide and repression mostly on the backs of Black people" (Garza 2014). Tbco5's change, however, attempts to invert the erasing "all," pointing to the marginalizing gaps in the ways #BlackLivesMatter has come to be contextualized in mainstream media. The student blogger uses #allblacklivesmatter with #equalityforall, #discussion, and #inclusion, but does so to index a quotation from Faithful's article that reads "#BlackLivesMatter is not #BlackCisMenMatter" (2014, 252)—protesting the erasure of Black trans/gender nonconforming lives from popular understandings of the movement's purview. The hashtags' relations to such a statement illustrates the possibilities these digital tools yield for coalitional Black resistance, viral Blackness, and Black annotation, upending the universalizing and whitewashing "all" of #alllivesmatter for an appeal to "broaden" mainstream interpretations of the movement. The student's potential awareness in their turn of phrase helps to show not only prospective futures that hashtag composition advance but also its rhetorically fluid and deep ecological promises for meaning-making/negotiation. Notably, however, the appeal to "equality" in #equalityforall, suggests work still to be done if the desires for viral Blackness lie in a Wynterian conception of systemic oppression.

"Tag, you(,) it"

Hashtag composition, as a form of remediated commonplacing tool, suggests much for writing/composition instructors whose settings afford students access to such technologies. As reading, hashtags join with previous relationships that a concept and/or interpretation might already foster in a social media space via deep rhetorical ecologies. As writing, they operationalize those relations to build upon them and advance/negotiate new(er) meaning. As note-taking, they offer archives of knowledge that stress collectivity and in-built digital communities that a student/writer can tap into. But these modes of engagement function simultaneously, animating these processes with critical thinking and creative expression to suggest hashtag composition's versatile application as an activity for writing classrooms and beyond.

Moreover, given the tool's culture/history, it reveals accessible avenues for antiracist energy and agency, particularly when contextualized in movements seeking public justice for Black folk, people of color, and other marginalized groups. While hashtags indeed also bring with them the constraints of public vulnerability, scrutiny, and/or un/intentional employment for neoliberal profit and oppressive ideologies, this chapter advances the notion of hashtags as a dynamic Black rhetoric and literacy tool in writing/composition classrooms. However, as its second section shows, the politics surrounding the tool remains just as vital as the tool itself—in fact, in the case of hashtags, it arguably highlights its cultural relevance.

As a marginalized literacy, hashtags can "suggest a fleeting yet nonetheless enduring coalitional moment as they manifest across space and time as performative political actions meant to protest temporally, spatially, and historically inflected racialized violences" (Prasad 2016, 67). Yet, they might express more. As a Black rhetoric, contextualized in an antiracist learning environment centering Blackness, encouraging viral Blackness and Black annotation, these tags sometimes present dynamic, deep rhetorically ecological windows for Black non/being with/in the fissures of Fanonian fracture. They might therefore help us grasp shifting Blackness and temporal instability in such grabbing, even while under the ever-surveilling gaze of white institutions and multinational corporations. Instructors should be mindful of their appropriation, destructive mutations, and co-optation in explicitly offering anti/racist cultural context for these tools in relation to anti/Blackness. They should enact an awareness of the ways in which the tags might undercut neoliberal value systems rather than strengthen them, if, of course, theirs is a project claiming antiracist motives. If not, destructive dominant cultures prevalent at historically white institutions can just as easily invert their agency to promote hegemonic "commonplace" ideology. We've heard the fake news. Let's unmake it.

3

"All my life I had to fight"

SHAPING #BLACKLIVESMATTER THROUGH LITERACY EVENTS

What does it mean to be Black in the United States today? Of course, there's no single, simple answer to that question. Yet documentaries, news specials, music, and even Black political leaders might try to give us one. In an age of Black Twitter, #BlackLivesMatter,[1] and sitcoms like ABC's *Black-ish*, the issue seems continuously raised. Is Cardi B Black? Is Meghan Markle Black? Who gets to decide? We know what Blackness is not—the public backlash to Rachel Dolezal's 'racial fluidity' has taught us that racial identity, though culturally fluid, still forces demarcating lines that distinguishes biological whiteness from Blackness.[2] Arguments abound as to why the widely accepted and used term "African American" implies that, at its core, the word "American" does not intrinsically include those in the United States of African ancestry—thus necessitating a hyphenating adjective. That term also fails to account for Black folk living in the United States who choose not to identify with the American nation, as well as those who do not have the privilege of that choice.[3] Hundreds of thousands of Black im/migrants in the United States, "documented" and "undocumented," fall into this category. Without even glossing the contested subject of cultural appropriation in relation to the primary question, we find ourselves in a sticky mess. But can we potentially turn to #BlackLivesMatter and its institutionalization to conceptualize means by which to read dynamic notions of relational, intersectional Blackness vis-à-vis state power in the post-Ferguson cultural moment?[4]

In March 2015, Cohen delivered "Whose Black Lives Matter? The Politics of Black Love and Violence," a public lecture at Midwestern State University (2015). She titles the third part of the talk "This is not the Civil Rights movement." Cohen uses the words and stances of activist Tory Russell of Hands Up United (interviewed on the PBS NewsHour in 2014) to explain #BlackLivesMatter responses to police brutality in the current cultural moment. The Black feminist scholar

DOI: 10.7330/9781646421473.c003

frames these responses as markedly different from the Civil Rights movement's approach to state violence, contextualizing the role that neoliberalist politics/ philosophies play into that difference. Russell pronounces:

> We more connected than most people think. This is not the Civil Rights move-ment. You can tell by how I got a hat on, my t-shirt, and how I rock my shoes. This is not the Civil Rights' movement. This is the oppressed people's movement. So, when you see us, you gon' see some gay folk, you gon' see some queer folk, you gon' see some poor Black folk, you gon' see some brown folk, you gon' see some white people. And we all out here for the same reasons. We wanna be free. We believe that we have the right over laws. I think the question we keep getting to is "What's legal?" We need to be talking about what's *right*. (PBS NewsHour 2014, emphasis mine)

The activist's assertion, in offering what Cohen describes as a "practical inter-sectionality," gives us a series of entry points into thinking about the modes in which #BlackLivesMatter works to produce/negotiate radical kinds of mean-ings through events. Paying attention to that meaning production/negotiation resists static, often oppressive institutional readings of race and Blackness. It demonstrates how we might both read and operationalize deep rhetorical ecol-ogies through (literacy) events in order to highlight the relation/ships between #BlackLivesMatter, history, and institutional power.[5] Moreover, the fractures in/between the non/being of Blackness coupled with their pulsating temporali-ties/histories conjure a lens for reading Blackness dynamically. Here I argue that the #BlackLivesMatter movement suggests the Black rhetoric of *inter(con)textual reading* as antiracist means.

Through this Black inter(con)textual reading, Russell highlights that connec-tions exist within the movement that are not readily noticeable—spotlighting the necessity for analysis of disparate events and non/beings within the movement to grasp its meanings, goals, and stimuli. The activist's reading urges us to be cogni-zant of interconnections between bodies, identities, movements, and meanings within deep ecologies. In other words, we should think of rhetorical situations as racialized, moving encounters between non/bodies always negotiating with other such encounters within larger contexts and histories—or ecologies. Elements in an ecology co-constitute its meanings/spaces through inter- and intra-activity (Barad 1996). Though feminist theorist Karen Barad names this concept "intra-action," I foreground Black feminist Wynter's (2005) ideas on sociogeny that these entangled (nature-culture/culture-nature) encounters between matter and meaning operate with/in notions of affect/desire determined by racialization. Here, in grappling with relationships between #BlackLivesMatter and the Civil Rights movement, Russell points to clothing: the camo baseball hat that reads "#Ferguson" in capitalized red letters, in relation to the black T-shirt (partially visualized) and shoes (not-visualized). On the one hand "#Ferguson" potentially alerts us to the significance of events following the shooting death of Michael Brown by Officer Darren Wilson and to digital assemblages on social media calling national attention to racial unrest in Missouri. On the other hand, the cap's camo pattern—especially in relation to Russell's T-shirt and the pronouncement of divergence from the Civil Rights movement—recalls the Black Liberation movement's militarization against state oppression in the 1960s and 1970s and material symbols associated with it. The histories of the Civil Rights movement, the Ferguson Uprising, the digital hashtag and its connotative connections, and the Black Power struggle interact through Russell's message and rhetoric to produce/negotiate the meanings of #BlackLivesMatter. Those histories are not always immediately inherent from the texts they produce/negotiate but become vital to understanding more fully the structural inter-/intra-/relations and intersections across, between, and underpinning racial power and Black meaning.

I continue to propose that within deep ecologies, those rhetorical interactions evolve continuously, but can be read through Fanonian fractures—where inferiority marks Blackness in contact with whiteness—and spaces around them that produce/negotiate moments/texts/shifts offering windows into Blackness' para/ontology. We perceive these bodies, texts, and/or non/beings (and their meanings) to be constantly shifting to understand rhetorical events and how they (re)construct cultural identity and connections in between identities. Those linkages—with/in spaces between Russell's cap, words, and "ways" of the body—engaged in rhetorical inter/intra-action might be considered relational, intersectional sites of meaning-making or knowledge production/negotiation of Blackness. How is Blackness gendered, classed, dis/abled, citizened, and/or sexualized in these moments? In doing the "wake work" that Sharpe calls for, I ask, "What does it mean to inhabit the Fanonian 'zone on non-Being' within and after slavery's denial of Black humanity?" (2016, 20). In Russell's insistence of having "the right over laws," we might re/turn temporally to wake work the hold of the Trans-Atlantic slave ship, the excess of Blackness' para/ontology—operating outside of whatever legal frameworks within which "Man" determines "man." In such social death across temporal deep ecologies, "We understand the compulsions of capital in our always-possible deaths. But those bodies nevertheless try to exceed those compulsions of capital. They, we, inhabit knowledge that the Black body is the sign of immi/a/nent death. These are accounts of the hold in the contemporary" (Sharpe 2016, 71). Through such accounts, we read how Black lives *matter*.

I should note, as Sharpe does, that "Wakes are processes" (21), so to read these fractures and the deep ecologies that they co-constitute and vice versa requires lens/es apt for such analysis: Black feminist relationality supported by the African indigenous philosophy of botho or Ubuntu. Alexander Weheliye's concept of "racializing assemblages," formulated via Wynter and Spillers's Black feminist relationality, "construes race not as a biological or cultural classification but as a set of sociopolitical processes that discipline humanity into full humans, not-quite-humans, and nonhumans" (Weheliye 2014, 4). Russell's description of the non/beings co-constituting the *movement*—through race, gender, sexuality, and class—demonstrates those ecological, relational "sociopolitical processes." Russell's thesis that "we more connected than most people think" animates the African indigenous botho, where interconnectedness and interrelations between non/beings stress mutual ecological responsibilities for environments. I strive to make Black lives matter by reading #BlackLivesMatter through its own terms, with/in its own environments.

In pinpointing the sites at which racial meaning is produced/negotiated within such processes, I invoke the field of literacy studies to remix aspects of the *literacy event*. The exigence for reading #BlackLivesMatter through literacy events motivates and characterizes Russell's motivations for protest: "We wanna be free." This desire, crystalized in Black feminist literacy as the practice of freedom (hooks 1994), the Combahee River Collective's conception that "if Black women were free, it would mean that everyone else would have to be free" ([1977] 2017, 23), and contemporary adoption of that motive by #BlackLivesMatter as a key philosophical tenet (Garza 2014) opens avenues for investigating these events as junctions for literacy. How might a motive to be free read/write/produce/nego-tiate meaning in such spaces? Using the literacy event in the workings of the deep rhetorical ecology offers a fundamentally fresh and complex way by which we might discuss meaning evolving with/in rhetorical situations.

Social phycologists Alonzo Anderson, William Teale, and Elette Estrada define the literacy event as "any action or sequence involving one or more per-sons in which the production and/or comprehension of print plays a role" (1980, 59). Linguistic anthropologist Shirley Brice Heath expands on that definition to underline that "in studying the literacy environment, researchers describe print material *available in the environment*, the individuals and activities that *surround* print, and ways in which people include print in their *ongoing* activities" (Heath [1982] 2001, 445; emphasis mine).[6] To reorient previous utilization to account for the dynamics of rhetorical ecologies across material and digital spaces, I pro-pose that we consider the literacy event in terms of print/textual as well as digital, bodily, and other communicative inter-/intra-actions. So, to use Heath's language of the literacy event in reading relational sites of meaning-making for Blackness within deep rhetorical ecologies, we should ask questions such as *What texts make up the rhetorical environments of the event in question? What identities and activities surround those texts and impinge on the ways in which its meanings evolve? And how do ongoing activities include that text or the individuals and activities that the text produces/negotiates?*[7]

In mobilizing these questions toward a Black feminist inter(con)textual analytic that demonstrates #BlackLivesMatter as a deep rhetorical ecology—one made up of ongoing fracturing literacy events that work to elucidate the relationship between Blackness and oppressive institutional power in the United States—I read three such literacy events. This chapter analyzes Garza's "Herstory of the #BlackLivesMatter Movement" (2014), Lamar's "Alright" (2015a), and Roberts's blacklivesmattersyllabus.com (2016) to consider how these events not only co-constitute the deep ecology of #BlackLivesMatter but also fashion a kind of rhetorical archive that continues the evolution of that ecology and its re/making of meaning. I choose these texts because they reflectively represent three central, yet fluid, stances on intersectional Blackness in relation to state power within the post-Ferguson moment: the *historical, populist,* and *pedagogical.* In media theory and cultural rhetorics, I bring an inter(con)textual approach to bear specifically through the deep rhetorical ecology, building on anthropologist Arjun Appadurai's calls for such a methodology of reading in *Modernity at Large* (1996), from which rhetorician Wendy S. Hesford draws in *Spectacular Rhetorics* (2011). In centering a Black feminist analytic and Black agency through my reading, I work dynamically in intersections between rhetorical theory and literacy studies.

Before approaching that analysis proper, however, the following section situates a tentative understanding of the *post-Ferguson* cultural moment,[8] predominantly as it relates to cultural moments chronologically antecedent to the emergence of the #BlackLivesMatter movement. That predominance emanates not primarily from the interests of this project, but from evolutions in these moments themselves. It also situates my upcoming rhetorical analysis of three literacy events within a framework that privileges Baker's notion of "critical memory" in Black modernity alongside Sharpe's (2016) wake work. Baker warns us that such memory reiteratively re/turns to the "illness, transgression, and contamination of the past" (1995, 3). Likewise, Sharpe tells us that "living in the wake means living the history and present of terror, from slavery to the present, as the ground for our everyday Black existence" (2016, 15). I pause to consider a few key chronologically anterior cultural moments playing into the evolution of one perceived as "post-Ferguson" in providing further ecological inter(con)text for my reading of #BlackLivesMatter. Such consideration illustrates how institutional confusion on race and Blackness along with *white public and institutional defensiveness* leads to notions of Blackness operationalized by #BlackLivesMatter's deep rhetorical ecology.

"Wouldn't you know / We been hurt, been down before"[9]

Russell's above declaration also suggests that the ways in which we have read Black resistance—and Blackness—in relation to systematic oppression in the past cannot be ahistorically applied to reading #BlackLivesMatter. The movement, unlike the Civil Rights movement, shifts focus from legal recognition as its motivating ideal. How institutions might come to the question of racial justice—for Russell, by asking "what's legal?"—forces us to reconsider exactly what white capitalist heteropatriarchal institutions confusingly promote as the meanings of race and Blackness in doling out that justice. If we look to governmental institutions, surely, we might find some "official" stance on the meanings of race and/or Blackness they operationalize.[10] The US Department of Commerce—the branch of the US government responsible for census data—uses the following as its definition of "Black": "a person having origins in any of the Black racial groups of Africa," while explaining that it allows individuals to self-identify on the category of race (Census Bureau 2020).[11] The Census Bureau's website, in addressing the question "What is Race?" cautions that "the racial categories included in the census questionnaire generally reflect a social definition of race recognized in this country and not an attempt to define race biologically, anthropologically, or genetically" (Census Bureau 2020). That definition, or rather lack of a definition, seems only to intimate a push against traditional white supremacist logics of racial categorization—that race does not equate to some biological/phenotypical, and therefore "natural" character—logics historically used to justify slavery in many forms. However, how the bureau's categorization of "Black" is *not* biological/phenotypical, anthropological, or genetic when the very description of it includes the words "origins" and "groups of Africa" is puzzling. From this contradiction on a governmental stance on race and Blackness, we begin to read the vexed and unconfident ways institutions deal with the concept for their own purposes. If the chief means by which the US government collects demographic data on its citizens (and noncitizens) mystifies the concept of race and places it within a framework gesturing defensively on questions about it, we might usefully consider other ways such defensiveness—what I call *white public and institutional defensiveness*[12]—at institutional and public levels usher in a resistant stance such as Russell's: one that overtly races, genders, and classes the ecological elements/relations of #BlackLivesMatter.

When I say white defensiveness, I refer to articulated responses that result from what whiteness studies scholar Robin DiAngelo calls "White Fragility" (2011). Such defensiveness manifests in "a range of defensive moves" triggered by white fragility, "a state in which even a minimum amount of racial stress becomes intolerable" (57). Whereas DiAngelo confronts affective defensive reactions on an intra/interpersonal level, the above definitions used by the Census Bureau operate on an *institutional* or *public* plane to attempt to "reinstate white racial equilibrium" (2020, 57) by anticipating white fragility and racial stress through defensive rhetorics. So, while Cohen contextualizes Russell's remarks as reacting to oppressive conditions of neoliberalism, I additionally link them to three important, intertwined cultural moments that arguably prompt white institutional (or public) defensiveness. These moments converge with several others to set up conditions for #BlackLivesMatter and its notions of relational Blackness post-Ferguson. They include—but are not limited to—the terrorist attacks on September 11, 2001, the election of President Obama, and the ideal of colorblindness in US society.[13]

While African American studies scholar Taylor's *From #BlackLivesMatter to Black Liberation* (2016) foregrounds the explosion of #BlackLivesMatter through a "culture of racism,"[14] focus here remains in ma(r)king the deep ecologies of these three specific cultural moments to highlight how their fractures evolve through contact with white institutional defensiveness arising specifically, but not chronologically, with/in the backdrop of colorblindness. In Russell's plea for "having a right over laws," I deploy these in concatenated, reflexive response to blacklivesmatter.com's (Roberts 2016) question/response "What does #BlackLivesMatter mean?" Effectively, this section uses critical memory of these events as a historical/temporal backdrop to "[broaden] the conversation around state violence" as a means to considering "the ways in which Black people are intentionally left powerless at the hands of the state" (Cullors 2018). Because of the institutional and public front of white defensiveness, as illustrated through these moments, such tensions promote an environment conducive to #BlackLivesMatter demonstrations of relational, inter(con)textual Black meaning-making as literacy events to counter white fragility.

Reductively, the events of 9/11 positioned the United States as nationally at odds with Islam and in some ways as anti-im/migrant, more pronouncedly than relations had indicated previously.[15] That positioning was undoubtedly racialized and citizened as the Western nation attempted to exterminate the threat identified with the Eastern religion both inside and outside of its "geographical borders." After September 11, 2001, the titular aim of the bipartisan End Racial Profiling Act of 2001—pursued by politicians aggressively earlier that same year—took a backseat to the perceived threat to national security that brown and Black folk in the United States represent. According to a Leadership Conference on Civil and Human Rights report,

> The federal government immediately focused massive investigative resources and law enforcement attention on Arabs and Muslims—and in some cases on individuals who were perceived to be, but in fact were not, Arabs or Muslims, such as Sikhs and other South Asians. In the years that followed, the federal government undertook various initiatives in an effort to protect the nation against terrorism. The federal government claimed that these counterterrorism initiatives did not constitute racial profiling, but the actions taken—from the singling out of Arabs and Muslims in the United States for questioning and detention to the selective application of immigration laws to nationals of Arab and Muslim countries—belie this claim. (Angulo and Weich 2003, 5)

The response to 9/11 thus complicated unfolding interrelations with the issue of institutionalized racism, with the terrorist attack providing justification for the intensification of racist methods of maintaining "safety."[16]

Because of the public "racial stress" resulting "from an interruption to what is racially familiar" (DiAngelo 2011, 57), the government sought fit to exasperate institutionally practiced discrimination as a defensive response. Such discrimination ramped up efforts at racial profiling, especially of those conjuring difference to whiteness in extremity, in im/migration, "antiterrorism" measures, public security, and policing. Because Blackness was/is formulated to "represent *difference in its raw manifestation*—somatic, affective, aesthetic, imaginary . . . a caricature of the *principle of exteriority*" (46), as Mbembe (2017) puts it, such profiling undoubtedly played into the deaths of Trayvon Martin and Michael Brown. As surveillance studies scholars note, the typical "disposition of US-led security measures and practices, and increasingly so post-9/11" (S. Browne 2015, 38) is to profile some by sorting them into risk categories, and then to project those categories by generalizing persons in them with its potential behaviors (Bigo 2008, 81). Public Blackness, "abnormalized by way of surveillance and then coded for disciplinary measures that are punitive in their effects" (S. Browne 2015, 17) in white public spaces, meant Martin's hoodie and Black teenage body in a gated Florida community were always already out of place demanding vigilante policing. White institutional defensiveness authorizes his murder. These events catapulted #BlackLivesMatter into the public sphere.

Barack Obama's rise to the US presidency in 2008 elicited notions that the country had somehow transitioned to a "post-racial society." Ironically, "the hope [to put racism 'behind' us] lay largely in the underlying representational politics that Barack Obama, a Black man, carried. That is, almost regardless of his political background and his experience, it was his [B]lackness that mattered" (Flores and Sims 2016, 206). Adding to the significance of President Obama's racialized identity, opponents (such as Donald Trump and the Birther movement) pointed to him as a Muslim and not a natural-born US citizen—the very identities of "enemy" born out of responses to 9/11. Race and Blackness, embodied nationally and problematically essentialized in the profile of one Black man, engaged in— as communication studies scholars Lisa L. Flores and Christy-Dale L. Sims call it—a "zero sum game."[17] So, while the election of President Obama made race and intersectional (via racing, gendering, and citizening) Blackness an unavoidable, ongoing national conversation, those discussions were often quashed by the office he held. Conversations on racism, particularly antiBlack racism, could be shut down more easily via white public/institutional defensiveness—it had found an inbuilt excuse. As president, Obama represented an invitation to exchanges on Blackness that were reductively dismissed by the very invitation— much in the way that the census frames race as a social construct but uses biology and genetics to ask respondents to read themselves. Yet that conversation remained volatile in the modes in which it would be initiated or not explicitly discussed. An air of public passive-aggressiveness, of defensiveness, often plays out in the rationale behind racial colorblindness that plagues efforts to discuss race in the United States.

What political scientist Naomi Murakawa calls "the problem of the twenty-first century" (2014, 7)—colorblindness—Taylor declares, "has become the default setting for how Americans understand race and race work" (2016, 73). Racial colorblindness refers to the ideal that race should not be a factor considered in an individual's potential for socioeconomic success (and "productive citizenship"). The concept is intricately linked to the rise of neoliberalism in the United States as both an economic agenda and a dominant cultural principle. The term "neoliberalism" summons the economic policies of Presidents Reagan and Nixon that began eroding the "social welfare state" through political policies and rhetoric of "freedom and choices": according to Taylor, "Nixon officials worked to narrow the definition of racism to the intentions of individual actors while countering the idea of institutional racism by focusing on 'freedom of choice' as a way to entertain differential outcomes" (63). Neoliberalism/colorblindness thus evokes a culture of vilifying those outside of the laissez-faire productivity model that (racial) capitalism promotes. Because state responsibility for the social welfare of its citizens has been corroded by free market economics and a culture of "every man for himself" for almost fifty years, those operating against/outside such a culture have and continue to be (acceptingly) marginalized.[18]

Neoliberal philosophies and practices have since been imbedded in and beyond most institutional spaces, policies, and cultures with/in white capitalist heteropatriarchal frameworks. The very philosophy breathes white institutional defensiveness into life through racially colorblind rhetoric. If to be American means to individually pull oneself up by one's bootstraps, then, conversely, freely made "bad choices" that "lead" to crime, poverty, incarceration and literal premature death, means that white fragility could be weaponized in the face of racialized language. Armed with white public and institutional defensiveness, white institutions could and have charged overtly racialized and overtly Black rhetoric as criminal, as terroristic. Reagan and Nixon's gifts that keep on giving grant the United States capacities to publicly talk about Blackness without talking about Blackness. The logics of colorblind approaches to race/racism, reified by the election of President Obama, add to the workings of historical antiBlackness and neoliberal epistemologies to demonize Blackness. By vilifying Blackness, then not allowing public conversations on it, rhetorics of white institutional defensiveness solidify Blackness' objectness, rhetoricizing Trans-Atlantic slavery's logics. #BlackLivesMatter slaps the hand that offers these "gifts."

Contextualized in this country's fraught histories of white supremacy built via antiBlackness, slavery, and segregation, "the new Jim Crow" of the mass incarceration of Blacks and Latinxs (Alexander 2012) provides an important additional backdrop to the post-Ferguson cultural moment. The problem of criminalizing these identities depends heavily on the notion of institutionalized/inter-/intrapersonal racial colorblindness. Civil rights lawyer, advocate, and legal scholar Michelle Alexander explains, "In an era of colorblindness, it is no longer socially permissible to use race, explicitly, as a justification for discrimination, exclusion, and social contempt. So we don't. Rather than rely on race, we use our criminal justice system to label people of color 'criminals' and then engage in all the practices we supposedly left behind" (2012, 2). The idea that individuals who and institutions that openly discriminate on the basis of race mark themselves overtly as counter to "American" ideals has found itself confusingly translated to imply—and even mean—that individuals or institutions should not *recognize distinctions* based on race. Both the former and the latter perceptions find themselves legitimized by the scientific dissociation between race and personality and thus feed into the neoliberal ideal that personal responsibility leads to material success in the United States. Colorblindness, thus, almost acts as a kind of trump card (hah!) in the game of white public and institutional defensiveness. Whereas 9/11 and the election of President Obama were temporally located markers of previous cultural moments, racial colorblindness' interconnectedness with fundamentally antiBlack "American" ideals weighs heavily on the current post-Ferguson cultural moment. This is not to say that we have moved past the influence of the two former events but, rather, to signal that they help fuel the latter deep rhetorical ecology.

All three cultural moments / deep ecologies remain integral with/in the (continued) shaping of where we stand on the question of cultural rhetoricity post-Ferguson, propelling us to consider what co-constitutes that rhetoricity through the following analysis of #BlackLivesMatter. Both the movement's expressed push toward "broadening the conversation around state violence" (Cullors 2018) and Russell's suggestion that "we more connected than most people think" (PBS NewsHour 2014) implore us to think through notions of Blackness in dynamic Black feminist and African indigenous inter(con)textual relations with institutions. In carrying out such analysis, I also contend that we reflexively engage in co-constituting the deep ecology of the post-Ferguson cultural moment.

We Might Not Overcome But . . .

In responding to calls, such as Corrigan's, for "new methods for racial inquiry . . . particularly around geographies of violence and resistance" (2016, 190), I operationalize Tori Russell's and #BlackLivesMatter's prompting for intersectionally relational, deep ecological readings of literacy events. I approach three literacy events (constellated texts), that give us insight into the meaning-making taking place in the #BlackLivesMatter movement: Garza's (2014) "A Herstory of the #BlackLivesMatter Movement";[19] the audio track (Lamar 2015a),[20] music video (Lamar 2015c),[21] and February 2016 Grammy performance (CBS Television Network)[22] of rapper Lamar's "Alright"; and blacklivesmattersyllabus.com's fall 2016 "Black Lives Matter Movement" syllabus, created by NYU instructor Frank Leon Roberts (2016).[23] We'll recall that they demonstrate historical, populist, and pedagogical relations between Blackness and state power. But the historical might better be re/visioned here as herstorical—conjuring not only the Black feminist epistemological tenet of Black women as knowledge agents (Hill Collins [1990] 2000, 266–269) but also the legacy of the Combahee River Collective's Statement alongside the Movement for Black Lives' "radical Black feminist praxis as its bedrock" (Ransby 2017, 181). With a primarily herstoric focus—that is, building from and upon histories/temporalities of Black feminist production/negotiation of meaning—the populist and pedagogical become the means to consider contestation of hegemonic notions of history that feed systemic power. To read ecologically and diachronically, my analysis of them moves around from text to text purposefully.

In such analysis of these sets of texts, my inter(con)textual readings take into account the points of encounter and disjuncture (intersections) between the texts and the associations that they set up in their unfolding. These intersections offer rhetorical encounters across texts within literacy events (each of the three centralized constellated texts) that operate in deep rhetorical ecologies with/in which meanings of Blackness are produced/negotiated. I prioritize (1) the inter(con)textual ways in which each literacy event overtly plays off and against each other, (2) how each references material that engages or centralizes the roles of Black women—particularly radical Black feminist women—and their work, (3) the events' referral to and enactment of histories and historicization, (4) how they critique the prison industrial complex, its cultural offspring, and consequences, and (5) the role of spirituality in connection to or against oppressive institutional (white capitalist heteropatriarchal) power at play in these literacy events.[24] Points of fracture where Blackness comes to be un/made with/in these ecologies via literacy events arise throughout, signaling the object-being of Blackness' potentials for meaning-making through Black inter(con)textual reading.

Going, Gon', Gone: #BlackLivesMatter Signifyin'

Due to its genre, Roberts's (2016) Black Lives Matter syllabus brings into conversation the two other literacy events. What's notable, however, are the modes

in which it engages with them and the material operating in the immediate ecological space of Garza's (2014) and Lamar's (2015a) texts. The syllabus constitutes institutional engagement with the radical (Garza's manifesto) and popular
(iterations of Lamar's track) with the pedagogical aims of producing/negotiating
knowledge. We can perhaps use the references across the three texts—how they
signify or are signifyin',[25] with/against each other—as an initial entry point.

Lamar's song, though not directly listed on Roberts's (2016) syllabus as a
whole assigned text to be read,[26] prominently features before all others through
a graphic display of its chorus's lyrics—if one scrolls http://www.blacklivesmat
tersyllabus.com/fall2016/ from the top of the home page at the syllabus's online
location, it comes into frame before all other info. In its graphic rendering "BE
ALRIGHT" appears larger than the preceding "WE GON'" against its black
backdrop, markedly using a black/white contrast. This contrast is reminiscent
of the word "Compton" in white on the black map of Africa in Lamar's Grammy
performance (CBS Television Network 2016), and could recall the black and
white aesthetic of Lamar's music video (Lamar 2015c). The differences in the
font size of the two pairs of words from Lamar's (2015a) chorus might highlight
being alright as a potential declarative goal of #BlackLivesMatter's racial politics, or a possible position that bodies participating in Roberts's (2016) class can
strive to occupy. The latter perhaps responds to a central question of the syllabus:
"How, when, and in what ways is it possible for us to stand in *formation* against
the treacherous legacies of capitalist patriarchal white supremacy?"[27] The goal of
the chorus's statement, however, seems to be a condition rather than a destination: the goal is not a *place* but rather a way/means of being, a kind of affective
ontology. Or maybe the condition and the destination warp into each other so
that marching, movement, and traction represent the modes in which one might
(em)body Blackness in relation to institutional power—perhaps the repeated
lyric summons an object/beingness, a how and a where, methods and temporalities. One might always already be moving away, progressing from, or destabilizing the place from which one comes or goes to in Blackness.[28]

Such a conception of Blackness might converse with Du Bois's (1903) theory
in *The Souls of Black Folk* of "double consciousness," where Blackness within a
white supremacist society involves an internal conflict of push-pull toward and
against an impossible ideal of whiteness. A possibility for relational Blackness
post-Ferguson, then, could hinge on a desire to resist and be apart from institutional and systemic white capitalist heteropatriarchal frameworks, while being
affectively okay with the knowledge of that desire's impossibility in the West. But
Lamar's (2015a) text, like Roberts's (2016) syllabus, wants to constantly interrogate that condition. Lamar's (2015a) chorus repeats its driving phrase six times,
four times prefaced by the racially classed/gendered addressee of the statement
"nigga," once without such an addressee and once with the question "huh?" The

chorus asks if the audience (referred to in second person) hears and feels its speaker before the framing sentiment, asking his (Black urban) audience to contextualize what being alright means to them. Lamar's (2015a) lyrics, like Roberts's (2016) syllabus, perhaps asks such audiences not only to be "woke,"[29] but also to routinely return to the question of what it means to be "woke." Yet could we also think through how the questions "Do you hear me? Do you feel me?" (Lamar 2015a) resuscitatively animate social death—the object-beingness of Blackness conjured through cyclical movement toward being alright, toward (em)bodying the historically commodifying but reclaimed rhetoric of nigga? Let's dig deeper.

Sociolinguist Geneva Smitherman in *Talkin and Testifyin* highlights the contraction "gon'" as one of a few emblematic "pronunciations in Black English that are used by a large number of black speakers [in the US]" (1977, 17). Smitherman explains that "here the *to* is omitted altogether, and the nasal sound at the end is shortened, producing a sound that is somewhat like an abbreviated form of 'gone'" (18). We might bring this omission to bear on Lamar's (2015a) lyrics in further questioning the destination/condition spectrum set up in the chorus's repeated line. Is it possible to conceive "going" alongside/against its phonetic referent (and past tense) "gone" in relation to a potential feeling of popularized urban Blackness? The going/gone interplay fractures meaning, temporality, and affect. It conjures "the wake." It invokes critical memory. The very end of Lamar's (2015c) music video seems to speak to its paradox when a white cop gesturally "shoots" Lamar, and he appears to be dead, but after a brief blank black-screen transition, he smiles up at the camera/sky. The sentiment of being rendered simultaneously dead to white institutional power, or the phonetic "gone," while very much alive in one's Blackness, or the articulated "gon'," reminds us of Weheliye's (2014) Black feminist search for generative meaning in "not-quite-human" and "nonhuman" spaces/bodies/beings. This condition *is* object-beingness. In the "disaster of recognition" (L. Gordon 2007, 11), the Fanonian fracture reveals a para/ontological Blackness: non/being with/in "the possibility of one's death as a legitimate feature of a system." Similarly, the lack of a preposition ("to") in Lamar's (2015a) phrasing could signal an acknowledgment that Black folk have the potential with/in the here and now (of the wake) to be "okay." But to arrive at such a position—which might seem impossible—they must involve themselves in a self-reflective interrogation, a narrative inventing, a world-making, as in the chorus's reiterative questions. In the syllabus (Roberts 2016), that inquiry comes by way of pedagogical work centered around these kinds of questions and texts. One such text—and a crucial text at that—is Garza's (2014) "Herstory."

While Lamar's (2015a) lyric graphically signifies a medial point of departure on the syllabus, Garza's (2014) may represent a grounding means of orientation/origin. Following the screening of the BET documentary Laurens Grant's *Stay Woke* (2016), on the first week of the syllabus to consider ways of "approaching" the

#BlackLivesMatter movement (Roberts 2016), the second session begins with Garza's (2014) article. The unit that it kicks off centers around the question "Who are they?" (Roberts 2016). Related readings for the week include several other sections of the #BlackLivesMatter website, an audio interview featuring Garza and fellow #BlackLivesMatter creators Patrisse Cullors and Opal Tometi, and the first chapter from Cornel West's (2004) *Democracy Matters*. The syllabus thus uses Garza's (2014) "Herstory" to direct understandings of the movement's provenance, as opposed to the way it uses Lamar's (2015a) lyric as a popular culture reference to acclimate readers/students to his destination/condition spectrum of (urbanized, and at points primarily masculinized) Blackness. Garza's (2014) manifesto, however, works in ways to push against Lamar (2015a) and his text to centralize the efficacy of Black queer women and their work. In addressing the use or appropriation of #BlackLivesMatter, Garza writes, "Straight men, unintentionally or intentionally, have taken the work of queer Black women and erased our contributions. Perhaps if we were the charismatic Black men many are rallying around these days, it would have been a different story, but being Black queer women in this society (and apparently within these movements) tends to equal invisibility and non-relevancy" (2014). Lamar's popularity might qualify him as one of these "charismatic Black men"[30] at whom Garza throws shade in wishing for political visibility and relevance for Black queer women's labor. Garza's stipulation that we be cognizant of what centering radical movements around these cis-het Black men and their texts means alerts us to the kinds of fractures that provide disjunctive opportunities for constructive meaning-making. Neither the #BlackLivesMatter movement nor its potentials for producing/negotiating racial meaning signal static conceptions of Blackness. What it might show us is the ways in which intersectional Blackness operates in relation to institutional power with/in the post-Ferguson cultural moment as reiteratively interrogating Black non/beingness or even "wokeness"—gendered, sexualized, classed, dis/abled, and citizened through its racialization.

A #BlackLivesMatter protest in Cleveland was the site at which public association between the movement and Lamar originated.[31] In July 2015, "attendees of a Black Lives Matter conference at Cleveland State University confronted transit authority police arresting a fourteen-year-old for allegedly being intoxicated on a bus" (J. Gordon 2015). Students at the university responded by repeating Lamar's chorus in resistance. According to *Fact Magazine*, "one of the conference attendees told ABC News Cleveland that people locked arms and blocked the street near the police cruiser while chanting [it]" (2015). Through the fracture with/in the deep ecology emerges new(er) Black meaning-making/negotiation, notably through (em)bodied Black relationality. Lamar became intrinsically linked to the movement and his popularity—and Grammy Award–winning success—a spotlight for issues related to #BlackLivesMatter's cause, spurred by the institutional abuse of a Black youth. So, despite Garza's (2014) overt reminder that the lack of attention paid to the Black queer women behind the movement is "hetero-patriarchal," public attention flocked to Lamar's (2015a) articulation of some of the movement's affects rather than in affirming Black queer work. That reaction is unsurprising, as the deep rhetorical ecologies being examined operate in, as Roberts puts it, "treacherous legacies of capitalist patriarchal white suprem-acy" (2016). So, while radical intersectional, relational Blackness might seek to position itself away from such legacies—as a destination it might be "going to" a difference place—the logics of Du Bois's (1903) "double consciousness" means that it remains a condition operating with/in/against white capitalist heteropa-triarchy. Public perception of those positions means that Lamar, through his liter-acy event, has the privilege to create meaning more widely consumed as (in effect, populist) Blackness—straight, (hyper)masculine, though urbanized, notions that feed capitalist frameworks—than Garza (2014), or even Roberts (2016).

For music critic and psychologist Adam Blum, "Alright" represents "a de facto, unofficial anthem of the Black Lives Matter movement," as he pronounces, that *To Pimp a Butterfly*, "will likely be remembered as an emblem of the cultural moment in which it was conceived, at the height of the initial swell of the Black Lives Matter movement" (2016, 143). Though Lamar does not candidly claim direct association with the movement, his response to questions regarding his stance in relation to it recognizes his role in shaping its deep ecological mean-ings. When specifically asked about the relationships between the song and the #BlackLivesMatter movement in a *New York Times* interview with Joe Coscarelli, Lamar explains, "It's a chant of hope and feeling" (2015). This assertion seems to argue for his song—particularly the chorus's lyrics—as (em)bodying emo-tions in conversation with intersectional Black queer activist affect in the con-temporary United States. Lamar's "hope" might trigger an affective conver-sion of the "bad feelings" of articulating injustice through narrative, moving away from the unhappy object of a protest chant to some happiness to come. Though, as Ahmed argues, if "in having hope we *become* anxious, because hope involves wanting something that might or might not happen" (2010, 183)—and historically has never happened (has Blackness ever really been "alright" in the Western world?)—then hope might be Blackened/queered with revolutionary unhappiness. Indeed, the Cleveland protests demonstrate how "revolutionary forms of political consciousness involve heightening our awareness of *just how much* there is to be unhappy about" (223).[32] Selling CDs, therefore, cannot make #BlackLivesMatter, but protest chants might ignite movement toward that mattering.

About the moment in which Lamar realized that the song had become caught up in the #BlackLivesMatter movement, he responds, "When I'd go in certain parts of the world, and they were singing it in the streets. When it's outside of the concerts, then you know it's a little bit more deep-rooted than just a song. It's more than just a piece of a record. It's something that people live by—your words" (qtd. in Coscarelli 2015). Lamar's (2015a) "words" become operational in the material lives of its consumers, with that consumption then playing out in ways such as protest-chanting. His particular expression "more than" suggests the generative capacity the song has to create/negotiate meaning in deep rhetorical ecologies. While Lamar's summation of "Alright"'s significance acknowledges its entanglement within capitalist strictures, when it takes on functional meanings in people's lives—as he sees it—its lyrics take effect/affect as the audience's. They are "your words," not just his. Those words then move with/from being caught up in one meaning/intention, as well as its urbanized, masculinized, and racialized identities—from a going to—to ways of being. The destination/condition spectrum represented in the line from the chorus and its apposite questions conceptualizes some anxious "hope and feeling" of interrogative, relational, Blackness post-Ferguson.

"Nothing to lose but our chains": Centering Race–radical Black Women[33]

As critical as Lamar's (2015a) phrase has grown for the movement, other chants by protestors and materials referenced particularly by Garza (2014) highlight the vital importance of race-radical Black women to #BlackLivesMatter and its making-meaning potentials. In Garza's contention that ahistorical/appropriative employments of the #BlackLivesMatter movement debilitate its potential for "transformative social change," the Black feminist activist references a quotation from Assata Shakur's (1973) "To My People" adopted as a protest chant. While prevailing white public and institutional defensiveness brands Shakur a "terrorist," Blackness postures otherwise. Shakur, a radical Black woman activist, a former member of the Black Panther Party and Black Liberation Army, escaped from a US prison in the late 1970s and fled the country in the mid-1980s. Her unapologetic, revolutionary stances/actions that cut against matrixes of oppressive institutional racism (most notably the criminal justice system), patriarchy, and gender normativity (both white and Black—the latter in relation to her dissatisfactions with the Black Panthers) serve as the underpinnings of Shakur's relevance to #BlackLivesMatter motives. Of Shakur, Garza (2014) writes, "When I use Assata's powerful demand in my organizing work,[34] I always begin by sharing where it comes from, sharing about Assata's significance to the Black Liberation Movement, what it's political purpose and message is, and why it's important in our context." In insisting on contextualizing Shakur's herstorical significance, Garza engages Shakur's biography, encounters, and relationships with Black activism as immediately impactful to the movement today. Shakur and "To My People" become an active part of the deep ecology, mobilizing feminist theorist

Vivian May's "history lessons" of intersectionality's "theoretical genealogy" (2015, 9–12) so that protestors cannot divorce themselves or their material identities from her/his/stories and other deep ecologies of Black liberation struggles that date back to the Trans-Atlantic slave trade, through to Jim Crow, and to the contemporary embattlement with neoliberal culture.

Although Shakur's (1973) writing does not overtly appear to be included in Roberts's (2016) syllabus, in his archive of videos from the material application of the syllabus—his Black Lives Matter Seminar at NYU in fall 2016—the chant appears as recited in class.[35] Members of #SayHerName (the African American Policy Forum) lead students in the chant "It is our duty to fight for our freedom. It is our duty to win. We must love each other and support each other. We have nothing to lose but our chains." #BlackLivesMatter protestors frequently use the chant in marches, and #SayHerName asks students to repeat their cries in a call-and-response format with deep roots in Black culture in the United States and beyond that illustrates the Black feminist importance of dialogue (Hill Collins [1990] 2000, 261). Placed ecologically alongside not only Garza's text but those written by Angela Davis, Lorde, Kimberlé Williams Crenshaw, and so forth, Shakur's text within the syllabus gives evidence of the centralized role of radical activist Black women—who adopt resistant intersectional Black feminist frameworks—in the production/negotiation of Blackness post-Ferguson. When their texts are mobilized in a classroom and verbalized in the streets as protest cries, Black women's voices interrupt the racist heteropatriarchy that fuels the destruction of Black communities in the United States. Those cries also (em)body feelings of Blackness, operationalizing a collective "we" (as in Shakur's [1973] chant) deeply entrenched in an ancestry of radical Black women's agency.

Lamar's (2015a) track might seem bereft of such Black women's voices as it adopts the traditionally urbanized, masculinized Black frameworks of the rap genre. Black women remain markedly absent in its music video's (Lamar 2015c) scenes of euphoria and elsewhere. They are palpably and unsettlingly missing. The character of Lamar's mother only shows up in the lyrics (2015a) in relation to his pronouncedly toxic gendered/sexualized masculinities. Immediately following lines about gratuitous enjoyment of prescription drugs, women's bodies, and money in the song's first verse, the speaker sends a message of love to his mother while affirming his penchant for the former. Lamar seems cognizant of how such a lifestyle might be self-destructive, apart from his back and forth with the materialist temptations of "Lucy" (who seems to be a stand-in for Lucifer—perhaps whiteness?). He highlights an awareness of his behavior four lines later in imploring his audience to send a message to the broader public of his self-defeat, possible madness, and succumbing to excess. The critique of wokeness mentioned earlier seems to be functional in this verse as well, though in this occurrence it works in acknowledging Lamar's concession to capitalistic heteropatriarchal "vices" and struggling to remove himself from them. Problematically, that relenting disables the speaker, as he's gone "cray," though it does intimate some relationship between the dis/abled Black body and these vices, providing gaps in which we might seek meaning, however fraught. His mother, nevertheless, seemingly represents the measure against which he positions those vices: his mother's love reminds him that his lust for prescription drugs and "pretty pussy" is ultimately self-destructive, while presenting rifts in the sexualization, gendering, and commodification of (Black) women. His mother's character perhaps motivates the statement on previous collective trauma, downtrodden-ness, and the sense of being lost in the track's pre-hook (that the chorus seeks to alleviate). Again, the dynamic push/pull of going/being appears relevant here—Lamar may desire a raging against such nadirs, against an object-beingness in engaging hypercapitalism—but that spectrum comes to our attention after this passing reference to Lamar's affect regarding his mother. Black women's roles, then, on the surface are minimized, but Black women's gendered/sexualized agencies appear to troublingly motivate Lamar's "anthem"—as object rather than subject.

Moreover, a Black woman's voice appears early in—and arguably central to—Lamar's track, through Lamar's signifyin' first line. The song opens by riffing off of Alice Walker's character Sofia in *The Color Purple*. Sofia tells Celie (her mother-in-law and narrator), "All my life I had to fight. I had to fight my daddy. I had to fight my uncles. A girl child ain't safe in a family of men" in response to Celie's advice to Sofia's husband to beat Sophia when defiant (1982, 38). Sofia explains that she's had to fight numerous men in her life (her father, uncles, brothers) but never thought she'd need to in her own home (one in which she seeks to hold some sociopolitical power). Sofia's outspokenness in the book stands against violence being perpetrated domestically (and arguably systematically) against Black women by capitalist heteropatriarchy. In the related film, Oprah Winfrey delivers the line as Sofia (Spielberg 1985). Through Alice Walker, Sofia, and Winfrey, Lamar (2015a) is signifyin' resistance to the white heteropatriarchy in his opening line, though Lamar's masculinist discourse reframes that resistance: "nigga" immediately follows the pronouncement. Through signifyin(g), the line "functions as a metaphor for formal revision, or intertextuality, within the Afro-American literary tradition" that explores the gap between literal and figurative uses of words or phrases for meaning production (Gates 1989, xxi). That "intertextuality" ecologically aligns the track's speaker (in 2015 post-Ferguson United States) with a fictional Black woman's rhetoric of noncompliance with her social position with/in a Black Southern US low-income household in the 1930s, which again plays into the double-consciousness of moving away from one's position in an oppressive system, while standing "alright" in defiance. While Lamar (2015a) does not manifestly pursue Garza's (2014) call for historicizing, acknowledging, and making visible Black women's work, through his metaphor the intersections between his experiences and Sofia's fracture the making of Blackness. The metaphor, I admit, remains troubling. By situating it in relation to oppressive Black masculinity quite conscious of the dynamics of capitalist exploitation—in the first verse's collapsing of indulgence in women's bodies and money in the speaker's salacious acme (Lamar 2015a)—we find that Walker's/Sofia's Black feminist declaration against physical violence can be muffled in service of the very frameworks it protests. But that fracturing also illuminates a self-referential (potentially self-reflexive) history-building that seemingly co-constitutes the spaces of critical memory for Blackness, particularly here in relation to the work/resistance of race-radical Black women. Fracturing possibilities through inter(con)textual reading, we note, open up multiple avenues for Black rhetoricity.

"By sharing where it comes from"[36]: Fracturing Historicity

A major point of encounter across the three literacy events arises from a focus on the historical. Garza's (2014) text, perhaps more than both others, frames itself in and resists the whitened, masculinized genre of history, as "Herstory," speaking not simply to events that occur—like the deaths of Trayvon Martin and Michael Brown—but around epistemological notions that underline the historicity of the #BlackLivesMatter movement's ethos. Additionally, it continues in the tradition of Lorde, who pushes against white feminist "assimilation into a western european [sic] herstory" (1984, 69), highlighting creative possibilities for social change in difference to lift up Black feminist herstories as necessary/legitimate. Garza (2014) writes in the lineage of the Combahee River Collective, who, according to cofounder Demita Frazier, view the genre as moving beyond manifesto. Frazier explains that "in publishing the [Combahee River Collective] statement and then continuing to remain unapologetic Black feminists over time despite everything just really tells the story . . . speaks the truth about the message that we were choosing to put out" ([1977] 2017, 131–132). Herstory writes and extends beyond that act through practical performance. The fracturing genre evolves through praxis by meaning-making in the Black feminist everyday to cycle back in the potentially fracturing present through the wake of Black being.

Garza's (2014) contextualization of Shakur, for example, calls attention to not only a herstorical figure's significance but also a powerful prevailing affect intrinsic to the thrust of the #BlackLivesMatter cause. Garza uses the example of Shakur's (1973) message to demonstrate a resistance against appropriative uses of the movement's meme/moniker—particularly as the work of Black queer women—contending that to "promote it as if it has no history of its own such actions are problematic" (Garza 2014). Similarly, Roberts (2016) begins his syllabus through historical framing. Its first "essential question" in the initial

week of the course is "What is the history of the Black Lives Matter movement?"
But Roberts does not only employ this frame for approaching the course matter; her/his/story runs through it. Later in the semester, in week 8 centering
on "Legacies of Rebellion," the unit on "Black Lives Matter's Protest Populism"
asks that students "pay attention to the vital role that commercial artists have
historically played in amplifying the concerns of black freedom movements"
(emphasis mine), while the legacy/background of the prison industrial complex remains key to the course's approach to its examination. Throughout both
the syllabus and Garza's (2014) "Herstory," her/his/story serves the dual function of illuminating contemporary oppressions and activist sentiments while
mobilizing the ongoing production/negotiation of relational meanings—as
#BlackLivesMatter operates with an astute awareness of how it works in its
ongoing her/his/stories.

Like Garza and Roberts, Lamar (2015a) proclaims the importance of past
wrongs and resistance to current injustices in his pre-hook. The rapper goes on
to place that line within an ecology that works to highlight being downtrodden
alongside feelings of self-conscious insecurity in being lost in the (white) world.
We re/turn again to the notion of movement, of going somewhere beyond the
stasis of (gendered) self-doubt. By the end of the pre-hook, we arrive at/cir-
cle back to the track's chorus, vitally framed with the conjunction "but" that
indicates how its gut feeling might interrupt those histories of insecurity. The
expressed hatred for police in the pre-hook underscores the criminal justice
system's role in that past, as Roberts (2016) likewise spotlights with his three-
week-long unit on the histories/cultures of the US prison matrix. Garza's (2014)
"Herstory" appropriately speaks to the roles police brutality and white vigilan-
tism play early on in the text. Lamar's (2015a) "hate," however, signals an affective
position in relation to those powers, highlighting the purposes emotion holds in
Black relationships, particularly urban Black masculinist relationships, with US
institutional power. With the track's opening reference to Walker (1982), Lamar
(2015a) rallies Sofia's histories of challenging abuse by the heteropatriarchy, while
changing Walker's (1982) character's "had" to present tense. While problematic,
Lamar's (2015a) signifyin' move to *make present* Sofia's defiance to physical/sex-
ual abuse in his first line fractures meanings of Blackness through the latter's cry
illustrating how in Black temporality "everything is now. It is all now" (Morrison
1987, 198). But we should mind the trauma of the fracture, of incorporating Black
women's (em)bodied resistance to oppressive power structures located in their
positions as relative to urbanized Black masculinity, where an appeal to a commonplace Blackness might possibly erase Black women's work. The potentials
of re/turning to a past that is now through inter(con)textual reading (in this
case through signifyin') must be navigated with a critical memory if our projects
mean to work against hegemony. Across and between these rhetorical encoun-

ters, history therefore becomes wrapped up in both affect, agential impetus, and pedagogical exigence with propelling immediacy, a present in a past tense and vice versa.

"In cages in this country": Blackness and the (School to) Prison Industrial Complex[37]

All three of these literacy events highlight the United States' oppressive prison industrial matrix. That system not only renders Black bodies disposable in relation to state power but also works to create a culture that filters in/to schools, neighborhoods, and ways of non/being. Roberts (2016) raises this issue as the first of the four "phenomena" set in relation to the #BlackLivesMatter movement in his course objectives. The syllabus mobilizes this particular phenomenon most explicitly for three weeks nearing the end of its span, following a unit on "Legacies of Rebellion." Placing this issue in close relation to histories of resistance allows for a long-view approach to the prison complex's relation to other systems of control that have sought to hold Black bodies (materially and culturally) captive in and beyond the era of chattel slavery. Roberts sets in motion three major texts: Alexander's (2010) *The New Jim Crow*, journalist Shaun King's (2016) twenty-five-part series on police brutality in the United States, and Angela Davis's (2004) *Are Prisons Obsolete?* The syllabus (Roberts 2016) also contains a short video on Shaun King's violent experience endured in high school in rural Kentucky—an experience that marked for him his Blackness in the racial schematics of the United States. Though that experience does not directly deal with the prison system or even the militarization of schools, its fracture allows for possible generative meaning creation/negotiation in #BlackLivesMatter's deep ecology. King explains that though not called a "segregated high school" outright, there was an "agricultural wing" of his school that was effectively whites-only. We might surmise that with such cordoned-off areas in a "public" place, whiteness functioned to set that space apart and not for Blacks, to racially "citizen" it as white. This meant that Black students were contained in other spaces—perhaps forcibly so—reenacting Jim Crow logistics that the prison system now animates, policed by culture. King then tells of being jumped by a group of white students and beaten so badly that he sustains multiple spinal surgeries as a result. Roberts's positioning of this video in the same ecological space as texts that interrogate the culture of Black imprisonment suggests that other institutions beyond that prison system operate along co-constitutive lines. When educational spaces coexist as carceral spaces that racially mark and de-citizen Black folk, how do such locations work to shape/produce/negotiate meanings of Blackness in the United States? That white students felt the need to police King's Blackness to the point of his near literal death illustrates the degree to which Blackness on its own accord stays set against/outside the "law" in the United States and remains surveilled as such, re/turning us far deeper into history than Jim Crow. Relatedly, Garza's (2014) "Herstory" critiques the prison complex in two ways that underline resistance to both the enculturation of its antiBlack philosophy and material imprisonment itself.

Garza spotlights the #BlackLivesMatter movement's antiprison stance in these ways on separate occasions in her "Herstory." First, when asked by another organization if they could incorporate "Black Lives Matter" into one of its campaigns, the #BlackLivesMatter movement declared that "as a team, we preferred that we not use the meme to celebrate the imprisonment of any individual." Though the requesting organization went ahead and used #BlackLivesMatter material in its campaign anyway, Garza's opposition to "[applauding] incarceration" suggests that even indirect associations with potential consequences of imprisonment are anti-#BlackLivesMatter. Garza proceeds to pronounce the movement's stance in relation to Black bodies legally en/slaved (or de-citizened) by the state. #BlackLivesMatter, Garza declares, "is an acknowledgment that 1 million Black people are locked in cages in this country—one half of all people in prisons or jails—is an act of state violence." This statement asserts the material, racial, and bodily realities of the prison system. It re/turns us to the reality that "US incarceration rates and carceral logics directly emerging from slavery into the present continue to be the signs that make Black bodies" (Sharpe 2016, 75). It underscores what Alexander's scholarship explicates in Roberts's syllabus and makes digestible—or perhaps indigestible—the very real implications of systematic oppression of Blackness in the United States: the mechanisms of white capitalist heteropatriarchy *subject* Blackness to hypercontrolled *object*ed-being.

Reading inter(con)textually Lamar's 2016 Grammy performance (CBS Television Network 2016) of "Alright" (along with the track "The Blacker the Berry" [Lamar 2015b]) in the same deep ecology as the syllabus affords further meaning-making possibilities for Blackness. Lamar enters the stage in a chain gang of imprisoned Black men, flanked by two prison cells with more locked-up Black males on either side of the stage (CBS Television Network 2016). The lyrics from "The Blacker the Berry" (Lamar 2015b) used to preface the performance of "Alright" very plainly critique white supremacy in the United States, while Lamar's costume and props specify how that supremacy functions.

Lamar spits to a second-person addressee about their hatred for, and plans to, destroy Black folks and their culture. In the previous line, he situates the politics of recognition alongside gendered, sexualized, (em)bodied meanings of Blackness when he raps about his Black phenotypical features, particularly drawing on the stereotype of Black men as well endowed. Lamar contextualizes Blackness and the imprisonment of Blackness in white culture at the intersections of hatred and destruction, summoning Fanon's suggestion that in the white male gaze, the Black man becomes a phallic symbol, with racial violence materializing sexual revenge for usurping the ideal of white "infinite virility" ([1952] 2008, 123).

Whereas Garza (2014) uses statistics and a stance on the cultural associations of #BlackLivesMatter to delineate her position on the issue, Lamar (2015b) uses his gendered/sexualized Black body in relation to the instruments of incarceration (chains, cages, jumper uniforms), to show how whiteness by way of the prison industrial complex and its contemporary manifestations of slavery might deliberately destroy his people, fashioning him into "a real killer." For US broadcast television, "nigga" transfigures to "killer." In the performance, Lamar therefore almost inverts the white defensiveness operating in the racialization of President Obama's body to confront directly the institutional oppression of Blackness (CBS Television Network 2016). In the deep ecological spaces between the three texts—between Garza's (2014) opposition and statistics, between Roberts's (2016) use of Alexander and Davis and alongside King's brutal attack in high school—we find means to generatively negotiate/create relational, intersectional Black meaning. The possible interconnectivity between these texts and the others explicitly enfolded with/in them suggest not just one way of being anti–prison system, but various means by which to (em)body/(per)form/demonstrate opposition to that system in relation to concepts of dynamic Blackness—from refusal to being associated with an organization to rhetoricizing the object-beingness Blackness (em)bodies in various gendered, sexualized ways.

On God, and Us: Black Christianity and Heteropatriarchy

But just as what immediately strikes readers of these three literacy events as visible across them, the relation/ships between Blackness and institutional power that seemingly defy inter(con)textual conversation deserve our attention. The relation/ships warrant our attention because material gaps across constellated texts do not equate to the absence of certain possibilities for Black meaning. Lamar's (2015a) "Alright," for instance, includes a general engagement with Christian themes in its lyrics, which seemingly does not stretch to the other apposite literacy events. After the opening play on the previously discussed lines from *The Color Purple*, Lamar writes about difficult periods and drops a biblical reference to Jesus's hometown.[38] Apart from that allusion, the formula that takes us into the chorus seems to put the weight of figuring out how to relate to the pressing issues of being Black in the United States on a higher power.[39] Elsewhere, mentions of temptations, encounters with the "preacher's door," and exclamations to God—such as the one that follows immediately the mention of Lamar's love for his mother to gender the spiritual relationship—punctuate the track. Most significant, however, Lamar struggles with "Lucy," the embodiment of temptation. The very last line of his track's poem-coda explains that the ubiquitous presence of this figure propelled Lamar to escape seeking reprieving solutions. But does this mean that the Black Christianity that sustains Lamar through the narrative of the lyrics proves insufficient to provide such answers?

Black Christianity seems to represent a core theme in the song, though it does not play a role in the music video (Lamar 2015c) or Grammy performance (CBS Television Network 2016). Its relationship to Lamar's mother's love appears to bolster its relevance for the speaker as a source of stability in the running/escape motif apparent through the track (Lamar 2015a). Yet, it remains unclear if the titular affective condition has stopped the running or the "going to" discussed earlier. We might make a conjecture that the faith in a Christian God articulated in the lyrics—especially as a contrast to the devil character, who seems to be the personification of capitalist heterosexual vices—motivates this escape or this "going to." The search for a state in which one can settle as "okay" parallels with a Christian search for salvation, though not in the sense that salvation will lead to "overcoming" (as in the Civil Rights' "We Shall Overcome"). Lamar's lyrics wrestle with Christian faith,[40] using it somewhat as a motivation for a continual search for self-acceptance. This one-on-one relation with a Christian God in Lamar's track seems set apart from institutionalized religion, which potentially escapes critique across these three literacy events.

But Roberts's (2016) syllabus does bring up Black women's complex relationship to the Black Christian church, notably in his unit on populist responses to #BlackLivesMatter. In this section, he assigns Beyoncé's (2016) *Lemonade*, which contains visual and verbal references to the Black Christian church. One article for that week, Candace Benbow's (2016) "Beyoncé's 'Lemonade' and Black Christian Women's Spirituality," touches on the multifaceted and often contradictory struggles between Black womanhood and the heteropatriarchal Christian church. Benbow argues that having been brought to the church by their mothers, Black women must seek ways to relate to the institution that do not repress their sexuality and render them the passive objects of Black men susceptible to abuse and absolute control in heteropatriarchal frameworks. In articulating her stance, she points to a "Lemonade syllabus" that seeks to affirm Black womanhood and their tools for freedom. Here we might take heed of the role of pedagogical apparatuses (syllabi) play in relation to populist literacy events (Beyoncé's *Lemonade*) and the relational meanings they produce/negotiate (articulations of Black women's gendered and sexualized positions vis-à-vis Christianity) in relation to histories (the Christian church as heteropatriarchal). Benbow ends, "Through 'Lemonade,' Beyoncé calls young Black women to reimagine their relationships in intimate and social spaces through constructing a relationship with God that makes self-love primary. Their mothers brought them to the faith. Now it must become their own." Though this text represents only one blip in the deep ecology of the #BlackLivesMatter syllabus, we can see how it might speak to and, in some ways, disrupt Lamar's (2015a) gendered and racialized contentions with God, faith, and Blackness. Although similar issues of self-searching and self-acceptance arise in Lamar, Black women's particular positions as always already having to fight (Walker 1982) (because of the particular intersectional matrixes of their oppression) mean that their relationships with Christian faith involve specific compounded and complex resistances; when, in heteronormative relationships, their husbands become representative of Black Christian authority, how might Black women engage that authority and Blackness, while moving away from systemic oppression?

Garza's (2014) "Herstory" does not seem to address these kinds of questions, though one might argue that they lack relevance to an explanation of the origins/ philosophies of #BlackLivesMatter. But, is the #BlackLivesMatter movement's rejection of "the hierarchical and hetero-patriarchal politics of respectability" (Ransby 2018, 3), critiqued in Garza's (2014) "Herstory," then, a rejection simultaneously of systematic Black Christianity? How can we square the institutional church with one-on-one confrontations with faith present in Lamar's (2015a) track and in Beyoncé's (2016) *Lemonade* (and raised directly by Benbow's [2016] critique)? Are these personal struggles with Blackness and Christian morals the means by which Black activism circumvents discussion on the role that the Christian church plays in oppression, resistance, or Blackness? Perhaps Garza's (2014) elision of religion in critiques of US institutions speaks to a move away from involving religion in Black activist work, which caused notable rifts within the Black community during the Civil Rights struggle. Media theorists/rhetoricians Amanda Nell Edgar and Andre E. Johnson analyze #BlackLivesMatter activists' use of faith, spirituality, and religion, finding that these things led participants to support the secular movement. Participants are not "non-religious" or "antireligious"; the movement's cofounders claim Christianity in nontraditional ways, and #BlackLivesMatter "has 'inspired and energized Black Christians' in Black churches" (Edgar and Johnson 2018, xxii). So, given these dynamics, how do we dis/engage with Black Christian spirituality when populist messages centered on Black resistance, like Lamar's (2015a) and Beyoncé's (2016), so clearly make it visible? How do appeals to self rather than system relate to neoliberal conceptions of racial identity that reify the former in service of the latter? Regardless of how we go about attempting to respond to these and other questions, the inter(con)textual reading of rhetorical encounters between these literacy events produce/negotiate them with/in the deep ecology of #BlackLivesMatter. Such reading helps us to not only see connections but also gaps, offering possibilities for meaning to create, fill, and exceed them, or compelling us to seek other texts, subjects, or rhetorical bodies as related foci for analysis. In these ways, Black inter(con)textuality reads/writes Blackness dynamically.

Conclusion: How "everybody gets free"[41]

So how does an argument for an inter(con)textual approach to deep rhetorical ecologies mark a demonstrative shift from other types of rhetorical analysis and/or meaning-making? How is reading one of these texts in isolation different from reading them with/in a deep ecological framework in which literacy events co-constitute a core focus? What do Black notions of temporality (Baker 1995; Sharpe 2016) in Fanonian fractures reveal for inter(con)textual readings of deep rhetorical ecologies to read otherwise? I contend that because our analysis focuses on relational interconnectedness in communicative and textual spheres, we could approach the literacy events in our primary frame with a sharp Black feminist relational awareness of how they speak to their environments and spaces in/between and across them, how they show the outside-inside-ness of Blackness in white worlds, how they mobilize a para/ontology. That conversation means being open and willing to divert our attentions to material not immediately relevant, pressing, or central and to considering how surrounding texts, meanings, and gaps can be sources for producing/negotiating meaning. Tangents, riffs, sounds from the next room might become drifts to follow in seeking meaning for the spaces in which we stand.

Shakur, for example, might not passingly appear important to populist meanings of #BlackLivesMatter or the conceptions of the post-Ferguson cultural moment, if we listened to Beyoncé's "Formation" or even Lamar's "The Blacker the Berry" track, for example. But in considering Shakur's relevance across these texts, we understand how her work (em)bodies relational race-radical Black activism—significant to conceptions of Blackness post-Ferguson in defiance of white (public and) institutional defensiveness. Shakur's intertwined relationships with other race-radical Black women like those on Roberts's (2016) syllabus, and even with Lamar's (2015a) mention of his Black mother, offer us paths to reading Blackness' multiplicity (in resistance to state power)—how it fashions and furthers Black meaning-making. By insisting on her/his/(s)toricizing, contextualizing, and demonstrating the importance of such women, this approach demands that reading be ecologically layered—and layered in ways that speak (to) power through a Black feminist relational method.

Inter(con)textual reading responds to the critical need for understanding Black con/texts not as just what is immediately relevant to a Black text's background and its specific time of production/publication. It summons also in what (wake-)works between them and around them, and in what histories worked with/in them contemporary deep ecologies re/imagine. In reading and producing meaning inter(con)textually, we not only (re)make meaning through a creative, generative process, but we also build upon rhetorical archives that came before us. Doing so means that we don't only have potentials for dynamic understandings of Blackness in interpersonal communication. We move closer to conceptualizing how Blackness (em)bodies the commodified object-beingness fueling the ever-expanding West, so we might conjure rhetorical technologies to destabilize it.

4

The Politics of Belonging...

WHEN "BECOMING A VICTIM OF ANY CRIME IS NO ONE'S FAULT"

On August 2, 2017, eleven days before a public white nationalist rally in Charlottesville, Virginia, turns deadly, I come upon the flyer below (figure 4.1). Stapled to a utility pole within a mile of Midwestern State University's main campus, its images and the word "NAZI" stop my usual walk toward the bus. The pole stands on the street where I live, right about where I was jumped by a wounded white vigilante three summers earlier. I think also about white supremacist posters found on campus the previous September. Enjoining with the "WE" that "MUST DRIVE" the "THEM" out, I want to resist the "ORGANIZING," to protect the "NEIGHBORHOOD" space, to possibly (em)body one of the four hands tearing the (still efficaciously arranged) swastika to pieces. I remain, however, wary of the imperative to "JOIN US." Who is the *us* of a white off-campus neighborhood? My conscious questioning of belonging to this neighborhood—a culturally white space—comes from the severe threat of my expulsion from it, a past incident of criminalization with/in it, in relation/ships to notions of exclusion tied historically to US territorial space, to the meanings of neo/Nazism, and my Black im/migrant body. As sociologist Nirmal Puwar highlights, "the moment when the historically excluded is included is incredibly revealing" (2004, 5). The poster fractures meanings.

I jolt aware of how that body relates to its surroundings in the moment of exclusion, forced to read it from a position of exteriority now invited in. Indeed, this "alienation is not an individual question" (Fanon [1952] 2008, 4). Black feminist theorist Wynter's (2001) sociogenic principle means that the moment of fracture ties the Black im/migrant body and its surroundings in learning once again what it is "like to be" Black; but what might be revealed of the internal workings of that principle by re/turning to it with/in these affective moments of encounter? The cultural reference to Nazism, iconography of white supremacy, my previous

 DOI: 10.7330/9781646421473.C004

FIGURE 4.1. *Anti-Nazi Poster (Photograph taken by author)*

experiences on this city street—these co-constitute a temporal object/subject developing from an intertwining and stitched-together reality with my environment. It is "a slow composition of my *self* as a body in the middle of a spatial and temporal world . . . [that] does not impose itself on me; it is, rather, a definitive structuring of the self and the world—definitive because it creates a real dialectic between my body and the world" (Fanon [1952] 2008, 83). Fanon describes carefully this being "in the white world": when a Black person "encounters difficulties in the development of [their] bodily schema. Consciousness of the body is solely a negating activity. It is a third-person consciousness. The body is surrounded by an atmosphere of certain uncertainty" (83). That "certain uncertainty," a navigation of the first person through a third, describes that fracture in the meanings of the campus's/neighborhood's deep rhetorical ecologies. What, though, makes up Fanon's "atmosphere" in the above anecdote, beyond the immediately called upon historically and temporally experienced? How do Black bodies dynamically come to being (or non/being) in white spaces vis-à-vis overtly political action? And how do policies and fractures with/in policy practice that white institutions implement play a role in that "certain uncertainty"?

My affective impulses to the flyer develop as they call up a fluid archive of relations to racism—the locative space of my home and street and the geographic and sociocultural deep rhetorical ecology of the MwSU campus. That reaction, put later into context with the Charlottesville attack and continuing histories of white capitalist heteropatriarchal hegemony in the United States, continue here to propel ecological/archival inquiry. Although "crisis" becomes "the archivist's moment," retorting to the flyer, I cannot practically mobilize rhetorician Jenny Rice's "inquiry as social action." For Rice (and the actor-network theorists from whom she draws), "where a question, exigence, or crisis exists, the inquirer's approach to this scene is not yoked with his or her own feelings." As a Black im/migrant—and therefore an understood threat to white nationalism—I do not have this privilege of taking "no account of how I am related personally to the scene of crisis" (2012, 174).[1] Such material embodiment with/in *deep* rhetorically ecological reading cannot be dichotomized for the sake of theorizing rhetorical agency or inter-/intra-/action, if analyzing lived experiences, particularly what it is "like to be" Black (Wynter 2001). Let's dig deeper.

This chapter turns to materials related to the practice of, and resistance to, institutional policy at Midwestern State University in 2016 via the framework of deep rhetorical ecologies while continuing to value autoethnographic engagement with/in those ecologies. I pay close attention to the temporal moment of 2016 in US race relations, a moment that sees the public reemergence of overt white supremacist propaganda and activity particularly related to / emphasized by Donald Trump's presidential election victory. By looking inter(con)textually at three sets of texts (or literacy events) produced through deeply ecological inter-/intra-/action at a historically white institution within this temporality, I expose how notions of Blackness become tethered with/in its spaces to deviance/disruption in response to crises of "safety." These crises of safety, I argue, arise as white (public) institutional defensiveness in these deep ecologies.

That illumination demonstrates how everyday practice of anti/racist policies make meanings that deeply affect and co-constitute non/beings precariously positioned at the neoliberal university. Deploying an African indigenous and relational Black feminist lens to such inquiry, I highlight notions of "deviance," of disruptive encounter, in complicating conceptions of institutionalized difference (or diversity). While the previous chapter adopts its #BlackLivesMatter analytic to interrogate the spaces of resistant meaning-making in reflectively reading that movement, this chapter adopts it in reading the historically white university with/in the post-Ferguson temporality. Here, analysis strives to further understand how Black students, instructors, staff, and their racialized assemblages in these educational spaces dynamically per/form Blackness in Fanonian fractures of deep ecologies in relation/ships with institutional attempts to address race issues sideways, colorblindly, and via concerns about safety. I zoom in particularly on Midwestern State University once again to locate possibilities for Black rhetorical agency within a white educational space, highlighting potentials for Black disruption as an antiracist rhetoric through what I call *rhetorical reclamation*.

In reading the politics of the everyday and how they come up against the institution through a Black feminist framework of relational intersectionality, I pursue Cathy Cohen's call for such directions in Black studies. Cohen outlines the transformative possibilities of spotlighting the nonexceptional and deviant and how we might think of Blackness beyond respectability, elitism, or public opinion, how "everyday contests over space, dress, and autonomy . . . pervade the lives of average Black people" (2004, 31). Centering the routine, highlighting the disruptive, and interrogating anti/racist policy practice offer avenues for challenging violent practices and epistemologies that reinscribe the very antiBlackness on which white heteropatriarchy and hypercapitalism always already build. To that end, I offer the concept of rhetorical reclamation via critical discourse analysis of daily workings of policy practice in relation to Blackness on white campus spaces. While white institutional defensiveness post-Ferguson produces conditions (via crises of safety) that continue to place Black bodies with/in those white institutions into precarious rhetorical binds, rhetorical reclamation offers means by which those bodies might creatively invert third-person consciousness to make Black agency with/in those conditions.

Literacy events relevant here respectively conjure different facets of MwSU's engagement with difference in relation to policy practice in a six-month period in 2016: via institutional anti/racist organization, jurisprudence, and protest. These events are (1) the "Black Lives Matter in the Classroom" symposium, a campuswide event series that took place April 1 and 4–5, 2016, represented here by the event's flyer and Carmen Kynard's (2016) keynote at the April 1 symposium (eventually put in conversation with a white supremacist poster found on campus in September 2016); (2) the operations of MwSU's Public Safety Department, exemplified by a series of "safety messages" via web posts between April and September 2016, together with publicity info for the department's Community Police Academy—an attempt at community outreach; and (3) a YouTube video of a heated interaction between students and administration at a sit-in protest at

an on-campus building on the night of April 6, 2016. The circulation of conspicuously antiracist and racist posters analyzed bookend the period, which saw the
shooting death of a Black teenager by the police in MwSU's surrounding city
in September. Amidst these national and local backdrops, the texts demonstrate
day-to-day processes of individual/institutional grappling with difference—
particularly Blackness—via policy practice. They illustrate both the white institutional defensiveness produced by the historically white institution in dealing
and not dealing directly with race and Blackness and, more crucially, possibilities
for locating Black object-being in rhetorical reclamation.

"There's *people* . . . in *this room* . . . who *live* here!"

While I take up surrounding texts in order to stress inter(con)textual reading, a
(print and electronic) flyer and keynote lecture, online safety posts and the publicity material for the Community Police Academy, and a protest video represent
the three core literacy events around which my study takes shape. My methodological approach resembles Ahmed's "ethnography of texts," as the cultural theorist follows around documents that "give diversity a physical and institutional
form" while also following around the actors who use them, to uncover what
diversity does/fails to do in educational institutions (2012, 12). Using a framework
of "multi-sited"-ness that stresses the moving, interconnected, and networked
meanings of a given concept, Ahmed's study offers the argument that diversity
documents often act nonperformatively in failing to enact the effects they name.
Likewise, I follow fluid notions of Blackness around to consider how that nonperformativity of institutional diversity commitments that Ahmed highlights in *On
Being Included* come up against the daily / lived effects / affects of them that Black
folk experience in historically white educational spaces. Deploying critical discourse analysis (Wodak 2001), I mine linguistic encounters and their contextual
exchanges with systemic power following studies using this method on discourses
of racism (van Dijk 1986), housing insecurity (Huckin 2002), and disability
(Price 2011), while instead paying specific attention to meanings/negations with
Blackness. Below, I ground us in these texts shaping relations to Blackness with/in
the deep ecology of Midwestern State during the six-month period in question.

~~~~~~

The Black Lives Matter in the Classroom events spanned several days (April 1, 4,
and 5, 2016) and coupled an interdisciplinary event with that generalized title
with a more specialized event titled Black Lives/Writers Matter run by MwSU's
English department. The former aimed to intertwine "arts, humanities, social
and political science perspectives to make visible and value Black life in [the
Midwestern state] and beyond through scholarly lectures, pedagogy workshops,

and community engagement" ([MwSU]BLMIC.org 2016). Framed publicly by conservatives as a question of whether the institution considered supporting the social movement as a "moral obligation" (Friedman 2016), the events drew support from a wide range of campus departments and organizations in support of diversity policy initiatives. These included MwSU's office for diversity and inclusion, academic departments, and various committees and programs.

The event's flyer—circulated on its website, as well as in print (posted throughout MwSU's campus)—includes the names of these supporters. Its white text sets these names in contrast with its dark background, and the names of sponsors along with location information constitute roughly half of the flyer. The flyer's image, set behind a citation, features prominently the faces of two Black women, with another Black individual obscured behind these two. All pictured in the image have raised fists, and the latter half of the word "FRUITVALE" arches behind them in bronze, in what appears to be community signage. The women wear gold jewelry and natural Black hairstyles, and the woman to the right of the image wears a black hoodie. None of these people appear to be looking toward the camera, instead looking to the street ahead of them. The URL citation for the poster is clickable on the electronic version of the poster (found on the event's website) and leads to an article about a student protest featuring a version of the photograph from which the poster's version seems to have been cropped. Centered directly above the flyer's image, the event title reads "#BlackLivesMatter in the Classroom Symposium."

On April 1, Carmen Kynard, then associate professor in English and gender studies at the John Jay College of Criminal Justice, delivers the lunch keynote for the Black Lives Matter in the Classroom Symposium. The lecture titled "'Ain't New to This': Black Lives Matter and the New Black Campus Movement," lasts about an hour and is followed by questions from the audience.[2] Kynard's talk centers around two narratives about her students of color set in relation to "the appropriation and neutralizing" of 1960s/1970s student protest into current institutional foci on diversity and inclusiveness; that contextualization interrogates how Black Freedom movements of the past find themselves situated in contemporaneous Black protest (Kynard 2016, 3). Through these stories Kynard emphasizes how her students' projects respond to shifting racial dynamics at public educational institutions, to the #BlackLivesMatter movement and to "new temporalities for cross-spatial, non-classroom-contained learning" (14). The Black feminist dares her audience to heed these students' examples, to match their creative energies in order to transform their contemporaneous university spaces.

~~~~~

Midwestern State University's Department of Public Safety posts alerts about violent crimes that occur in campus areas via its emergency management system and its website. According to that department's annual report, "Public Safety

Notices are issued by the University Police . . . Timely Warnings/Public Safety Notices provide information about crimes that have already occurred but still pose a serious or continuing threat" (Department of Public Safety 2017, 24). I analyze alerts publicized in the six-month period between April 1 and September 30, 2016.[3] Though the department records seven such alerts in the six-month period, members of the campus community sometimes receive emails and text messages containing additional reports and information that do not always correlate with the publicly posted information.

The alerts posted on the department's website contain news on crimes ranging from sexual assault to theft that describe suspects via racial and gender markers, as well as through clothing and bodily descriptions. They also provide tips on how members of the campus community might respond, thwart, or prevent victimhood. The alerts present some standard language across messages reasoning on victimhood, offering resources, and contact info, including the phrase *"becoming the victim of any crime is no one's fault,"* which appears in all but one post (emphasis mine; Department of Public Safety 2016e; 2016f; 2016g; 2016h; 2016i). While the reports remain consistent in certain respects on the kinds of information provided (date, time, and location data feature in all messages), the ways they describe suspects and sometimes victims differ significantly across alerts. These notices enact the Jeanne Clery Disclosure of Campus Security Policy and Campus Crime Statistics Act of 1990 that requires federally funded institutions to disseminate information on campus crime (Legal Information Institute 2018).[4] According to the safety department, the criteria considered before issuing such notices include "Did a crime occur?"; "Did a crime occur on campus property or on other Clery reportable property?"; "Is the crime a Clery reportable crime?"; and "Is there a serious and continuing threat to the campus community?" (Department of Public Safety 2016a).

The Department of Public Safety (2016b) at MwSU runs a four-week program intended to afford "eligible community members an idea of what it's like to protect and serve on campus." In its publicity material, the department stresses its commitment to "diversity," explaining that the academy also affords the university's police force "yet another opportunity" to learn about the campus community's issues. The sessions offer participants information on the police force's policies and practices in the form of discussions and role-playing, and it concludes with a "ride-along." Beneath this textual description, the publicity page for the program displays graphics and blurbs of the activities involved in it, which notably include the image of red handcuffs with the text "Handcuffing and suspicious persons calls" and a red circular "fingerprint" with "Process, fingerprint and photograph prisoners." Along with descriptions of who might be eligible for these sessions, an accompanying video advertises some of the program's highlights. Testimonials by three participants—a Black man, a Muslim woman of color,[5] and a white woman—intersect scenes of "role-playing" sessions. The video also contains police officers' explanations of the program's aims and philosophy.

On the night of April 6, 2016, a coalition of student groups, collected around a mission to "#Reclaim[MwSU]," engage in a sit-in protest of university administration, emphasizing their silencing, the corporatizing of the university's food and energy investments, and MwSU's support for anti-Palestinian companies as issues in need of attention. To that end, students demand thorough and detailed access to the university's budget and financial investments and for administration to be responsive to social justice efforts (Wainz 2016). The coalition included antisweatshop, pro-Palestinian, and pro-Black groups, among others. The student-led resistance occupies the seat of the university's president from midafternoon on April 6. Later that evening, when folks outside the building attempt to provide food for the students in the building, police prevent them or the food items from entering. The conversation recorded in the YouTube video artifact follows that incident. The video circulates on social media (such as YouTube and Facebook) and news websites with various titles, including "Coalition for Black Lives Told to GTFO at [Midwestern] State" and "[MwSU] Administration Threatens Expulsion Against Students" (Keep[MwSU]Public 2016).

In the video, six students (who include five students of color and five women) sit in conversation with two white male university officials. The men explain to the students that they must clear the building by 5 a.m. or they will be removed in adherence with the university's Student Code of Conduct. When questioned by students as to what exactly that removal means, the official describes in detail how they will be physically uprooted from the premises. He goes on to describe that the removal will not only result in their arrest, but also their expulsion from the university. When asked by students why such action would be necessary, the white official in the foreground describes the student group as "threatening" and "disruptive." He cites the earlier altercation with police: "Do you remember when you all made the rush down there and chanted to folks outside the doors a minute ago? That scared people [thrusts index finger in reproach]." When the group asks, "Who?," if it scared the "police officers with guns," the official contends that protestors refuse to understand their position; the students "would scare employees wanting to do their work." In his paternalistic tone, [MwSU's] senior vice president of administration urges the group to make "good decisions." When asked why "students" will not be allowed access to university space (beyond 5 a.m.), the official says the building is not open to "disruptive people." Even when protestors offer video evidence that the altercation used to reason them as a threat shows that designation invalid, the senior vice president contends that they have a disagreement and underlines his mandate. According to journalist Mary Morgan Edwards, "the final group of about 25 left at about 12:30 a.m., an official said" (2016). The event makes local news and results in heightened police presence for the next day or so around the university president's office.

~~~~~~~

In the previous chapter, I theorize a Black Lives Matter framework of inter(con)textual reading to mobilize the Black feminist process of literacy as the practice of freedom (hooks 1994). Inter(con)textual reading flows like rhetorician Banks's theory of "mixing," where through "selection, arrangement, layering, sampling, beat-making," and "blending" texts, contexts, temporalities, and histories surrounding my back-beat, I create "new and renewing possibilities" in analysis (2010, 35). I again take up that methodology that understands these "back-beat" texts under analysis as literacy events. Linking rhetorical theory with literacy studies through critical discourse analysis, conceptualizing rhetorical situations as literacy events offers means to dynamically understand the fluid evolution of meaning in deep rhetorical ecologies; it places focus on how texts' environment, histories, conjured temporalities, and contexts inform/impact their meanings. We'll recall underlying questions that mobilize that reading, remixed from Heath's ([1982] 2001) methodology of studying literacy events: *What texts make up the rhetorical environments of the event in question? What identities and activities surround those texts and impinge on the ways in which the environments' meanings evolve? And how do ongoing activities include that text or the individuals and activities which the text produces/negotiates?*

Continuing Threats:
White Institutional Defensiveness and Rhetorical Reclamation

Over the six-month period surveyed, all seven online safety posts (Department of Public Safety 2016d, 2016e, 2016f, 2016g, 2016h, 2016i, 2016j) contain the word "black." It appears 24 times, 13 as a racial descriptor and 11 to describe clothing or hair, all in relation to "suspects." Each time these posts narrate a body "black," the description contains a gender marker; "male" occurs twelve times. Safety posts elaborate the descriptor "black" with "light skinned," "dark skinned," "young," "with dreadlocks," "skinny," and "with a light complexion." Clothes associated with the word include "hoodie," "shorts," "jacket," "pants," "sweat pants," "sunglasses," and "high top shoes." The campus "community" might therefore imagine those "considered to be of a concern and/or a continuing threat" as Black, Black and male, and wearing stereotypically urban hairstyles and clothing. As Black feminist Simone Drake highlights when emphasizing this issue at the selfsame university in a 2016 monograph: "On a campus with a total African American student pop-

ulation of 5.33 percent or 3,630 students, in a state whose African American population is 13.7 percent or over 1.5 million people, and at a university with a total
enrollment of 64,868, notices that consistently identify black male suspects, in the
minds of many, render all black males on campus, whether they are students, staff,
faculty, or guests, as suspects" (2016, vii). Drake even details action taken by a staff
member at the institution to create their own internally circulated alert about a
Black man wearing a backpack around certain academic buildings, one of which
houses the department of African and African American studies. The staff member
responsible lets their audience know that they have notified campus police about
the issue. In analyzing the vigilante mimicking of the "official" alerts, Drake notes,
"For many, then, there is a logical equation between black maleness and pathol-
ogy" (viii). Black maleness, along with the continual use of the descriptor "black"
in detailing criminality (Department of Public Safety 2016d, 2016e, 2016f, 2016g,
2016h, 2016i, 2016j), renders those (em)bodying both constructs as incapable of
being law-biding and therefore a threat to safety in these historically white spaces.

The alerts demonstrate criminalization on MwSU's campus, one of several
processes transforming the likenesses of certain identity categories into criminals. This criminalization results directly from what Black feminist S. Browne
details as "racializing surveillance," a "technology of social control where surveillance practices, policies, and performances" mark what might be in/out of place,
moments that "reify boundaries, borders, and bodies along racial lines" resulting in discriminatory treatment (2015, 16). Such processes not only stigmatize
bodies but also precarious rhetorics embodied by and co-constituting their Black
assemblages—here rhetorics associated with deviant Black maleness. These messages might fracture Blackness into the wake of Trans-Atlantic slavery (Sharpe
2016), particularly echoing detailed runaway slave advertisements "defining the
slave" and, as a result, Blackness "as out of place" (S. Browne 2015, 72) in the afterlives of Trans-Atlantic slavery. But these processes apply not only to Black males,
as they also summon Blackness proper, a likeness, para/ontological images, and
resultant imaginaries, with references to dreadlocks, hoodies, and dark clothing.
The relation/*ships* evoked animates Spillers's idea of "oceanic ungendering," a literal suspension in the Middle Passage, an "analogy on undifferentiated identity"
(2003, 214). Spillers highlights that "under these conditions we lose at least gender difference in the outcome, and the female body and the male body become a
territory of cultural and political maneuver" (2003, 206). Sharpe, likewise, reads
the criminalization of Black women by New York City's stop-and-frisk tactics,
where Black women were frisked by male officers, justified by wearing clothing
common to crimes and having "suspicious bulge" (2016, 85). Indeed, one officer, an Inspector Royster, claims "Safety has no gender" (Ruderman 2012). In
the ecological temporalities that fractures animate, Blackness, invoked as the
deviant as in MwSU's security posts, becomes formless (here in terms of white

heteronormative gender distinctions) under the white authorial gaze as a means to the end of (re)establishing safety.

In so fracturing us into the wake of Blackness' non/Being with/in this deep ecology, notions of "community" border and boundary. S. Browne again (re)minds us of how the circulation of runaway slave advertisements assumed a white audience both "consuming at once the black subject, imagined as unfree," while producing "the readers of such advertisements as part of the 'imaginary community' of surveillance: the eyes and ears of face-to-face watching, observing, and regulating" (2015, 72). Those safety posts overtly mark these Black rhetorics as neither a part of, nor a present unwanted part of, who and what *belongs* in this particular historically white institution's spaces; Blackness represents an out of place non/being in such an ecology. The posts shape and racialize a white "campus body" through these hypervigilant, antiBlack senses. The notices co-constitute (and geographically close off) campus spaces as belonging to the "campus community," a white body defined through a mutual concern about "continuing threat" (Department of Public Safety 2016d, 2016e, 2016f, 2016g, 2016h, 2016i, 2016j). But notice how this threat works through the (em)bodied and the *imagined* to re/produce fear of Blackness as the specter of cultural criminality. As evidenced in Drake's (2016) vigilante's actions, white cultural imagination conjures Blackness via the ghostly figure of the Black male—even while gendered amorphous. As in Darren Wilson's projection of Michael Brown and Susan Smith's case of drowning her two sons,[6] this figure augurs "a specter, *the* specter" of crime (Sharpe 2016, 82; emphasis in original). Blackness in white imagination, manifested in historically white spaces, co-constitutes that para/ontological atmosphere of certain uncertainty with/against which white "community" becomes defined.

The department itself attempts to more clearly articulate who can make up this community through their aptly named "Community Police Academy." In promotional material, sections on "Who May Attend" and "Responsibilities of Participants" gesture at who the department considers "eligible community members." The former warns, "Please do not apply if you have been charged with or convicted of a felony" (Department of Public Safety 2016b), reinforcing the non-humanness/exclusion/de-citizening of criminalized/incarcerated people. From this statement, we know that the program does not include those criminalized by the US racial caste system as in need of knowledge about campus police's operations or as belonging to campus spaces. These exclusions reinforce the racing of such spaces by white institutional defensiveness through policy. Colorblindness's normalization in interrelation/ships with the stigmatization of the prison industrial complex make possible the general palatability of such statements.

The visual of a rounded fingerprint with the invitation to "Process, fingerprint and photograph prisoners," along with another of handcuffs advertising "Handcuffing and suspicious persons calls" as part of the "Community Police

Academy" program's highlights further categorize whom the department sees as in-/out-side of the campus community. The following statement on participant responsibility stipulates that clothing and other (em)bodied rhetorics play a part in who/what the department accepts as belonging: "Participants are expected to conduct themselves in a manner that will reflect credit to themselves, the university and the agent/organization. This includes personal appearance." The safety department's criminalization of Black skin, clothing, hair, and those (em)bodying Blackness (phenotypically and culturally) through security posts intimate what kinds of "personal appearance" or "conduct" might exclude identities—particularly Black identities—from eligibility in campus community: persons embodying ranges of racialized descriptors such as the "black male approximately 25 to 30 years old . . . 5'11" to 6'0" tall with a medium build, medium complexion, a tattoo on his right shoulder and wearing a white t-shirt and black shorts" (Department of Public Safety 2016f). The safety posts characterize such "personal appearances" as threating to the "safe" environs of the historically white university.

Almost predictably, however, publicity material for the outreach program conjures "diversity" as a trope with which it works diligently. The first line of the program's detailed description reads, "[MwSUPD] is committed to serving a diverse population of students, faculty, staff and visitors" (Department of Public Safety 2016b). Yet race remains a kind of spectral, amorphous presence through the program's attached promotional video. Although it features testimonials from a Black male employee (classed by captions as "HR Manager" in the "Office of Business and Finance") and a Muslim woman of color (a third-year student), notions of race and/or Blackness never overtly show up in publicizing the sessions. Those notions, nonetheless, function tellingly and perniciously in what appear as directorial and programmatic decisions to invert stereotypical scripts of those deemed deviant and dominant. The video thus portrays the Black male participant handcuffing a white male assailant—the latter notably (still) dressed in a gray hoodie, with that object reiterating the "personal appearance" of this community's out-group. The white woman detective described as "Community Police Academy Coordinator" in the video reveals that "the program is . . . uh . . . written for all ages, genders, and types of people." Her use of age and gender as markers of difference along with general hesitation in her statement and the phrase "types of people" suggest a tense sidestepping of race and racialization around issues (of police/civilian interrelationships) very much plagued by dynamics of racial identity/Blackness post-Ferguson. The video and related publicity material represent institutional white defensiveness by the historically white university, where the institution attempts to alleviate any potential racial stress that might arise in white audiences and "community" members through a series of defensive maneuvers. So, while the Department of Public Safety's security notices race Blackness as deviant and a "continuing threat" to safety (Department of Public Safety 2016d, 2016e, 2016f,

2016g, 2016h, 2016i, 2016j), it defines "diversity" through a shy away from racial difference that reinforces dominant and potentially stereotypical racial scripts.

The YouTube video of #ReclaimMwSU's student protest documents a discussion of what constitutes such a "threat" at the historically white university (Keep[MwSU]Public 2016). The more vocal of the white administrators in it deploys language of "violation" to depict the behavior of the protestors, explaining that in order to "have dialogue" the administration desires, and for such dialogue "to extend beyond tonight," the sit-in must desist. He explains that the activists "are violating the Student Code of Conduct as dictated by [the university president]." Contextualized in a paternalistic, condescending tone, which Fanon notes as a marker of white male rhetoric toward Black folk ([1952] 2008, 19), empowered deployment of language such as "dictated" registers as sinister with the impending threat of police force (Keep[MwSU]Public 2016). Although he explains that "this is your university"—almost to claim a shared belonging of the space—the administrator demands that the students leave the space by 5 a.m. to protect the university staff who work in the building (the proper, *safe* functioning of the neoliberal machine). An off-screen protestor asks directly, "How are we threatening them?"—the question spotlighting underlying tensions between authorities and the students' numerous Black and brown bodies. When the administrator explains that protestors' previous behavior (an attempt to obtain food) "scared" people, they probe, "Who did we scare?" "The policemen with guns?" The protestor's clapback in the exchange overtly calls into question the (over)policing of Black bodies at MwSU that buttresses historical scripts of such bodies as disruptive threats to white security, as always already out of place; Black beings "fit the description of the nonbeing, the being out of place, and the noncitizen always available to and for death" (Sharpe 2016, 86). Like the email notices and the vigilante response that Drake (2016) narrates show, being a criminalized racializing assemblage at the historically white institution elicits rhetorical and weaponized police/vigilante response.

After various overlapping exchanges, the white male administrator, frustratedly asks, "Are you telling me that we need guns to protect ourselves?" (Keep[MwSU] Public 2016). In making such an assumption, his inquiry turns the "fault" of criminalization on to those criminalized because of their antiracist assemblage. Such a move resembles the public vilification by media coverage of several Black people whose deaths became associated with Black Lives Matter protests: the ideology that #IfTheyGunnedMeDown exposes. When the other white male administrator attempts to deescalate the tension in the room by again stating that the very presence of their bodies in a campus space would "scare employees," an off-screen voice wonders, "Students would scare employees?" Using racially unmarked language to classify folks as "students" and "employees" through their questions, the activists deploy universal language to gesture at the problematics of that very (colorblind) language. The racial stress for the white institution caused by an assemblage of Black and brown bodies and affects heightens the perceived threat to the safety of whiteness. The protest (em)bodies the deep ecologically affected ghosts of Blackness, haunting white notions of safety. The administrators there-fore defensively summon the Student Code of Conduct as a policy that might quell such stress and snuff out racialized insurgency. Later, another voice probes: "Are you saying this university building is not open to students?"—the query emphasizing *the politics of belonging* in campus spaces, confronting the institution with the challenge of actively defining its fictitious borders, rather than drawing on the negation of Blackness to do so. They seek an adjective since their nouns do not seem to stick signification. The more vocal white administrator responds: "It is not open to disruptive people." In deeming the group disruptive—and nota-bly "people" rather than students—he rhetorically joins with the safety notices in determining who and what might be a part of, not a part of, and a threat to the stability of whiteness and white spaces and by extension its institutions, while evoking the language of white institutional defensiveness. Anyone can be "dis-ruptive," just as Nixon's administration claimed that every/anyone had "freedom of choice" in the United States.

But in response to the marker "disruptive," one Black woman quite audibly notes, "Some of us are people of color, so . . ." slapping her knees, as the administra-tor looks away from the group in nonresponse to the point. Her calling out of the racial dynamics of the situation puts racialized dynamics inherent in their treat-ment on blast. The administrator's telling look away from racialization evidences the "intense silent resistance," that "speaking the truth-of-racism-to-power tends at [historically white educational institutions] to be met with" (Kynard and Eddy 2009, W35). In the fracture between them, the protestor *rhetorically reclaims* pos-sibilities for Blackness and its meanings by illustrating the unsaid of the email notices: Blackness at/for the historically white institution equals disruption to security (Keep[MwSU]Public 2016). Difference, instead of signaling "diversity," spotlights deviance. The student protestor rallies race conceptually in critiqu-ing the very idea of racialization, in *anti*racism. Whereas the Community Police Academy video represents the tense defensiveness surrounding the acknowledg-ment of race as a marker of difference (Department of Public Safety 2016b), the Black woman protestor makes clear the unsaid notion that Blackness disrupts the functioning of white institutions when not incorporated unmarked into its fabric or public practice of institutional policy (Keep[MwSU]Public 2016).

More than a reassertion of cultural ownership over gestures, performances, and objects, these reclamations involve public exposure of racializing Blackness, in upending its stigmatizing energy for rhetorical means and as marginalized literacy. Here lie the rhetorical possibilities in Fanonian fracture. Such agency functions/flows relationally, with potentials for social energy and discursive power through Black feminist and African indigenous frameworks for agency that conceive it as simultaneously, fluidly, individual and collectively interconnected (Chilisa 2017). In the Black woman's "some of us" she racializes her body *along with, in between, and across* the protesting assemblage, mapping herself in/directly through the group's interrelations. That fracture, possible through the rhetorically exteriorized co-constituted self, also mobilizes a past that is not a past by reanimating Black being in the afterlives of slavery. While in the "sensitizing action" of the fracture, "the goal of the [Black being's] behavior will be The Other (in the guise of the white man), for the Other alone can give [them] worth" (Fanon [1952] 2008, 119), rhetorical reclamations forge otherwise possibilities with/in its affects/temporalities/meanings as *actional*. In that moment, the Black non/being, "preserving in all [their] relations," their non/beingness and para/ontology with/in their deeply ecological environments, "prepares to act" (173). That action may take on an interchangeable range of rhetorics to hurl Blackness as object-being at the white institutional frame, as with Black autoethnography, hashtagging, and inter(con)textual reading in previous chapters and Black disruption in this one.

Rhetorical reclamations bear similarity to the rhetorical theory of "recognitions in between," forwarded by Wendy S. Hesford (2015) via Arabella Lyon (2013), as they also "represent the temporal present," while pointing "to the moment of relationship among rhetorical actors where future political potentials are formed" (Hesford 2015, 552). Hesford argues that recognitions in between spotlight the limitations of classical liberal and neoliberal recognition logics and generates alliances not possible via those logics (539). The rhetorical theorist offers #BlackLivesMatter die-ins as sites of collective recognition, "where recognition exists in between bodies and identities . . . to connect those who came before with those who come after," highlighting "a shared history of struggle and hope" (552–553). In the case of Black rhetorical reclamations, however, the Fanonian fracture, the temporalities of the wake, specifically transfigure Blackness into non/being as deviation and always already living in the aftermath of slavery. These reclamations thus cull the particular plasticizing commodification of Blackness, through object-being, in a rhetorical otherwise made possible through histories of antiBlackness. Rhetorics of the Black student protestor here revitalize a push for Black freedom through (re)claiming a social death (in identifying the assemblage "disruptive") in the ways that #BlackLivesMatter reiteratively draws on the idea that Black lives do not matter in asserting that they do. The movement's cling to Black feminist thought (and insistence in the *Black* of #BlackLivesMatter) and the protestor's reclamation mobilize to invert the philosophical, hermeneutical, legal, and material control of Black women's (em)bodied rhetorics dating back to Trans-Atlantic slavery that conjure Black women as carriers of Blackness (and thus deviance).[7] Black feminist rhetorics invert a denial of agency to expose the white racializing power structure. Through the wake work of the fracture, these relations (might) emerge between/across called-upon histories/contexts/temporalities with/in Wynter's (2001) sociogenic principle in the Black woman's retort in distributively energizing deviance back at the administrators' racially colorblind logic.

While Lyon points out that "any act in-between is not easily owned or attributed" (2013, 58), rhetorical reclamations ground their own specific cultural temporalities and histories. Such gestures, performances, and objects mobilize their historiographical/temporal rhetorical agency. Yet, what Hesford argues of #BlackLivesMatter die-ins as recognitions in between also applies to rhetorical reclamations as they "put forth an understanding of agency based not on autonomous, atomistic self, but grounded in social interdependences" (2015, 553). The Black rhetorical reclamations outlined in this chapter and project proper work through such ecological inter-/intra-connections in Black feminist and African indigenous notions of agency to destabilize white institutional defensiveness, which has become standard operational procedure for white institutions. They deploy Cohen's (2004) appeal for disruption/deviance to be reconceptualized as generative for transformative possibilities for Black folk in their social deaths and object/being-ness. Rather than reactionary posturing aimed squarely at rehabilitating white culture, these reclamations alternatively cull Black histories, temporalities, languages, and literacies as Black invention. They, in ways, use the epidermalization of Blackness for Black contagion.

Kynard's keynote for the #BlackLivesMatter Symposium, likewise, calls out the neutralization of Black protest in aid of notions of inclusivity, instead focusing on how her students act as "practitioners" (2016, 2) to push against these institutional moves/motives. Through their experiences and projects, such as her student Andrene's creation of the e-portfolio website "Pretty for a Black Girl," Kynard demonstrates how Black insurgency operates in the classroom to invert neoliberal value-systems of literacy. The rhetorics of Andrene's website undercut degrading racist stereotypes, Black women's struggles with colorism, and the marginalization of Black vernacular. For instance, Andrene's section headings draw from Black cultural vernacular: "Burning through the Cerebral Cortex," in particular, references Oprah Winfrey's description of Black women's problematic and oppressive histories with hair straightening. In demonstrating how students of color innovate through what Kynard calls "vernacular technocultural competence" (14), the Black feminist's keynote works to turn the heteropatriarchal capitalist project of offering Black bodies space in white institutions back at those institutions. Unlike the stigmatization of Black bodies by safety notices, and distinct from imagery of Black protest for publicity, the keynote—following Spillers—strives beyond the historical use of Black folk as "raw material" for white means (14). Kynard's student example protests hair-straightening practices and colorism—that have destructive historical and ongoing consequences—through "Pretty for a Black Girl," operating in online and the keynote presentation's temporalities, while signaling how Black student protest extends (and has historically extended) sociopolitical possibilities for subverting literacies dressed up as racializing surveillance like the e-portfolio. The keynote thus acts as its own kind of rhetorical reclamation co-constituted by those of Kynard and Kynard's students.

The presentation not only emphasizes Kynard's students' projects and experiences to inform disciplinary fields and universities on re/shaping education from multiple knowledges, but also focuses on the energies of cultural expressions (and modes of expression) deeply engrained in Black cultural temporalities. The presentation's focus on Kynard's student's cultural force in critiquing matters such as Black hair and language—along with pro-Black attitudes grounded in the Black Freedom movement and Black feminist ideology—ephemerally reclaims space in the white institution for subversive energy. Such energy comes through student resistance to dominant cultural forces, rather than institutional policy practice. On the flip side, the poster for the symposium, through its images, represents similar cultural expressions in its display of Black clothing, hair, and embodiment. The flyer foregrounds young Black women's roles in the Black Lives Matter movement, Black power fists, and a black-and-gold color scheme (in clothing, jewelry, and even the backdrop signage). The listing of eleven institutional organizations that cut interdisciplinarily across the campus use as much of the flyer's space as the image, endeavoring to signal an ethic of resistance grounded in the work of Black women and supported by a coalitional range of allies. However, while the poster utilizes these rhetorics to publicize presentations such as Kynard's, their appropriation by the selfsame university that marks Blackness as a ghostly threat potentially renders the visualized Black student protest's agency moot. These images, in white cultural imagination, possibly reinscribe notions of Blackness (beyond the white community) commodified as deviance in the white gaze, while selling wokeness as white progressiveness.

On the surface, the visuals for the Black Lives Matter in Classrooms Symposium run opposite these widely circulated criminal perceptions of relational Black assemblages and that arise from safety notices (Department of Public Safety 2016d, 2016e, 2016f, 2016g, 2016h, 2016i, 2016j) or those definitions of diversity at MwSU more subtly represented through Community Police Academy (Department of Public Safety 2016b) material. They draw on the same kind of specificity in representing Black bodies as the notices: not only through skin color, but, importantly, through dark clothing—a hoodie in particular—natural Black hair, and dark shades. The images, indeed, belie the conception of Blackness as criminal specter that results from the circulation of the safety department's posts. But although they publicly provide visions of Black student protest circulated widely at the historically white institution, their use by the institution's eleven listed funders runs the risk of co-opting such imagery for those funders and the institution's public and financial benefit. And while the Black Lives Matter Symposium flyer does similarly mark its visual rhetorics racially—not (color-blindly) shying away from racial identification—the poster lists the symposium's institutional supporter, its office of "diversity" and "inclusion," close to the top of its allies, opening up potential readings of neutralized, objectified Blackness in nonperformativity for institutional benefit.

Universal Whiteness, Feelings, and the Question of Black Antiracism

That white male administrators' visible turn away when confronted with race by the Black woman protestor's rhetorical reclamation, along with his earlier characterization of the protestors to diffuse the situation—he calls the protestors "smart kids"; he wants them to "make good decisions" (Keep[MwSU] Public 2016)—(em)bodies and reflects a general attitude of refusing to acknowledge the racialized dynamics of criminalization by white institutions. In such refusal, the racial stress caused for empowered white assemblages by such situations often results in language of universalized morality such as "smart" and "good"—language signaling white institutional defensiveness—here couched in the infantilizing rhetorical finger-wagging of paternalistic "care." That language exemplifies the "more subtle forms where [Black student protestor's] political activism is downplayed so as not to create conflict" (Kynard 2013, 239). The video advertisement for the Community Policy Academy deploys comparable rhetoric, as its coordinator skips over race as a marker of difference (immediately after highlighting age and gender) to claim: "everybody will be successful in this program" (Department of Public Safety 2016b). Race and Blackness—and by extension difference, such as with the ungendering of Blackness in the pursuit of white "safety"—do not matter so long as some universal good is achieved. As Ahmed explains via an interview with a research participant on the politics of "perception data,"[8] "diversity work becomes about generating the 'right image' and correcting the wrong one . . . about *changing perceptions of whiteness rather than changing the whiteness of organizations.* Changing perceptions of whiteness can be how an institution can reproduce whiteness, as that which exists but is no longer perceived" (2012, 34; emphasis in original). The video, therefore, naturally, fails to highlight the exclusionary politics used in determining who might constitute the "everybody," whereas the eligibility criteria use the language of "conduct" and the prison industrial matrix to mobilize its white institutional defensiveness (Department of Public Safety 2016b).

Similar to the video, though, campus safety notices use the standardized statement: "Becoming the victim of any crime is no one's fault" (Department of Public Safety 2016e, 2016f, 2016g, 2016h, 2016i, 2016j). Though significantly undercutting a culture of victim-blaming that can be particularly damaging when campus crimes like sexual assault face publicness, the statement comes attached to all but one of the Department of Public Safety's posts speaking to "any" violent crime. In an attempt to exculpate and soothe its audience from the racial stress of its tense power dynamics, the sentence places victimhood in a subjectless, cultureless vacuum. No one is at fault; you are "smart kids"; "everyone will be successful" (Keep[MwSU]Public 2016). It also, despite attempts to eschew "blame," potentially exonerates all readers and consequently the institution of social responsibility for the spaces in which "crimes" occur. Who is the "one" that is free from fault (Department of Public Safety 2016e, 2016f, 2016g, 2016h, 2016i, 2016j)? Should audiences understand violence as randomly occurring in campus spaces and not tethered to bodies, interactions, or cultures? Or is it that responsibility is shared among all of the readers of the message (the "campus community") and therefore not falling on any *one* person? Like the nonperformativity that Ahmed characterizes as inherent in institutional language on diversity (2012, 117), the message's defensive posture tries too hard to soothe racial stress for the white community and almost becomes a nonmessage. What it does, however, arguably—by not tethering blame to any/body in particular—is leave such blame to the ghost of Blackness, that spectral criminality not belonging to this community, that certain uncertainty of para/ontological Blackness.

The ambiguity of the statement is then complicated with the following, which appears on all seven posts: "We remind you to increase your overall safety by being cautious and looking out for one another; being aware of your surroundings and looking assertive; walking with a trusted friend or co-worker, when possible; if a situation makes you feel uncomfortable or unsafe, choose an alternative" (Department of Public Safety 2016d, 2016e, 2016f, 2016g, 2016h, 2016, 2016j). If the former interpretation of the initial statement is read to mean that no person or institutional body is at fault for violence on campus, then the tips that follow belie that notion. The final statement, which flatly offers alternative "situations" to discomfort and danger, also puts some responsibility on members of the "campus community" for their bodies, interactions, and cultures. Of importance, however, "one" and "you" as subjects come after very specific third-person racialized, gendered descriptions of persons involved in violent altercations. This shift sets up a binary between a racialized "they/them" and a generalized "one/you," a *Black or right* scenario, a contrast between heavily gendered, classed, racialized language regarding Blackness. The seemingly colorblind, vague tips—the rhetoric of institutional white defensiveness—on maintaining the safety of this "one/you" highlight the coded language of those tip-toeing pieces of advice. Such language resembles that of workplace cultural competence training courses, where "racially coded language reproduces racist images and perspectives while it simultaneously reproduces the comfortable illusion that race and its problems are what 'they' [people of color] have, not us [whites]" (DiAngelo 2011, 55). These rhetorics have the

FIGURE 4.2. *White Supremacist Poster (Photo Credit: Mike Bierschenk)*

insidious potential to continue to mark Black bodies in white educational spaces as disruptions to a universalized white comfort, as has historically been the case.

In late September 2016, faculty in the historically white university's department of English bring the department's attention to white supremacist posters found throughout academic buildings at Midwestern State. The posters, which bookmark the end of the six-month period under analysis, visually illustrate the vagueness of white nationalist heteropatriarchal ideology found in standardized statements about "fault" and boilerplate language used by white administrators to paper over relational, intersectional resistance (Department of Public Safety 2016d, 2016e, 2016f, 2016g, 2016h, 2016i, 2016j; Keep[MwSU]Public 2016).

The mandate "SERVE YOUR PEOPLE," while superficially straightforward, raises several questions, most significant: To whom does the poster direct its message? Since the group claiming ownership of it, Identity Evropa, openly identifies as white supremacist, then "your people" might well be understood as white people at the educational institution. However, what the poster leaves unclear is the particular subject of the imperative. Who is the understood "you" that should "SERVE YOUR PEOPLE"? The institution? White faculty? White staff? White students? Identity Evropa's goals to "promulgate the idea that America was founded by white people for white people and was not founded to be a multiracial or multicultural society" (Anti-Defamation League 2018) along with the grayscale image of Julius Caesar attached to the alphabetic text suggest all of the above—a centralized message from a centralized dictating power—but the poster's ambiguity leaves the possibility for any of the above. It aligns with the them/you binary dynamics of the university's security posts. Like victimhood being "no one's fault" (Department of Public Safety 2016d, 2016e, 2016f, 2016g, 2016h, 2016i, 2016j), suggesting some *other* collective as possibly responsible for crime, the poster suggests service of white people as *some one's* responsibility in relation to the inclusive "YOUR" people, a singular duty. In Wynterian terms, whiteness in the form of the white heteropatriarchal male (and his apposite institutions) overrepresents the genre of universal Man (Wynter 2003)—The you, in relation to the third-person them (re/calling Fanon [1952] 2008) here—targets universal Man, signaling whiteness.

Conversely, the Black Lives Matter Symposium material, through Kynard's (2016) keynote, frankly calls such amorphous, ambiguous appeals to the universal—as with "All Lives Matter"—into question. Kynard's keynote touches on this issue in discussing white male students' feeling the need to ask why race might be important, noting the risk inherent in response as a Black woman instructor prone to complaints based on racial stereotypes (of being overly aggressive and "extra"). As opposed to the white supremacist appeal to absolute dictatorial rule or the deployment of universalized colorblind language, Kynard's (2016) keynote spotlights Black students' projects that protest continuing histories/temporalities of oppression—highlighting the specific rhetorical potentials of marginalized bodies in university spaces. Moreover, its centering of student protestors situates the keynote as possibly more immediate to a potential college audience than the static, decontextualized Louvre sculpture of Nicolas Coustou's Julius Caesar. Situated in their own histories, Kynard's students' projects conjure their "central role in reshaping schooling" (Kynard 2013, 239) that continue to be ignored. Meanwhile, the white supremacist appeal to centralized rulership and as a message from above to below (via the angle of the photograph) speaks to the material processes that constitute white authority at the historically white institution. The white administrator's message surrounding the violation of the Student Code of Conduct is "dictated" from a similar angle (Keep[MwSU] Public 2016). The "variably subtle" (Anti-Defamation League 2018) directive to "SERVE YOUR PEOPLE" aimed at a vaguely understood audience aligns with (invisible) notions of whiteness in security notices.

The word "white" appears only three times in the seven such notices to describe clothing ("pants," "shoes," and "Nike logo"), while the world "color/ed" appears only once in the description of clothing (Department of Public Safety 2016d, 2016e, 2016f, 2016g, 2016h, 2016i, 2016j). No ethnicity descriptors occur in the alerts. Racialization with regard to deviance on MwSU's campus occurs only with reference to Blackness, nuanced in terms of gender, age, and clothing. These security posts clearly mechanize antiBlackness through Blackness' conjured threatening spectrality. The notices do not describe a number of individuals featured in the them in terms of race but only by gender, however (perhaps because they are deemed crime "victims"). This move eerily echoes the Community Police Academy coordinator's mention of difference via age and gender only (Department of Public Safety 2016b). In the six-month period surveyed in safety posts (Department of Public Safety 2016d, 2016e, 2016f, 2016g, 2016h, 2016i, 2016j), the sharp contrast of all suspects being marked "black," with all other described individuals being racially unmarked, reinforces the ubiquitous invisibility of whiteness in US culture "against which difference is constructed" (Lipsitz 1998, 1). Whiteness, thus, need not "acknowledge its role as an organizing principle in social and cultural relations" (Lipsitz 1998, 1) while also not being particularly tethered to certain bodies or clothing (Dyer 2005). Although statistically persons described as "black" make up 100 percent of those described as "suspects" in the alerts (Department of Public Safety 2016d, 2016e, 2016f, 2016g, 2016h, 2016i, 2016j), results of a search of the safety department's daily crime log from the six-month period, which rendered 1,522 reports, do not describe those reporting or involved in crimes using race—only gender, profession, age, or name (Department of Public Safety 2016c).[9] The editing of what appears in security notices directly circulated to the campus community, then, offers a specific, racialized Black picture of what criminality and security threats look like on this particular campus. That picture, when rhetorically reclaimed in Black protest by those deemed deviant, as in the Black woman protestor's statement "well some of us are people of color, so . . ." (Keep[MwSU]Public 2016), might be mobilized as Black rhetorical agency in Black feminist antiracism, as also evidenced by Kynard's (2016) symposium keynote.

Public backlash to that symposium centered around the idea that the white institution postulated engagement with the Black Lives Matter movement as a "moral obligation" for students. The conservative news website *Campus Reform*, in an article notably titled "[Midwestern State] encourages students to participate in Black Lives Matter movement," undercuts the symposium's "claims" that antiracism efforts mean to counter structural racism—and thereby "help" the white institution's public perception and functioning—by citing the institution's African American president and a conference on hip-hop culture held at the university (Friedman 2016). By framing the event in relation to the university president's race, as a part of a larger drive to focus on Black culture, and splicing parts of the symposium's material on the question of "moral obligation," the article implies a kind of "Black takeover," racing coalitional antiracist efforts as Black. It plays on white fears, using white feelings as a means to justify racist backlash. The news article suggests that the university as a singular entity "encourages" participation in the movement—in its title—and wants students "to endorse the aims of the Black Lives Matter movement"—in its first line. Another such article uses the word "heralding" to describe MwSU's publicity of the event, framing it in relation to the July 2016 shooting of Dallas police officers and other academic institutions' engagement ("from kindergarten to college") with the social movement (Kline 2016).

Conservative reaction to institutional antiracist efforts at the historically white institution thus intimate those efforts as the replacement of whiteness. This very concept of replacement underlines "the new white supremacist slogan 'You will not replace us,'" a phrase "adopted and popularized" by Identity Evropa (Anti-Defamation League 2018, n.p.). As pop culture critic Jeff Chang explains in recounting the rhetoric of the Trump presidential campaign in 2015 and 2016, "Racial apocalypse is the recurring white American narrative in which the civilizers, the chosen people meant to fulfil their destiny, are overrun by the savages, the barbarians who embody chaos and ruin . . . The end of whiteness is one of the oldest, most common Americans tell to scare ourselves" (2016, 14). These fears evoke policy stances and practices that either avoid the subjects of race and Blackness (through colorblindness) or manipulate them as objects for the purposes of institutional gain, as demonstrated in the Community Police Academy's video ad (Department of Safety 2016b)—stances that exemplify white institutional defensiveness.

Such a threat, even understood via "peaceful" demonstrations like student sit-ins, "scare employees who are wanting to do their work," as posited by white university administrators in the footage of the on-campus protest (Keep[MwSU] Public 2016). That the historically white institution would publicly "endorse" Blackness through symposia, hold discussions on the morality of social in/justice, or even acknowledge that "disruptive students" (Black and brown students) belong in university spaces causes public racial stress. That racial stress manifests itself in individual "white responses"—which "include anger, withdrawal, emotional incapacitation, guilt, argumentation, and cognitive dissonance (all of which reinforce the pressure on [institutional diversity programming] facilitators to avoid directly addressing racism)"—is what Robin DiAngelo describes as "White Fragility" (2011, 55–56). The Nixon administration's decoupling of racism from institutions to make it a one-on-one issue trickled through to contemporary neoliberal culture means that far-right journalists can call upon these responses as tactics for maintaining the status quo. Further, when institutions create policies or policy statements that posture defensively on the subject of race and Blackness, they enact these affects through rhetorics of institutional white defensiveness.

Such public or institutional defensiveness often arises in ways that deflect attention away from evidenced injustice or articulations of being by Black folk, instead placing emphasis on individualized (white) feelings. In the promotional video for the Department of Safety's Community Police Academy, for instance, much work goes into describing the feelings that arise for police officers in the act of doing their job (Department of Public Safety 2016b). The program slyly allows these descriptions to come from people of color—primarily a Black man but also a Muslim woman of color—rather than the police themselves. The video first frames the academy as responding to public perceptions of police; a white woman officer atop a horse explains, "We're gonna talk about that fear." The video does not explain who has what fear, or why, or how it might be historicized and racialized. It leaves questions of how exactly the program confronts that fear, instead addressing it through articulating the affective experience of police via Black and brown bodies. But, as the security posts remind us, the specter of Black criminality structures who the subject "we" (as in "we're gonna talk") of the community includes.

After the program coordinator explains the "memory you'll never forget" from "doing something hands-on," footage of the Black male staff member splices in: "High stress, high stress absolutely," he explains. As scenes of him apprehending a white hoodied male cut in and out, he continues, "You're caught between several emotions." He cuffs the white "suspect" while his voiceover contends "You don't have a lot of time to, uh, to think about what you wanna do . . . and as you assess the situation, you cannot hesitate." Through the experience of a Black male middle-class staff member, the safety department provides an account that asks its audience to empathize with police officers, humanizing them through multiple affects—"high stress," "several emotions," "cannot hesitate"—while not once mentioning the hardware the program equips the man with for the role-playing exercise. The video also fails to clearly note why hesitation becomes an invalid option in the situation. Through the scene the Black man holds a gun and handcuffs while wearing a safety vest, all co-constituting his assemblage. "It really gives you a very good understanding of what law enforcement goes through," he concludes. The video's focus on (empathizing with) the feelings of police, its unracing and sidestepping of the acute problem of racial profiling and police brutality in the post-Ferguson cultural moment, and reactive use of Black and brown bodies to potentially defend impulsive (and possibly lethal) actions by the police illustrate the pernicious ways in which institutional white defensiveness employs the language of feelings and universal humanity to articulate in/difference—and in some ways dismissal—toward antiBlack social injustice and state violence.

University administration also utilize such tactics and language to invalidate student resistance (raced, deviant, and disruptive) at Midwestern State. In the protest video, for example, students point to cell phone videos of the altercation with police that allegedly "scared people" to validate their nonviolent belonging to university space (Keep[MwSU]Public 2016). The white male administrators dismiss the videos based on the "fact" that "people who were here, who work past five o clock, left early tonight . . . You know why? They were scared you guys were going to do something." The less vocal white administrator (in the background) states, "That's the truth, you guys, that's the truth." White truth marked "universal" re/presents the only valid truth, as Black beings, historically, lack "the possibility of universalism that comes with reason" in the face of Enlightenment rationality, as Mbembe notes (2017, 86). Therefore, when an off-screen protestor asks if administrators would change their positions if students could "prove" via video evidence that there was no "rush" to the doors deemed "scary" and the reasoning behind the threats of the students' removal (and nonbelonging), the white administrator in the foreground admits, "No, I wouldn't change my position" (Keep[MwSU]Public 2016). Much like the idea that videos documenting (sometimes lethal) violence by police against Black people and people of color have failed legally to prove injustice both post-Ferguson and prior, the administrators regard the criminality of the "disruptive" (Black) assemblage to be inherent and indisputable. Much like Darren Wilson's fear of the overwhelming "Hulk-Hogan-like" strength of Mike Brown, white capitalist heteropatriarchy adjudges those deviant as always already non-law-abiding, placing importance on white feelings, impulses, and appeals to universal reason to unmake Black lives.

See(k)ing Black Possibilities

So, what, if any, alternative possibilities exist for Black folk who live and co-constitute these deep rhetorical ecologies? How might they navigate these spaces in the historically white institution to create generative or perhaps transformative potentials for Blackness? Just as Black folk at Midwestern State have the "option" not to dress in hoodies, in dark sunglasses, and in black clothing and not to wear natural hair, as those criminalized in safety notices—though, of course, they cannot change their biological skin color—the white administrators in the video afford students the "option" of leaving (Keep[MwSU]Public 2016). They miss the important objection that these Black and brown students have to their "philosophy," the latter being that if deemed disruptive, as the administrators put it, "we are going to take you out." "People live here," the most vocal Black woman protestor proclaims; "there's *people* . . . in *this room* . . . who *live* here!" Instead, the administrators offer the "option" of leaving or, they say, "our police officers will physically pick you up and take you to a paddy wagon and take you to be arrested"; the students will be "discharged from school also." The possessive adjective "our" before police indicates the relationship between university administration and its safety services. Despite attempts at dialogue by protestors, the white male administrators wield the force as a weapon to vanquish their resistant rhetorical agency, since "we don't have an agreement" on video evidence according to the more assertive white male administrator. The protestors' Black and brown push against the neoliberal university, considered a "disruptive" threat to security, must be expelled—it does not belong.

Neo-Nazi Andrew Anglin, who attended Midwestern State for a semester in 2006 (O'Brien 2017), declares the university administrators' actions in the video a victory for the state—it made him "proud" to be from it (Anglin 2016). Indeed, as Kynard spotlights, "blatantly racist public forums" often question Black student protest's transformative potentials (2013, 239). Anglin (2016), moreover, races the protestors' "Black" on his now publicly defunct website the Daily Stormer.[10] He tellingly titles his article "[MwSU] Administration Tell Black Lives Protestors to GTFO or Get Arrested and Expelled." The now infamous neo-Nazi's involvement with the organization of the rally that mobilized hate into murder in Charlottesville, Virginia, demonstrates the very real, dangerous white supremacist entanglement in these deep rhetorical ecologies at historically white universities—involvement that the utility pole flyer at the beginning of this chapter directly spotlights and attempts to push against. In addition to the implications of a neo-Nazi endorsement of such behavior, however, the ideologies of administrators at Midwestern State—hidden in plain sight through white institutional defensiveness publicly exposed through the video's rhetorics, put in Black feminist inter(con)textual relation/ships with other notions of Blackness at the historically white institution—reveal much about racialization and anti-Blackness in such spaces. The video, arguably, demonstrates what happens when Black student protest comes up against the enactment of policy (here, in particular, the Student "Code" of Conduct) (Keep[MwSU]Public 2016). Further contextualized with the national attention garnered by Black student protest at the University of Missouri in late 2015, the video of student protest at Midwestern State shows tensions not only at a regional but also at a national level; "nearly one hundred universities and colleges would receive demands demonstrating for racial equity . . . during the 2015–2016 school year" (Chang 2016, 34). Eventually, the "Black Liberation Collective, a national network of Black student activists" would emerge from various disparate campus struggles (Ransby 2018, 80).

The student protestors in the video, especially the Black woman in red, offer a practical Black feminist framework for undercutting the manifestation of oppressive whiteness in these white spaces (Keep[MwSU]Public 2016). When she emphasizes that "there's *people* . . . in *this room* . . . who *live* here!" she illuminates the disconnect—the generative fracture—in between and along life and work.

In direct contrast with the white administrators' continued logic that "scared" white employees "don't want these kinds of things happening at their jobs, don't want to be exposed to this," she calls attention to her (em)bodied Black (student) precarity in simultaneously living *and* working in such spaces, while doing antiracism through disruptive rhetorical agency. Like her earlier declaration that "some of us are people of color, *so* . . ." she reveals the dynamics of the rhetorical situation that racialize, gender, and class the space across and in between rhetorical actors with/in the deep ecology through rhetorical reclamation. Again, her rhetoric draws not on a "transparent I" of Western Man (Ferreira da Silva 2007) but in summoning herself outside of herself, as a part of a disruptive collective through Black feminist relationality, with (Blackened) spatiality being an interconnector to a now: "There's *people* in *this* room . . . who *live* here." The agency the protestors exhibit through such literacies—the Black feminist notion of literacy as the practice of freedom—continue a tradition of what Kynard calls "vernacular insurrections." Black communities use these insurrections' "expressive" "counterengeries" . . . "not only as counterhegemonic, but also as affirmative of new, constantly mutating languages, identities, political methodologies, and social understandings that communities form in and of themselves, both inwardly and outwardly" (2013, 10–11). Linking up with the historical tradition of Black student protest that Kynard illuminates in her monograph, the MwSU protestor's Black rhetorical reclamations confront the dynamics of post-Ferguson US race relations and widespread stances and rhetorics mobilizing institutional white defensiveness. While those race relations still render Black identity criminal through mechanisms like safety notices in white campus spaces, rhetorical reclamations animate Blackness in the face of the antiBlackness always already co-constituting it in the afterlives of Trans-Atlantic slavery.

The Black Lives Matter in the Classroom Symposium poster represents other such fractures: in the spaces between the white university and racialized disruption, between the symposium's temporal moment and its histories, between institutionalized ideas of "diversity" and activist visions of social justice, and between communal literacies and academic conversation. Because of these fractures in bringing Blackness under contact with (and in ways in service of) whiteness, it grapples with histories of capitalism, always already racial capitalism (Robinson 1983) from which "a predominantly white institution derives social or economic value from associating with individuals with nonwhite racial identities" (Leong 2013, 2154). But unlike the doctoring of photos by the University of Washington to improve its admissions profile in 2000 (Chang 2016, 16–20), the poster does not attempt to integrate Black images into an already prescribed visual of centered whiteness. It still, though, positions imagery of Black student protest in the ecological contexts, histories, cultures, and imaginations of white institutions that have long worked to snuff out such photographed resistance to provide illusions of safeness for white audiences, parents, students, and alumni. The institution, of course, simultaneously gains from racial capitalism—it is a "systemic phenomenon" (Leong 2013, 2154)—even while the ways the poster deploys Blackness undermines a historical practice of tying together impressions of diversity and excellence spearheaded by the University of California at Berkeley and the University of Michigan in the 1980s (Chang 2016, 17). So, despite setting in relation Black feminist rhetorics and the disruption of Black student resistance with institutional sponsors, the poster and the symposium it publicizes nonetheless wrestle with the prospect of counteracting the efficacy of Black protest by rendering it a rhetorical object for the purpose of promoting institutional diversity.

Nonetheless, the flyer confronts its audiences (and its historically white spaces) with visual connectors to histories of the Black liberation movement. The poster also draws significantly on the online archive of #BlackLivesMatter activism by using the digital phraseology in publicizing the name of the symposium. "#BlackLivesMatter" conjures connections to #ICantBreathe, #IfTheyGunnedMeDown, and other intertwined online movements and their ever-evolving archive.[11] In the electronic version of the poster, a hyperlink visibly mapped onto its image leads to a further captioning attribution of the photograph that centers student activism: "Students participate in a Black Lives Matter protest in Oakland, California, January 19, 2015. (look2remember)." The link signals the poster's "hypermediacy," while "remediating" digital rhetorics of student protest (Bolter and Grusin 2000). The link also provides an article on the possibilities of understanding relationships between the Black Lives Matter movement and Black communists in Alabama during the Great Depression (Jaffe 2015). The connections made via the poster's link—between the symposium at the historically white institution in the Midwest to Black workers in the 1930s South and Black student protestors at Oakland's Fruitvale Station in 2015 (together with the cultural memory of the police shooting of Oscar Grant in 2009)—demonstrate digital potentials of Black feminist relationality ([MwSU] BLMIC.org 2016). The student e-portfolio analyzed in Kynard's (2016) symposium keynote, however, shows more fully these possibilities through student resistance to dominant cultures, as opposed to ones so closely (and inherently) tied in/to a historically white institution's neoliberal functioning.

Kynard's centering of the student's agency also does work to flip normative power relations between student/instructor. The example of student work becomes the means by which rhetorical reclamation arises, with Kynard taking the position of interlocutor. In pushing against white conceptions of phenotypic attractiveness, Kynard's student's dynamic uses of Black vernacular, her focus on and imagery of Black hair, and her use of a Lorde quotation as a defining footer demonstrate how the very genres of academic discourse might be rhetorically reclaimed in Black agency in public digital spaces. Those fluid, relational meanings of Blackness in Andrene's project counteract the safety notices' individualized descriptions that criminalize Black bodies and play into dangerous, stereotypical scripts about Black folk at the particular campus, such as the menacing shadow of the "Young black male wearing a black hoodie with a white Nike logo and black sweatpants" (Department of Public Safety 2016g). Instead, the keynote's focus on a Black woman's student protest employs digital relationality to evolve histories that co-constitute Black feminist antiracism through Black rhetorical reclamation (Kynard 2016).

Kynard also shared some context on her contemporaneous teaching situation in her keynote by telling the story of a group project between four Black and brown students that became compromised when one Black Dominican student disappears. His absence, assumed to be related to his undocumented immigration status, results in Kynard being asked by her students to step into his role in the group. The coalitional efforts by group members—both inherent in the assignment design and emergent through "a ripple effect in the hearts, imaginations, and lived opportunities of multiple people" (2016, 8) that one student's disappearance causes—exemplify Black feminist ethics of empathy and equity. Kynard's sense of responsibility to "represent" for the missing student, like her centering of Andrene's e-portfolio, cuts away at hierarchical distinctions between teacher and student that neoliberal institutions tend to reinforce through an education-as-commodity principle. Coalitional frameworks that the keynote analyzed, shared, and enacted illustrate the political imaginaries foregrounded by Black feminist thinkers like Hill Collins, how "it is possible to be centered in [Black women's] experiences and engaged in coalitions with others. In this sense, Black feminist thought works on behalf of Black women, but does so in conjunction with other similar social justice projects" ([1990] 2000, x). The coalition of student groups behind the #Reclaim[MwSU] movement in the video likewise reveal relational, intersectional resistance efforts. The student groups involved include "the International Socialist Organization, United Students Against Sweatshops, Real Food Challenge, Committee for Justice in Palestine, Sierra Club Student Coalition, Still We Rise, and [MwSU] Coalition for Black Lives," (Wainz 2016)—all working toward calls for transparency from the white university in its operations. In both the video's and the keynote's rhetorical reclamations, Blackness, though variously positioned as disruptive/deviant by the institution, works through these quotidian, relational, historiographic, temporal, collective forces in a multiplicity of literacies to reveal white supremacy in its contemporary practical manifestations.

"Remembering / we were never meant to survive"[12]

I call attention to the ways in which Black rhetorics and literacies engage with day-to-day interaction with the practice of policy at a historically white institution in order to conclude a project aimed at centering those Black ways of being (otherwise). In defining Black rhetorical reclamation through reconceptualized Black disruption as a means to resist institutional white defensiveness, I draw together ideas presented in earlier chapters, while particularly explaining how such reclamations push against aggregative white institutional defensiveness in policy practice at Midwestern State University. Rhetorical reclamations reveal means to interrogate those relations, to think of the fractures between them as actional, mobilizing the deep rhetorically ecological approach to read/write/think Black meaning-making and institutional power dynamics. They offer rhetorics for generative Black being in Fanonian fractures that pose further questions and spur future meanings, allowing evolutions in deep ecological meanings to continue.

While the exigence of this project lies in potentials for Black beings in rhetoricizing various Blacknesses that may be put to various means and ends, I choose to chip away at destructive antiBlackness at historically white educational institutions through such reclamations. I join with Cacho (2012), Kynard (2013), and others in operationalizing them for legal scholar Derrick Bell's philosophy of "Racial Realism." In doing so, "we must simultaneously acknowledge that our actions are not likely to lead to transcendent change and, despite our best efforts, may be of more help to the system we despise than to the victims of that system we are trying to help. Nevertheless, our realization, and the dedication based on that realization, can lead to policy positions and campaigns that are less likely to worsen conditions for those we are trying to help" (1992, 378). By spotlighting those who are deemed as threats, disruptive, deviant, and socially dead, by emphasizing those who are raced, gendered, and classed as precarious, I suggest, instead of seeking the end of the tunnel or even its light, rhetorical reclamation as a move that *rearticulates* the situations we are put with/in Black non/being.

Through this Black feminist rearticulation (Hill Collins [1990] 2000), owning disruption/deviance and, in ways, social death, as a fundamental with/in Blackness, as Cohen (2004) envisions, might fuel versions of Blackness that seek to argue otherwise with/in Blackness' in/fungibility and para/ontology. While white institutions and publics deem Black bodies an excess to commodify and control, mapping that deviance onto extant cultural scripts, fracturing meaning in white spaces might re/cast these scripts by re/turning Blackness unto the white institution opening new(er) avenues for struggle. Bell reminds us, indeed, that "confrontation with our oppressors is not our sole reason for Racial Realism" (1992, 378). I'll admit, it's not my primary motive; I often daydream of never knowing US racial politics, of remaining content with my little islands. But "Continued struggle can bring about unexpected benefits and gains that in themselves justify continued endeavor" (378). And that fight to rhetorically reclaim involves risk. But when even authorities and publics turn "white" modes of evidence (videos, statistics, surveillance technologies, etc.) on Black bodies as inadequate in the face of white fear and racialized modes of protection of white spaces, then Black bodies must find opportunities in navigating, reshaping, and non/being (in) the fractures afforded. So, I inhabit those in-between/across spaces when conjured with these disruptive rhetorics and literacies, in the words of Audre Lorde, by "remembering/we were never meant to survive" (1978, 32).

Conclusion
De Ting about Blackness (A Meditation)

I came into the world imbued with the will to find a meaning in things

FRANTZ FANON ([1952] 2008), *BLACK SKIN, WHITE MASKS* (82)

I re/turn to my island home for the first time since earning my doctoral degree
from Midwestern State and starting my first tenure track job. Some tings hav-
en't changed. In the place we call the "droiyn" room—what would translate to
a living room[1]—I sit among objects: a wooden sofa set I bought my mother the
Christmas I worked my first job (or as my brother calls them "de Foodmasters
chairs"); photos from my childhood, some in dilapidated aging frames, glass broken, Scotch tape visible and one dangling—turns out I rarely smiled in them—a
graduation photo with a bearded grin, dreadlocked, roped, medaled, pride in a
native son hugging my Black mother; a set of curtains I know very well—they
signify no season, is not no Easter curtains, if yuh ketch me. I open an email from
a white administrator colleague. She asks to see the syllabus for my fall "Projects
in Black Rhetoric" undergraduate course, one never before taught at the historically white institution where I now work. But we're a good three weeks from the
beginning of the semester. She wants to see if 25 percent of my course is "global"
to market the course to other departments: how "transnational" will Projects in
Black Rhetoric be? I mull over how to measure transnational Blackness (to sell it).

I think: how does the white university measure me? . . . "And then I found
I was an object in the midst of objects" (Fanon 1952, 82); in the wake of the
fracture, I dig deeper. What does my Black im/migrant non/being mean in per-
centages to them, to me in a temporality so unlike the "Cathedral of Learning"?
"And already I am being dissected under white eyes, the only real eyes. I am
fixed," echoes Fanon (87). I re/turn under racializing surveillance with/in temporal relation/ships to technologies like "ships' registers in which African lives

DOI: 10.7330/9781646421473.C005   **133** were recorded as units of cargo, or listed alongside livestock on slave auction notices, and census categories, estate records, and plantation inventories that catalogued enslaved people as merchandise" (S. Browne 2015, 42). And have we, Black beings, then, not always been "transnational" tings in the West? Existing in the nowhere-land of the slave ship, transitory, belonging to whichever nation bought us without really be(long)ing? As Black feminist Katherine McKittrick recounts, "new world blackness arrives through . . . accounts, price tags, and descriptors of economic worth and financial probability" in the "mathematics of unliving" (2014, 17). And like the (now cultured as) buzzword "transnational," do we not try hard to measure Blackness in words, in terms, in cultures? How Black are you in these fractures when raced an object, much less an unhappy object? De ting about Blackness is that thing that also surrounds it, co-constitutes it with its ghosts.

The word "ting" in Trini/Trinbagonian usage metonymizes in/discretion, as a verb, noun, pronoun, what have you. It is not uncommon to say/hear: "De ting nah!"; "By ting and them"; "Yuh know, de ones they use to ting with." Growing up, we were schooled out of this word through British English. Nouns, pronouns, and verbs have particular functions. Be discrete. Describe what you see in front of you so that others may also understand. But still, we understood a parent sayin "pass de ting nah" pointing with mouth and pursed lips, and you knew when your brejrin or sistrin say, "das de ting self!" you were on the right track. Ting then became heavily gendered/sexualized with age and experience. "Bad tings" (promiscuous/unruly young women), "bess tings" (attractive young women), and a host of other adjectivized "tings" evolved "tings" in adolescence to shape young boys and girls into (de)meaning heteronormative projects. De ting is, ting still paradoxically kept its amorphous shape, still means what you want it to mean with an elasticity I have yet to find in other words. Only "being" comes close. But I want to pause for a second to think of nouns as verbs in particular. What does the fracture between a static "ting" transformed *actional* into being glean for how we think of language? To think through Fanon ([1952] 2008), what "will" will "find a meaning in things"? What can an object-beingness, as I've described throughout *Black or Right*, do for Blackness?

Via Spillers and Moten, Sharpe comes to the idea of "anagrammatical blackness," in the literal and "in the metaphorical sense in how, regarding Blackness, grammatical gender falls away and new meaning proliferates": "So, blackness anew, blackness as a/temporal, in and out of place in time putting pressure on meaning and that against which meaning is made" (2016, 76). This conception of the transformative potentials for Blackness is at the heart of what I call rhetorical reclamation in deep ecologies. If we think/read/write to make Blackness by using the possibilities of the fracture *to be actional*, to (em)body/(per)form its out of place-ness as object-being, we can see avenues for Blackness beyond the

measuring containment of surveillance, outside of its non-Black and Black policing (yes, we often do this, too; think quickly of the game "Black Card Revoked").

Being that out of place-ness, even ephemerally, means occupying the Fanonian
"atmosphere of certain uncertainty" ([1952] 2008, 83) in the ecological ghosts of
Blackness, how ever. It means co-constituting a para/ontological Blackness. In
those temporal, historical fractures between Black non/being, we can find that
out of place-ness. In Trini culture, the phrase "fass and out of place," as in "you
too fass and out of place," might be hurled at someone minin yuh business, or
overstepping a line by being "boldface." S. Browne points to possibilities in this
phrase and also to the Jamaican "facety," meaning "obtrusive, audacious, and 'not
knowing one's distance'" (2015, 72). Browne invites us to understand this phrased
idea as rejecting the colonial "lived objectification," as refusals to stay in one's
place (72). As a means of channeling the ways in which Blackness in wake of
fracture can rhetorically reclaim by using the space where it is objectified *to be
out of place*, to make rhetorics to hurl back at the white heteropatriarchal window
of viewing ourselves (Du Bois's Veil) in Fanonian epidermalization, let's re/turn
to Ferguson for a (cultural) moment.

> his same old body. ordinary, black
> dead thing. bring him and we will mourn
> until we forget we are mourning.
>
> and isn't that what being black is about?
>
> DANEZ SMITH (2014), "NOT AN ELEGY FOR MIKE BROWN"[2]

Ferguson, Missouri, in the US cultural imagination has come to signal many
things. Some think of damage, harm, and violence. But not always to the living.
Some summon Ferguson not as a place but a temporality: "Users on Twitter felt
like they were *participating* in #Ferguson, as they tweeted in real time about the
unfolding events, rallied supporters to join various hashtag campaigns . . . and
monitored live streams where they could bear witness to the tear gassing and
arrests of journalists and protestors" (Bonilla and Rosa 2015, 7; emphasis in original). Ferguson fractures open, lets us see and go where we shouldn't—in digital spaces, between individuals and institutions, between Michael Brown and
Darren Wilson. Black feminist historian Barbara Ransby (2018) re/tells, "Wilson
told Brown and his friend Dorian Johnson not to walk in the street. They talked
back at him telling Wilson they were almost at their destination" (47). They never
got there, at least not together. Always going while gone, Black being, fracturing 'gon' "mourn/ until we forget we are mourning" (D. Smith 2014). "Brown
fit the description" (Ransby 2018, 47) as Black beings tend to. "Things escalated
from there" (47), as the amorphous specter of Blackness in white imagination
means that property broken should only be broken by its *rightful* owners. When
"things escalate," they must be put back in their *rightful* place. Rightful, meaning,

in contemporary usage "Of a person: having a legal claim; legitimately entitled to a property, position, or status; holding by right or custom" ("rightful" 2020). Is it possible for the socially dead, the always already criminalized, the undocumented im/migrant, the Black being in the afterlives of slavery, of delegitimized custom, to *be* rightful, to claim an adjective "of a person"?

We know now how overpoliced Ferguson is by its white authorities; we don't need stats. Brown's "same old body. ordinary, black/ dead thing" (D. Smith 2014) lay "to fester in the hot summer sun for four and a half hours," protected by threats of dogs and guns (Taylor 2016, 153). Crowds gather and residents make a memorial of things, "teddy bears and memorabilia," in place of the place where Brown's body once was. A cop's dog pees on the memorial. Later, Brown's mother shapes "rose petals in the form of his initials," and "a police cruiser whizzed by, crushing the memorial and scattering the flowers" (154). How do we re/member things always out of place? In anagrammatical Blackness, there's no way to arrange things to signify, "As the meanings of words fall apart, we encounter again and again the difficulty of sticking the signification" (Sharpe 2016, 77). When the spirit, the word, cannot rest it haunts. Ferguson itself attests. Even its hashtag means unwilfully. And "Just as residents rebuilt the memorials for Mike Brown within hours every time the police tried to destroy them, the same dynamic held for the protests" (Taylor 2016, 156). If it was the destruction of property with/in the Uprising that police cared so deeply about in contrast to Black non/being, why then destroy the marker of Black memory, every time it re/emerges, (per)forms new shapes?

Narrative can exert control over pasts, over history, can turn some/things deadly into saintly. But Ransby explains the philosophy in the #BlackLivesMatter theory that "there did not have to be a correlation between 'sainthood' and Black citizenship. This was an important shift in the discourse about who is or is not a sympathetic victim of injustice. Brown did not have to be a church-going, law-abiding, proper-speaking embodiment of respectability in order for his life to matter, protestors insisted" (2018, 49). But could his death *matter* as well? These qualities attached to the deviant that make being unworthy, Cohen (2004) suggests, ought to be where Black study places focus. Brown might then become a subject of politically queer analysis when we disengage with normative epistemologies (Cohen 2015). Think otherwise. How can we find narrative for these who speak differently? Whose language falls away in the wake of history? #BlackLivesMatter wants us to theorize a world in which the tag should fold in on itself, where we wouldn't have to use it by using it. How might we tell its story, especially in the spaces between Black non/being? #IfTheyGunnedMeDown imagines a literal social death—that space between the first- and third-person Fanon goes on about (1952, 83). #HandsUpDontShoot, likewise, means the criminalized recognize the system, putting verbed, adjectivized, into the passively constructed. The logics of grammar and words again fall away. What's fluid—between, across, outside—is where it's at. Going is already gone for unruly tings.

In late September 2014, a couple months before a jury rules Wilson free, "Mike Brown's memorial was doused with gasoline and ignited" (Taylor 2016, 157). This time / we cannot mourn until we forget. The insistence on desecrating the ways we re/member tell us we can't. The "Black dead thing" whether body or in place of a body still cannot be in place. Under the white heteropatriarchal gaze, belonging won't be a physical space, and here's where we must find potentials in Black para/ontology. For if a hoodie can make the Black non/being criminal, then let's use its ghostly body to find some shape with/in it to be, otherwise. Rhetorical reclamation radiates not in the symbol of the hoodie as a product/commodity but in the shapes it can shift to make ghosts mean ghastliness, that otherwise. How then can we see the possibilities in the para/ontologically meaning that Blacknesses of Black being in the fracture?

> One night in bed yuh sleepin
> Next night is a wake that yuh keepin
>
> SINGING SANDRA ([1999] 2001), "VOICES FROM DE GHETTO"[3]

I tie the Black rhetorics offered in looking with/in and through Blackness in the historically white university and beyond together through the processes/literacies of *rhetorical reclamation*—and its associated means, "rhetorical reclamations"—in the previous chapter. Rhetorical reclamations turn the fracturing space of Fanonian epidermalization (animated in the afterlives of slavery) back at the white heteropatriarchal window, through which Black non/beings make themselves *other/wise* to possibly hurl rhetorics back at that white pane. They make Blackness precisely when/where objectness commodifies it or renders it potentially socially dead. "Reclamation" and "reclaiming" in this sense, should not evoke the mainstreaming of a term or its neutralizing incorporation into some kind of positive-through-negative affective conversion that happened some time in the past giving us present agency. We should think of reclaiming, maybe, like the relation/ships that Trini calypsonian Singing Sandra ([1999] 2001) above suggests between sleeping, "waking," and keeping in de "deviant" "voices from de ghetto." These languages, these acts, and their in-betweens co-constitute the process of rhetorical reclamation, where to be doing one might also do the others, recognizing the process, Black non/being, as transient. Black sleep rhetorizes wake keeping as Black wake keeping rhetorizes sleep: now is a past that is a present; it have no day/dey in between.

Although the word "Black" "has been held up by some (but not all) linguists as a premier example of reclamation because it can now be used referentially, without risk of insult or self-abnegation" (Chen 2012 65), I'm not sure that, in white institutional spaces in the United States, we might be as comfortable with it as these linguists are. While Geneva Smitherman wrote of "Black's widespread use accepted cross-racially" (1977, 35), I'd argue that neoliberalist ideologies/practices reverse whatever "normalization" might have been palpable in the 1970s. My current job position was offered in "African American" rhetoric, and I myself have been referred to by this "politically correct" nationing adjective by white folk. Neither citizened African nor American, I wince. #BlackLivesMatter's universalizing spinoffs testify to white public and institutional defensiveness undercutting ideas about *Black*'s neutralized reclamation.

But rhetorical reclamation, see, resists assimilation. The act of re/claiming here summons the "claim" of de ting as a question, a demanding request; the re of de ting represents a turn "once more." To turn once more to a demanding question in the process of possibly meaning, then, in the moment of fracture, rhetorical reclamations pulsate Blackness' potentialities through deep ecologies in the United States (and the West broadly construed). But the fracture is always moving, so how do we translate Blackness' para/ontology without falling short?[4] We can't. Yet still, we struggle. Opportunities stew in the means by which we do, the processes, so we look to the rhetorics of re/turning in the fracture for the spaces we might sojourn for Black non/being. Possibilities for rhetorical reclamations run through the analysis of Black rhetorical technologies of each chapter of this project. Black autoethnography, Black hashtags, Black inter(con)textual reading, and Black deviance/disruption represent these reclaiming means.

In creative analysis of one's condition, in reclaiming the Black feminist mandate that "poetry is not a luxury" for Lorde (1984, 36), Black autoethnography positions Black non/being in relation/ships with culture (dominant, subversive, or otherwise). "Nameless and formless" (36), autoethnography like/as poetry illuminates when rhetorized to tell the story of the thing and its "quality of light" (36), often caricatured by the very rhetoric of storytelling; it (per)forms, dances, as the Black athlete or the Black entertainer might be expected to in the US white gaze. And like these figures, the politicizing of that (per)forming, well, it's usually not welcomed, usually out of place: "shut up and play!" In white educational institutions, (per)formed token service as the Black being often means playing in the pocket—game managing. But autoethnography gets outta pocket. In the bind of institutional "diversity"—of being the number, not the figure—it means being with/in the fractures of deep ecologies to meaning-make by telling one's story otherwise, otherwise. It grasps the ghosts of Blackness—that we don't wanna see, want to keep under the bed, the bad dream of non/being Black, the sleep in wake keeping—to dance Césaire's "jail-break dance" (qtd. in Fanon [1952] 2008 54).

Hashtags connect. They (per)form more of a place than a being, while being a place, while being a being. As a technology of our digitized zeitgeist, they mean while referring elsewhere. Put to antiracist Black and Black feminist use, though, they split things open, they decode (Conley 2017), call attention while carrying away. They re/present things, places, beings, conditions, while marking time, conjuring a "feeling of shared temporality" (Bonilla and Rosa 2015, 7), but are they really that feeling? They might be. But they also conjure the what's-left-behind, affecting the spot of the memorial, like Mike Brown's, where mourning mourns in an unforgetting re/membering. Black hashtags used to rhetorically reclaim reopen spaces to question the being of Blackness, as in the Black feminist "#YouOKSis?" or Eric Garner's dying "#ICantBreathe." The spaces of these Black tags corral while opening up, define while differing, and in some cases might "empower" through their definitions as Lorde urges in the "The Master's Tools Will Never Dismantle the Master's House" (1984). They afford pedagogical possibilities to mean with/in the context of Blackness, where avenues for antiBlackness no doubt exist, but in showing us those alleys, they help us learn. While #BlueLivesMatter might infuriatingly appropriate and equate racial identity with an occupation, reinscribing racial capitalist white supremacy, it also makes visible, rearticulates, what we knew was already there for all to see. Now we know how to find and not find what we want to find and what we don't want to find. More important, though, rhetorically reclaiming tags do the dual work of exposing the white window while moving to break that white p/l/ane: #BlackLivesMatter tells us that Black beings matter while showing how they historically/temporally/affectively don't, how even language might fail to explain:

that feeling, that's black.
\ \

(D. SMITH 2014)

Inter(con)textual reading asks deep rhetorically ecological questions. By thinking through the meanings produced/negotiated through the African indigenous framework of botho/Ubuntu to mobilize the Black feminist ethic of literacy as the practice of freedom via hooks (1994), Black inter(con)textual reading as a methodology reveals generative intersections for those meanings, places where we can do rhetorical reclaiming. #BlackLivesMatter prompts us to ask these sorts of questions through its Black queer feminist politics re/turning to the wake of the Combahee River Collective's work. As cofounder of that collective Barbara Smith suggests, "There's so many things to say about Combahee" (2017, 43). Fuh real, in its wake Combahee reveals opportunities for us to say / make / think / arrive at / depart from so many tings. Smith goes on, really digs in, declaring, "We need more dialogue about the history and the ongoing organizing of people who claim and share these politics" (43). That's the kind of dialogue that deep ecologies might make happen when we think through just what it means to chant Shakur's "We have nothing to lose but our chains" (1973) alongside Lamar's "Alright" (2015a). The intense histories, temporalities, affects, meanings of these texts, their counter/public commonplace phrases, and the beings they conjure in use demand our attention. What does it mean for Black lives to matter when flowers to re/member the Black dead get peed on in Ferguson streets, when Walker's (1982) "all my life I had to fight" gets paired with Black masculine hype, and/or when the ways "Black mainstream culture has gotten into the fuckery of white mainstream culture is ridiculous" to a Combahee cofounder (Frazier 2017, 133)?

Black inter(con)textuality helps us to see cracks in white heteropatriarchal windows that double consciousness for Blackness, to see in those fractures where Black meaning might take us to mean beyond frameworks for legal recognition or capitalist assimilation. Simultaneously, those fractures show us the frame, the pernicious white public and institutional defensiveness, that operate as a constraining background with/in which antiBlackness remains mundane. Growing up, I was always warned that "yuh hafta read to write," and this Black methodology collapses the two into its process-based moves toward antiracism, while incorporating gesture, thinking, clothing, movement, and other ways of (per)forming Blackness into the mix toward Black feminist justice. In making intersections that question as Black inter(con)textuality does, we relation in ways that draw clearer the where and how of rhetorical reclamation.

In the now of wake keeping, that reading methodology opens paths toward revealing the daily operations that un/make Blackness in white institutional spaces. In/security concerns materialize routines that afford white supremacy means to re/animate old tropes in dominant cultural imaginations of Blackness as criminal specter. Those deviant ghosts—that disrupt in showing up to "scare" workers who just wanna do they jobs, they "don't want to be exposed to this" (Keep[MwSU]Public 2016) when Blackness occupies white spaces—do more to speak Black non/being than diversity's "non-performative" language (Ahmed 2012). When just the word "Black" haunts criminal, schemes dreadlocked, tatted, and hoodied, means that cops must underline how "high stress" they job is, "high stress, absolutely," through the mouth of a Black body (Department of Public Safety 2016b), we play, unwillingly, the dangerous game of measuring whose feelings make a real gun pop and a fake gun real. Through Cohen's (2004) embrace of deviance, though, rhetorical reclamations reveal sites of the sleeping wake, of fracturing Blacknesses out of place, boldface, that might break the p/l/ane of white institutional defensiveness.

Blackness, transitory, could peep through. Rhetorical reclamation, to continue this fracturing space metaphor just a lil further, might be conceptualized as the kind of "black hole" that Black feminist historian of science Evelynn Hammonds (2004) theorizes via fellow Black feminist Michelle Wallace's (1990) hold of astrophysics to discuss the hegemonic negation of Black creativity. In reading Black women's sexualities, Hammonds explains, "we can detect the presence of a black hole by its effects on the region of space where it is located," while calling

CONCLUSION: DE TING ABOUT BLACKNESS (A MEDITATION)

for "strategies that allow us to make visible the distorting and productive effects" (2004, 310). In *Dark Matters*, Browne evokes this idea to shatter the surveillance of Blackness, "being that nonnameable matter that matters the racialized disciplinary society" (2015, 9). I follow Black feminists Wallace, Hammonds, and Browne with Black inter(con)textuality to suggest its technologies of reading that make partially visible Blackness' para/ontology, with rhetorical reclamations the black holes unfolding possibilities for "distorting," "productive effects" (Hammonds 2004, 310). Black feminist relationality, activism, and theory conjure these boldface capacities.

But Black autoethnography, Black antiracist hashtags, Black inter(con)textual reading, and generative Black deviance only represent some means for rhetorical reclamations. These should be understood on a larger spectrum of rhetorics of Black non/being that *call out* with/in fracture. Brittany Cooper (2018) in *Eloquent Rage* teaches us in conversation with Lorde (1984) that Black feminist calling out can be from a place of messy rage, a process as opposed to something precise. I want to situate these processes (autoethnography, hashtags, inter(con)textual reading, generative Black deviance) on a range of rhetorical reclamations spanning from something like rhetorical silence to the kind of "cancelling" thrust we might see on Black Twitter, digitized/(em)bodied/in between. These reclamations crystalize in an otherwise kinda Black being that uses its amorphous, co-constitutive, para/ontology for a range of potentialities that can resist for many operative ends, or not. They take up a space outside, but inside material spaces as "its energy distorts and disrupts that around it" (Browne 2015, 9), like Hammonds's idea of the black hole, like being inside the white institution while being somewhere outside it too. These reclamations lie with/in knowing you're the ghost of slavery conjured to maintain the white heteronormative equilibrium but *to fuck with it*. In re/claiming otherwise in that space, rhetorical reclamations make Black matter that permeates the deep rhetorical ecology, resisting the very commodification of Blackness that has the potentialities to make us see that "anti-Blackness is the fulcrum around which white supremacy works. Right?" as #BlackLivesMatter co-founder Alicia Garza (2017) asserts. They repeatedly force hard questions that we cannot always answer neatly, that we may not always hurl specifically, or just ask more questions, for the same or similar causes. But that's okay. We're here to try to crack/open spaces for Blackness, to virally spread Fanonian epidermalization to *infect*—meaning to *dis-ease*, to contaminate, to *take hold* of and/or to be communicated to ("infect" 2010)—*otherwise* the socially dead, the dead yoked to the socially dying,[5] and objectified Black non/beings.

There is little more dangerous than a willful thing

R. A. T. JUDY, "ON THE QUESTION OF NIGGA AUTHENTICITY" (1994, 225)

These technologies, and the larger spectrum of rhetorical reclamations, allow us to hurl Black being in what I have described throughout as a kind of "object-beingness." I talk of Blackness' para/ontology, of using otherwise the objecthood and its "certain uncertain" surroundings that come from the historical conception of it as always already means, for fueling colonialism and racial capitalism. As Mbembe re/minds us, "Clearly, not all Blacks are Africans, and not all Africans are Blacks. But it matters little where they are located. As *objects of discourse* and *objects of knowledge,* Africa and Blackness have, since the beginning of the modern age, plunged the theory of the name as well as the status and function of the sign and of representation into deep crisis" (2017, 12; emphasis mine). Let's dig deeper into that crisis to think through what the object-beingness of Blackness through rhetorical reclamations in deep ecologies might mean for new materialist frameworks of objects' mattering. Through an African indigenous relational recognition of the living and nonliving and the Black feminist intersectional politics mobilizing the entanglements of being in hegemonic systems, we might peep how Blackness means through this "object-beingness."

Jane Bennett's *Vibrant Matter* and studies that genealogically follow seek "to give voice to a thing power" (2010, 2). "Instead of focusing on collectives conceived primarily as conglomerates of *human* designs and practices ('discourse')," Bennett emphasizes "the active role of *nonhuman* materials in public life" (1–2; emphasis in original). In rhetorical theory, work like Laurie Gries's *Still Life with Rhetoric* (that analyzes the distributive meanings of memes) animates these investments to consider "reality to be collectively, materially, and semiotically constructed via a variety of actants that have equal ontological footing. New materialists thus acknowledge the vital and transformative characteristics of matter—characteristics typically reserved for humans alone" (2015, 6). My objection to the re/animation of these lives of objects rests not in the attempt to give dem time/space/matter attention. On the contrary, I strive throughout to consider the co-constitution of Blackness with objects, spaces, matter, and so forth. My problem lies with the premise of ideas of the nonhuman in a binary opposition to the human in Bennett, and Gries's specific claim of "equal ontological footing" (6). As the opening epigraph to *Black or Right* from Fanon points out, Blackness' being has "no ontological resistance" in its construction relative to whiteness ([1952] 2008, 83). Wynter extends, pronouncing that to even think "ontological sovereignty," we must engage a totally different version of the human and our theories thereof, which orthodox thought (re)produces (Wynter and Scott 2000, 136). To claim equal ontological footing for humans, nonhumans, animals, and objects, then, suggests that Black beings now, but not always, classed "human" exist on a flattened plane of reality where ontology can be conceived of on the same terms as white Man. But what happens when we theorize Blackness from the Fanonian "zone of non-being," from Moten's claim

that Blackness' history is one of objects resisting (2003, 1), from a re/turn to
Mbembe's idea that Blackness "constituted the manifestation of existence as an
object" (2017, 11) in its conceptualization by Europeans? What happens when
we re/turn simultaneously to the "deep crisis" of signification that Blackness
conjures (12), to Sharpe's anagrammatical Blackness where words fail to "stick"
signification (2016, 77)?

Aimé Césaire (1972) calls "thingification" that process by which European
colonizers hail(ed) their humanity/superiority by re/inventing the colonized
as objects through the colonial encounter, by destroying the colonized's past.
Fanon, likewise, throughout his oeuvre, illuminates how colonizers "make the
native an object in the hands of the occupying nation" (1967, 35), while also drawing on white notions of the Black non/being as "animal" ([1952] 2008, 86). But
I want to be careful here to mark distinctions between dehumanization, objectification, and bestialization. While these things certainly overlap, easy conflation
of them undoes understandings of the processes that Black feminist relationality
knows as disciplining beings into humans, not-quite-humans, and nonhumans
(as Weheliye 2014 shows via Wynter and Spillers). Because Black feminists
like Wynter, Spillers, Lorde, and Hill Collins, among others, through relational
frameworks visibly expose the concatenated ways Black women's subject positions complicate objectification as well as the genre-ing of beings (Wynter in
particular) in relation to the "human," the terms flow more than interchange-
ably. Mel Y. Chen's (2012) mobilization of "animacy hierarchies" (Silverstein
1976) in linguistics to evoke "horizontal relations between humans, other animals, and other objects" (Chen 2012, 50)—in thinking through racial mattering and Karen Barad's agential realism's focus on the "material-cultural" (1996,
179)—complicates new materialisms along these lines, but not in specific relation to Blackness, Black object-being, or the workings of Black social death. But,
Z. I. Jackson (2020), through challenging the human-animal divide by noting
that "the animal" emerges not as a result of, but *through* histories of antiBlackness, gives us pause on dehumanization, because the African's humanity through
abjecting animality "is ultimately plasticized" (23). *Becoming Human* makes clear
that posthumanism puts Blackness in space of the unthought, presupposing all
humans privilege over all animals (16–17). Yuh see, as Black performance and
literary scholar Jayna Brown suggests, the "we" of universal positioning in new
materialism must be situated historically (2015, 327). I push here, then, to re/iter-
ate the question(s): if given the history of/Blackness "is a strain that pressures
the assumption of the equivalence of personhood and subjectivity" (Moten
2003, 1), and, if in the United States and elsewhere, "Black people ejected from the
state become the national symbols for the less-than-human being condemned to
death" (Sharpe 2016, 79), have Black beings ever really *been* human? Was Mike
Brown *being* in the Ferguson street and (not on the sidewalk) an "object" out of

place for Darren Wilson to put in place? Was Mike Brown's *being* left to lay in the same street for hours dead not an object in place for the white heteropatriarchal gaze? Was Mike Brown's memorials *being* peed on, driven over, and set ablaze not objects subjected to antiBlackness?

I propose that rhetorical reclamations, which derive from Black feminist relational methodologies of knowing and being, self-reflexively pose these kinds of questions in transiently occupying an object-beingness in the fracturing moments of Fanonian epidermalization. In those spaces, somewhere on or off Chen's (2012) horizontal spectrum of animacy, with/in or out/ of Z. I. Jackson's (2020) possible "everything and nothing" of anti/Black ontological plasticity, Black being hurls itself as object to ask the above questions (and others like it). Framed via Ubuntu, the recognition of interrelative co-constitutions between the living and nonliving means that these reclamations can spotlight the cracks in non/being *to be otherwise*. In that para/ontology, in Black disruption's generativity, its polysemy, a multiplicity of possibilities arises for Blackness to mean and how Blackness could mean. To what specific antiracist ends those meanings might be put, well yuh talkin a whole setta other questions.

My final prayer:
O my body, make of me always a [being] who questions!
FRANZ FANON, *BLACK SKIN, WHITE MASKS* ([1952] 2008, 181)

Since I endeavor, through the Black rhetorics evoked with/in deep ecological encounters in white institutional spaces, to open up spaces for meaning, to ask questions, before we "pause for a cause" leh we think through some possible ends to which these technologies of rhetorical reclamations might be put. These suggestions do not intend to boundary the potentialities of these rhetorics, but instead to call attention to the various fluid ways (and ways in-between) the technologies of rhetorical reclamation might be deployed for quotidian Black non/being in white spaces couched in various Black philosophical traditions. These range from Black humanism, to Black posthumanism, Afropessimism, Black antihumanism, racial realism, and, of course, the deep ecological spaces with/in between.

To suggest rhetorical reclamations be used for a Black humanist project does not plead to locate them as rhetorical technologies fueling assimilation into a liberal multicultural humanity or its afterthoughts. De progress narratives could salt.[6] As should be clear by now, these Black rhetorics do not fund or hope for recognition from state institutional apparatuses, for pro-Black/Black separatist entrepreneurship, or for what might result of rhetorics longingly reading the Black past in modernity via "nostalgia" as Baker identifies (1995, 1), which might desire attempts to re/cover some lost agency or elevated social status.[7] While #BlackLivesMatter does admittedly thrust to affirm Black humanity (Garza

2014; 2017, 166), the movement eschews these kinds of moves that rally around traditional notions of Black freedom (and their respectability politics), instead centering Black queer feminist ethics that feed the "call out" element radiating beneath the full spectrum of rhetorical reclamations. In practice, then, the clap-back energy of these rhetorical technologies can very much seek, through Black feminist materialist and humanist means, antiracist ends that broaden categories of human. Black autoethnography, Black hashtagging, Black inter(con)textuality, and generative Black deviance derive from the Black feminist relational episte-mologies and #BlackLivesMatter contexts with/in their deep rhetorical ecolo-gies. We might even envision #BlackLivesMatter and the Movement for Black Lives as striving (in some, but not always all, ways) to usher in Wynterian "new genres of being human" that always already disarticulate human being from the white heteropatriarchal genre of Man through epistemological rupture (Wynter 2007, 112).

Calls for what might be characterized as a Black posthumanism sometimes evoke Wynter, as in Conley's (2017) argument for Black feminist hashtags via Weheliye's "assemblages of freedom" (2014, 137) that deploys Wynter's and Spillers' Black feminist relationality to read racializing assemblages. Greene Wade centers Wynter in formulating a Black feminist posthumanist viral Blackness "to shift and/or erode borders/boundaries that inhibit the free flow of blackness" (2017, 35). Both Conley (2017) and Greene Wade (2017) formulate Blackness outside of the understood categories of human as Man via digital and in-person assem-blage; re/call the specific political potentials of Black hashtagging in chapter 2. Pritha Prasad (2016) likewise underlines the "coalitional possibilities" via Black Twitter through #BlackLivesMatter-related tags like #IfTheyGunnedMeDown and #AliveWhileBlack. But ventures abounding through Black autoethnography, inter(con)textuality, and the potentialities of Black disruption skewed otherwise also open up notions of Black being co-constituted by its temporalities, its spati-alities, its specters. Rhetorical reclamation conjectures in and past the boundar-ies of attempted Black ontology to imagine dynamic kinds of Blackness, always shifting with possibility with/in and out of any one Black body.

The object-beingness of Blackness' fractures speak to conditions of Black social death, lets us in/to the wake of Trans-Atlantic slavery, colonialism, the wretched temporal underbellies of the now that is a past, an Afropessimist con-dition. In Sharpe's (2016) wake of Fanonian epidermalization, Spillers (2003) reveals the "oceanic ungendering" (214) of Blackness when conjured criminally as ghosts haunting the white university as disruption. We might sneak in these opportunities to see how that deviance can reflexively illuminate the pasts of slavery in the stop and frisk that fails to afford Black bodies notions of heter-onormative gender relations, making us pure property. Black hashtags might also reveal the depravity of the pasts where #ICantBreathe evokes lynching control over Black non/being to teach what enslavement means in twenty-first-century terminologies. Autoethnography could uncover the always already of criminalizing the Black body as out-of-place commodity in the deep rhetorically ecological contexts of plantations and house and field slaves at the white university, along with those spaces' un/bodied technologies of control. Meanwhile Black inter(con)textuality offers fracturing questions that might wake the Black body out of its deep neoliberal contexts to show us what's really good, ya feel?

Rhetorical reclamation might seem foreign to Black antihumanist ends, but not when Black autoethnography can show how "Blackness is coterminous with Slaveness," through the fracturing experiences of anti-Blackness that lead Frank B. Wilderson III (2015) to his points on Black non/being. While he claims historicity and redemption as antiBlack, and that Humanist narrative precludes Blackness from its arcs because Blackness lacks "the psychic and/or physical presence of a sentient being . . . *ab initio*" (2015, n.p.) Wilderson gets in/to this place through analyzing his story of experiencing antiBlackness from a Palestinian friend, uses his own poetry to get to the heart of these declarations. The metaphysical nothing that Calvin Warren (2018) claims of Blackness to argue its ways outside of being in *Ontological Terror* parallels the Blackness of the Fanonian fracture and may be what deviance means as specter. If the Afropessimist, Black antihumanist, or nihilist strives to expose antiBlackness for ending the West as we know it, to emerge, or not, out of being into something otherwise, then rhetorical reclamations could throw that very Black non-being at the white heteropatriarchal window desiring to completely destroy it. To use another metaphor, Black antihumanism could use viral Blackness to spread awareness of Fanonian epidermalization (through, say, hashtagging) for its own contagious ends. The technology of inter(con)textual reading, then, may uncover for them the fracturing cracks at which to hurl, the gaping wounds in which to infect, non-being, breaking the antiBlack window, poisoning its body to reveal "there is no place like Europe to which Slaves can return as Human beings" (Wilderson 2015).

At the end of the previous chapter, I suggest my particular theoretical stance toward practicing these rhetorical reclamations through racial realism (Bell 1992). That posture evokes struggle not for its outcome but for the factors determining struggle, for its processes and the reasons that prompt them rather than its anticipated products. In situating rhetorical reclamations in this way, I could summon autoethnography to engender Black being's catharsis, to work toward antiracism, to expose antiBlackness, and/or to provoke policy change. Engagement with Black hashtags might conjure being in relation/ships with others, forging the interconnectedness of Ubuntu to respect, to heal, to call out, or other/wise. Within this framework inter(con)textual reading fosters its question-making perhaps to offspring, to make realist struggle see itself moving in a variety of directions, to cut away at easily received popular messages about Blackness that might, after all, play into hegemonic meanings of it. You might ask: Who doesn't wanna, at least once, bump "Alright" without thinking about racialized hypercapitalism? Listening/reading/thinking/writing through inter(con)textuality, though, might force us to check ourselves for the things we might be complicit with. To the racial realist, Black deviance/disruption generates meanings of non/being in the world that can chip away at antiBlackness one crack at a time; who knows if the white p/l/ane will break? The acts, though, might be worth each fracture's distorted Black light.

> How are we beholden to and beholders of each other in ways that change across
> time and place and space and yet remain?
>
> SHARPE, *IN THE WAKE: ON BLACKNESS AND BEING* (2016, 101)

And it's in these questions of what those Black holes might help us otherwise be, even in deeply antiBlack ecologies, de tings about Blackness that we can't really explain or see in signs, significations, languages, or faiths, when nouns, verbs, adjectives fall away, what metaphors can we leave to describe the way for some being else, some other/wise, coming behind? I'm trying to unwind. I try to undiscipline. I'm trying to mind fractures to find the kind of rest that keeps me waking up as de ting about Blackness always outside of me, asking, other/wise/.

> The true leap, Fanon wrote at the end of his *Black Skin, White Masks*, consists in
> introducing invention into existence . . .
>
> WYNTER, "UNSETTLING THE COLONIALITY OF BEING/
> POWER/TRUTH/FREEDOM." (2003, 331)

Notes

Introduction: "It ain't that deep"

An important note on slashes (/): I use slashes to enjoin terms throughout, not to suggest that both sides of the slash mean the same thing or are interchangeable, but as semantic denotation of the space in which meaning fractures polysemically with/in, in-/out-/side, across, and between terms involved in such an equation. Most prominently, I employ the term "produce/negotiate" in relation to meaning in this project. In that conception, I mean to include not only ideas of production and/or negotiation, but also ideas that exist within that spectrum of meaning unable to be situatedly expressed by either term. As Black feminist writing practice, slashes here commune with moving texts like Ntozake Shange's (1982) choreopoem *for colored girls who have considered suicide / when the rainbow is enuf* and Christina Sharpe's (2016) more recent academic monograph *In the Wake: On Blackness and Being*. As Shange explains, of scenes from *for colored girls*, "what people say and how people use language do not necessarily mean what they are conventionally assumed to mean" (Lester 1990, 762). See Neal A. Lester, "At the Heart of Shange's Feminism: An Interview" (1990). Theorizing movement in spaces in between, along, in/side, and out is central to *Black or Right* and in considering significant meaning that does not and cannot occupy static, linguistic/culturally articulated frames. More than anything, this project *projects possibilities.*

1 I tell autoethnographic stories from memory, sometimes re/creating speech, acknowledging that stories change through re/telling; however, where available, I use emails, text messages, published materials, and written notes to augment these re/tellings.

2 In reference to the epigraph from Ahmed (2012, 2).

3 All character and institutional names apart from my own are changed throughout this project as a courtesy to the folks animated in it.

4 I capitalize "Black," "Blackness," and related terms throughout as a grammatical move signaling a centering of Blackness.

5 I prioritize ideas of affect mobilized in cultural studies drawn from the work of Audre Lorde and Sara Ahmed. The latter explains that "to be affected by something is to evaluate that thing. Evaluations are expressed in how bodies turn toward things" (Ahmed 2010, 23).

6 I recognize the im/possibility, then, of speaking of the 'paraontological,' without operating on some received ontological plane.

7 While Z. I. Jackson tackles Western scientific and philosophical discourse to tease out Blackness in relation to bestialized humanization, underscoring how through enslavement and colonization discourses on "the animal" emerge as both human and nonhuman forms (rather than the opposite) (2020, 23), I focus on rhetorical tussling with the plasticity of Blackness in antiBlack spaces.

8 Although related to Jenny Edbauer (Rice)'s approach to rhetorical ecologies— and consequently building off of her terminology—the description of the concept above acts as more of a corollary than a borrowing (Edbauer 2005). While I agree that we should "look towards a framework of affective ecologies that recontextualizes rhetorics in their temporal, historical, and lived fluxes" (9), this project departs from the way in which Edbauer (Rice) performs ecological readings. She describes elements within these ecologies using the term "testimonies," which goes undefined. While I attempt to clarify these elements, I also prioritize power dynamics and race work that she sidesteps, by pinpointing instances which I describe as fractures. By paying attention to these dynamics, I pursue ecological reading that resists the (cultural and ontological) flattening of ecological elements and subjects.

Additionally, I note here that my concept of 'deep ecologies' deploys language associated with (and ideas superficially similar to) the environmental philosophy and activist movement, emerging in Western thought in the 1970s, without inherent endorsement of this movement's ideologies. Agreeing with Ramachandra Guha that the deep ecology environmental movement potentially mobilizes Eurocentric bias through anthropocentrism, therefore ignoring Western overconsumption and militarization, offers potentially imperialistic frameworks, and appropriates and oversimplifies Eastern philosophies, I look to African indigenous understandings of conscious, mutual, and intertwined relationships between humans, nonhuman animals, and their material environments through botho or Ubuntu. See Guha (1989), "Radical Environmentalism and Third World Preservation: A Third World Critique."

9 Deep rhetorical ecologies acknowledge antiBlackness as foundational to their functions and politics. I draw on Sharpe's notion of 'weather' as the antiBlack totality of our climates (2016, 104), requiring adaptiveness, "the atmospheric condition of time and place; it produces new ecologies . . . The weather trans*forms Black being" (106).

10 I summon the economic connotations of produce/negotiate intentionally, as they highlight how the very concept of Blackness always already operates within/from a history borne from racial capitalism, objectification, and colonialism—one in which "Black" signaled a commodification of a human resource (see Mbembe 2017).

Rather than offer boundaries/borders for reading such ecologies, I'm more concerned with potential overlaps in the conditions/temporalities for knowledge production. So, for example, if we were to read the racialization of the Black Lives Matter movement, we would inherently be caught up in mulling the rhetorical aspects of the Movement for Black Lives. The Occupy Wall Street movement, however, might offer conditions or temporalities that suggest possible deepening of the rhetorical ecologies being read, so I don't bracket myself off from delving there or elsewhere.

11 Remixed from Shirley Brice Heath's ([1982] 2001) conception in chapter 3.

12 Following folks such as Jeffrey Grabill and Stacey Pigg (2012) in rhetoric/communication and writing studies scholarship.

13 In an Aristotelian framework, ἐνέγεια (enérgeia) situates 'being' as simultaneously act (*enérgeia*) and potency (*dýnamis*), explained in his *Metaphysics*, according to physicist Robert Lindsay as a "realized state of potentialities," dealing, though, with the capacity to bring about something else. See Robert B. Lindsay (1975, 16–32) Historian Philip Mirowski adds that the Greek philosopher uses the term in multiple senses: in his *Ethics*, Aristotle uses it as 'activity' as opposed to disposition, in his *Rhetoric*, he uses it in the sense of "vigorous style." According to Mirowski, Aristotle also deploys *enérgeia* to differentiate activity from potential, while also implying the interminable transformation from the possible to the actual. See Mirowski (1989, 13).

14 This body includes, but is not limited to, work by Geneva Smitherman, Keith Gilyard, Beverly J. Moss, Jacqueline Jones Royster, Adam Banks, Carmen Kynard, Vershawn Young, Staci Perryman-Clark, Marsha Houston, Olga Idriss Davis, Aimee Carrillo Rowe, Karma Chávez, Bernadette Calafell, Lisa Flores, Kent Ono, Andre Johnson, C. Riley Snorton, Darrel Wanzer-Serrano, David Cisneros, Dexter Gordon, Tom Nakayama, Lisa Corrigan, Catherine Squires, Ralph Cintron, Eric Pritchard, Abe Khan, Morris Young, and other key figures who examine critically marginalized rhetorics, communication practices, and literacies in these fields.

15 This includes work by, but not limited to, Krista Ratcliffe (2005), Asao Inoue (2015), Timothy Barnett (2000), Jennifer Beech (2004), Wendy Ryden and Ian Marshall (2012), Frankie Condon (2012), Matthew Jackson (2006), and so on.

16 See *White Privilege: Readings from the Other Side of Racism*, ed. Paula S. Rothenberg and Soniya Munshi, now in its fifth edition (2016), for other foundational texts in whiteness studies.

17 As Diana Coole and Samantha Frost contend, materialist frameworks "are congruent with new materialist ontologies inasmuch as they understand materiality in a relational, emergent sense as contingent materialization" (2010, 29).

18 Likewise, in Black studies, Sharpe (2016), following Saidiya Hartman, emphasizes how the autobiographical example counters a "violence of abstraction" (Hartman 2008, 7) by looking to one's emergence via sociohistorical processes as a window into those very processes (Saunders 2008, 7; Sharpe 2016, 8). In cultural studies, Ahmed points out that "migrant memoirs . . . give texture and complexity to the migrant experience, to the ways in which hope, fear, anxiety, longing, and desire shape the decisions to leave one's country as well as the experiences of arriving and becoming familiar with a new country" (2010, 154). Autobiography, aesthetically, might be potentially considered autoethnographic given the consideration of sociocultural power alongside personal reflection. Chapter 1 more fully unpacks the relationships between these narrative modes.

19 Undergirding this deployment of Black feminist thought, the philosophies' five epistemological tenets remain essential to this study. Patricia Hill Collins ([1990] 2000) outlines these as lived experience as criterion of meaning, the use of dialogue in assessing knowledge claims, the ethics of caring, the ethic of personal accountability, and acknowledging Black women as agents of change.

20 I replace the names of institutions where my analysis takes place for the purpose of anonymizing the vulnerable people of color mentioned in this study. Replacements (both in-text, in notes, and in references) are marked with square brackets "[]."

21 Where X represents a condition, such as "cool," or "strugglin'."

22 White institutional defensiveness arises from public stances or policy implementation by white institutions/media that move to preempt or skirt racial stress or even the subject of race to protect white feelings. Contextualized in the age of neoliberal narratives of "post-raciality" and colorblindness in institutional operations, that defensiveness subtly manifests itself in several ways including through policy, diversity initiatives, media displays, and day-to-day rhetorical encounters. For example, my undergraduate university—in grappling with how to snuff out the idea that such racial tension, racist ideology, and violence do, in fact, survive into the twenty-first century—illustrates this defensiveness, as it asks students to simply unplug from the social media network citing capitalist values (career advancement) as validation. White institutional defensiveness serves as an ever-present backdrop for the Black rhetorics explored in *Black or Right*. Chapter 4 provides further examples.

23 Brian Street defines literacy practices as modes of reading and writing connected to broader sociocultural patterns in its use (2000, 21).

Chapter 1: "Are you Black, though?"

1 Reprinted with the kind courtesy and permission of the *Village Voice*, where "Power" was first published.

2 Tangentially: ScHoolboy Q's membership in the supergroup Black Hippy—which includes Kendrick Lamar—and his tracks' intermittent focus on social justice issues arguably mark him this way in popular culture.

3 I use "autoethnography" to refer to autobiographic stories contextualized within the theorization/study of culture (ethnography) for knowledge production/negotiation. Tony Adams, Stacy Holman Jones, and Carolyn Ellis mark autoethnography distinct from autobiography due to its academic audience (2015, 36–37); however, Pratt's explanation (noted here) points out that autoethnography might address multiple audiences. I lean on Pratt here to open up possibilities for knowledge production/negation with/in/beyond the academy.

4 As critical race theorist Lisa Marie Cacho stresses, "criminalized populations and the places where they live *form the foundation* of the U. S. legal system, imagined to be the reason why a punitive (in)justice system exists" (2012, 5; emphasis in original).

5 Though institutions border spaces for control and commodification, I argue those spaces operate with/against such bordering. "Off-campus areas," even while signaling separation, are inculcated in an institution's ecological meanings, since they remain rela-

tionally, geographically, and linguistically tethered to it. My study aligns with feminist geographers' "notions of space as paradoxical, provisional, contradictory, fragmented" (Reynolds 2007, 20).

6 She even wrote me a private note after the semester to thank me for helping her understand her (racialized) identities and experiences. Thank you, Shaina!

7 Ratcliffe uses it to initiate her antiracist 'rhetorical listening' but then turns to "academic research" to "explore further" (2005, 37).

8 I neither mean to essentialize Blackness or the role of the Black graduate/instructor, nor to provide any kind of guidelines for the future negotiation of that position.

9 I look to ways that we may consider Black masculinity, in particular, nonmonolithically: beyond binaries of exceptionalism or victimhood, toxically straight or stereotypically queer. I follow Simone Drake (2016) in approaching the study of Black masculinity through Black feminist frameworks, imagining possibilities for intersectionality, complexity, and accountability. This project thus follows on work in rhetoric/communication and writing studies like Eric D. Pritchard's (2017) that operates at the intersection of race and gender/sexuality studies. I acknowledge able-bodied, straight, cis-gender male privileges, hoping to dismantle a tradition of their misuse. In centering Black women's scholarship, I theorize Black masculinity in this chapter to work against essentialization of difference, both in the United States and transnationally.

10 Such as Wendy S. Hesford in *Framing Identities* (1999) and Mike Rose in *Lives on the Boundary* (1990).

11 I include these texts to show a (three-decade) trajectory, acknowledging that there are many other examples.

12 While traditional griots use oral performance, autoethnography's performativity/ reciprocity allows readers spaces to relate and respond (Calafell 2013, 8), dis/identify, riff, and clap back, offering deviations from standard fare in research/academic writing. As Barbara Christian spotlights, "people of color have always theorized—but in forms quite different from Western logic . . . [Our] theorizing (and [she uses] the verb rather than the noun) is often in narrative forms, in the stories we create, in riddles, in proverbs, in the play with language, since dynamic rather than fixed ideas seem more to our liking" (1987, 52).

13 The US tradition dates back to Black knowledge-making by former slaves through autobiographic writings and speeches.

14 For more on the rhetorical, historical, and linguistic politics of the word/concept "nigga," please see Kermit Campbell's (1997) "Real Niggas Never Die," Gloria Naylor's (1986) "A Word's Meaning Can Often Depend on Who Says It," Vershawn Young's (2007) chapter "Nigga Gender" in *Your Average Nigga*, and/or Randall Kennedy's (2003) *Nigger: The Strange Career of a Troublesome Word*. My project here focuses more, instead, on the rhetorically ecological radiations of the word in the context of the historically white classroom than on the particular word's politics proper.

15 This heading re/calls attention to the epigraph to this chapter from Lorde (1974).

16 This charted history is inherently somewhat reductive. I choose Black scholars who represent the analytic for which I argue and speak in some way to my project's politics, welcoming further engagement with this history.

17 For further descriptions of these environments, see Young (2004, 2007).

18 Later in Du Bois's (1903) text, in "On the Meaning of Progress" and "Of the Training of Black Men," he switches roles from student to teacher/education theorist, still engaged in critical reflection of how the color line works to dismantle attempts at Black education.

19 Black autoethnography shares similarities with Kimberly Benston's "black autocritography" (2000, 284). However, I contend the former centrally analyzes the materiality of peoples and cultures (as opposed to literature) and represents more than slippages in other writing genres.

20 Young's (2007) second chapter features his poem "shiny," interrelating analysis of it. I extend this aspect of Black autoethnography.

21 Liberal Arts College is a four-year public liberal arts college established in the late sixties in the US Northeast.

22 At the time, I didn't own many dress clothes, both because they were unnecessary for the job I held and because that job paid close to minimum wage. I distinctly recall making between US$6 and $7 an hour, while being restricted to working no more than twenty hours per week due to my nonresident alien status. Naturally, the photograph does not necessarily highlight the material realities of the situations that lead to the "success"—at least superficially—celebrated by it. The related article, with a chance to do just that, also does not.

23 Both incidents occurred within a one-mile radius of each respective campus.

24 Chapter 4 delves deeply into analyzing such notices.

25 Originally published by the *Academy of American Poets* website at: https://www.poets.org/academy-american-poets/ohio-state-university-poetry-prize-2016.

26 Groups of about six classes make up a work group. Six instructors grade from their group's assigned pile. A classroom instructor thus has under a 20 percent chance of grading their own students' work.

27 "Raff" in Trinidadian dialect is a verb meaning to pull an object away (usually from another person) violently, to potentially abscond with it.

Chapter 2: Composing Black Matter/s

1 Certain tags have indeed been identified as "Blacktags," such as #onlyintheghetto and #ifsantawasblack—racialized hashtags deployed and circulated by Black Twitter users (Sharma 2013). Sanjay Sharma argues, however, that "as digital objects, Blacktags reveal the contagious effects of networked relations in producing emergent, racial aggregations rather than simply representing the behavior of an intentionally acting Black group of Twitter users" (48). This chapter engages with the utilization of hashtags for (education about) Black virality and annotation in ways that counter neoliberal value systems of literacy/agency, stressing the racial enculturation of tags for their resistant Black capacities.

2 Pritha Prasad's "Beyond Rights as Recognition," in particular, illustrates them. Prasad examines how specific tags (#IfTheyGunnedMeDown and #AliveWhileBlack), through "the embedded, distributed modes of collectivity and community they offer[,]

can create critical posthuman coalitions and affirmative bonds" (2016, 52). Prasad's study aligns with the abovementioned critical race scholars in theorizing racialization in these spaces by looking to tags as field sites for research, but through an exploration of hashtag's rhetorical capacities, the article intimates prospective follow-up work in writing studies.

3 Greene Wade (2017) characterizes this thrust as Wynterian, in order to create new genres of the human in order to untangle Blackness from (Western) Man.

4 These are, naturally, condensed and particular histories. For more on the role that printed commonplaces played in the formation of ideology in the Western tradition, see Ann Moss (1996); for a view of how commonplaces and "common" writing shaped early American thought systems in particular, see Susan Miller (1998).

5 Miller (1998) analyzes the writings held in the archives of the Virginia Historical Society in the 1800s. These include commonplace books, family histories, lists, narratives, and so forth.

6 See, in particular, Miller's chap. 4, "The Class on Gender" and the analysis of Thomas Massie's commonplace book (1998, 163–70).

7 Examples include the sometimes-problematic institutionalization of Black studies as an academic discipline and the growing practice of 'multicultural' or 'diversity' requirements in university general education course requirements.

8 One might argue that the Conference on College Composition and Communication (CCCC) policy statement on "Students Right to Their Own Language" (1974) helped spark such changes and that statements like the National Council of Teachers of English/CCCC's Black Caucus "NCTE Statement Affirming #BlackLivesMatter" (2015) evidence continued change in these fields.

9 This history is not to suggest that dominant ideology could not be undercut by commonplace book use but to give a broad picture of how writing/composition tools through their design and implementation in the classroom and beyond can inform and reinforce such ideologies.

10 Facebook represents the only exception, where a greater proportion of surveyed Hispanic internet users (73%) used Facebook than Black users (70%) (Pew Research Center 2018).

11 Similarly, a 2015 special issue of the journal *Feminist Studies*, "Teaching About Ferguson." articulates "the meanings of the [Ferguson/Black Lives Matter] moment" and their unfolding conditions for their latent pedagogies (Nash 2015, 2).

12 I recognize that such discussions come with varying degrees of risk dependent on the identities of instructors and students, as well as surrounding contexts. I mean to suggest that hashtags can be a means by which such risks might be pedagogically confronted, and in the third section of this chapter I explain how the "Tumblr as Commonplace Book" assignment navigates some of the complications that arise in race talk—especially in historically white spaces.

13 In the proceeding section, I analyze my writing assignment "Tumblr as Commonplace Book," in which I pick up hashtag composition as a means of using digital commonplacing for pedagogic purposes of engaging in viral Blackness with potentials to subvert rather than reinforce cultural hegemony and its antiBlackness. I don't suggest,

however, the latter as impossible. The above history of commonplacing suffices to argue otherwise. Before delving into that analysis, though, I sketch the digital environment for the assignment (another deep ecology at work in this educational hashtagging)— Tumblr—in the remainder of this section.

14 Jacobs' (2012) article originally inspired my assignment, which later developed to focus on hashtags. The article does not discuss the role of tags in the commonplace book / Tumblr comparison, however, nor does it consider the racialized dynamics of tag use.

15 No safeguard, of course, exists from the possibility of offensive or violent responses from other Tumblr users once a blog is set as public on the website. That possibility remains a distinct constraint of public/digital writing exercises. For example, in a 2019 graduate course, my students were followed by a white supremacist Tumblr account.

16 In this section, I examine my students' application of the "Tumblr as Commonplace Book" social media writing assignment that operates as a reading/writing/note-taking activity scaffolding other projects for the course throughout the semester. Before looking at student examples of hashtag usage for their relational Black feminist meaning-making potentials, I unpack the assignment and contextualize the course for which the assignment is crucial.

17 Chapter 3 unpacks the term "cultural moment" and the moment termed "post-Ferguson."

18 Similar to a retweet, Tumblr's "reblog" feature allows users to repost content on their blogs while giving credit to the original poster. Re-posters may add additional data below the reblogged post.

19 I specifically ask students not to use part or full real names in the URLs for their blogs. For the purposes of maintaining further anonymity (and in accordance with International Review Board–exempt status), I have coded the blog titles tcb01–tcb41.

20 Students are also encouraged to use content such as GIFs and video stills that already exist on the site on or the internet.

21 Across each semester, the racial demographics were as follows: in the autumn 2016 semester, 15 students identified as white, 2 students identified as non-Black students of color, 4 students identified as Black; in the spring 2017 semester, 15 students identified as white, 4 students identified as non-Black students of color, and 1 student identified as Black. Students self-identify through an autoethnographic reflection exercise early in each semester.

22 I read three students' posts using this same image to show how different meanings might be made from the readings of the same text.

Chapter 3: "All my life I had to fight"

Quoted from Alice Walker's (1982) *The Color Purple* (38).

1 I use #BlackLivesMatter here (and throughout) to refer to the hashtag as well as the social movement, choosing to contextualize that use based on chapter 2's arguments about the meaning-making potentials of the hashtag.

2 Rachel Dolezal was a former Spokane, Washington, president of the National Association for the Advancement of Colored People and a former instructor of Africana Studies. In 2015, she lost both positions after it became public that she had falsely claimed to be African American. Because (based on biological notions of race), she is white/Caucasian, her presentation as a Black woman and identification as such on documents led to the eruption of a debate on "racial fluidity." General sentiment was that Dolezal's racial identification was offensive to Black folk, as she adopted the histories and cultures of Black womanhood and alleged race-based hate crimes against her.

3 As someone who identifies as such, I acknowledge that this implicates my reading of Blackness and #BlackLivesMatter. I, thus, prioritize the term "Black" as opposed to "African American."

4 By "cultural moment" I mean the contextual, yet dynamic, backdrop within which we consider social relations during a sociopolitical and historical period that relates to, but can differ from, other such periods. Certainly, earlier histories/historical events play a significant role in contributing to proceeding cultural moments. But I argue that reframing and recontextualizing those histories due to significant events and cultural shifts within certain geographical spaces allow for spills from/between one cultural moment to another. Cultural moments can vary by location, but thinking transnationally, I classify such moments through highlighting issues that arguably move in and out of widespread (news and social) media-driven narratives. Cultural moments represent very deep rhetorical ecologies.

5 I mean to ask with/in this particular fracture ("relation/ships"), by conjuring the Trans-Atlantic slave ship, Sharpe's question: *"If the crime is blackness, is the sentence the circuit between ship and shore?"* (2016, 57).

6 Whereas these scholars tend to focus on the interplay between oral and written communication, and if "participants . . . learn whether the oral or written mode takes precedence in literacy events" (Heath [1982] 2001, 445), our attention lies with the prioritization of interactivity in the production/negotiation of meaning.

7 Whereas Street (1999; 2000) and Janet Maybin (2005) propel conversations regarding literacy events toward readings of literacy practices, I privilege the event because I do not work with the notion that I study cordoned-off "communities." Street (1999) extends the conversation around literacy events in proposing his notion of "literacy practices" to point to the importance of "social practices and conceptions of reading and writing" (1). He seeks to alleviate what he sees as the descriptive nature of literacy events, as opposed to a focus on the meaning construction. For Street, the idea of literacy practices, on the other hand, "attempts to handle the events and the patterns of activity around literacy but to *link* them to something broader of a cultural and social kind. And part of that broadening involves attending to the fact that in a literacy event we have brought to it concepts, social models regarding what the nature of this practice is and that make it work and give it meaning" (2000, 21). Literacy practices, then, might seem more applicable as a concept to the approach that this chapter takes. Maybin's contention of their importance might be of relevance. She explains that "the taking on of more complex ideas about discourse and intertextuality" allows for scholars "to more clearly conceptualise the pivotal role of literacy practices in articulating the links between individual people's everyday experience, and wider social institutions and structures. It also enables them to explore issues of power, through examining the relationship between micro- and macro-level contexts" (2005, 197). The issue with looking toward literacy practices within the deep rhetorical ecologies at hand in this project, however, lies in the assumption that that attention lies with a defined, sociological community. Deep rhetorical ecologies refuse such boundaries.

So, while I indeed mobilize issues related to individuals' relations to social power and draw from Street's (1999, 2000) (and others') efforts to consider social practices and cultural discourse, I emphasize the literacy event. This emphasis highlights the particular fracturing in events radiating with/in deep ecologies.

8 In using the term *post-Ferguson* I do not suggest that we have somehow transcended the events of the Ferguson Uprising of 2014. Rather, my employment of the term seeks to center the cultural moment that follows the Uprising as distinct from moments prior. We might understand "post" as closer to the literal "after," with the imposition to re/turn (through critical memory [Baker 1995] and wake work [Sharpe 2016]) to the salient role that the Uprising plays in events following it. As historian Barbara Ransby argues, "In the wake of the Ferguson uprising, Black freedom organizing overall took on new agency" (2018, 76).

9 This section heading uses lyrics from Lamar's "Alright" (Lamar 2015a).

10 I do not mean to suggest here that the census is the one place where the US government defines all its ideas of race and/or Blackness. I use it as an example to emphasize the preponderance of confusion with/in government institutions on these ideas. Because demographics are wielded freely as weapons in Eurocentric analyses of race in the United States, I highlight the methods for the collection of those statistics here as a counterpoint.

11 This "self-identification" seems to be an implied affordance, rather than a stated constraint in collecting official data.

12 I call this defensiveness "white institutional defensiveness" because of the convergence of power used by institutions (and people) to deploy and promote racial supremacy of whiteness via antiBlackness: Eurocentric and now neoliberal (within the last half century) ideals established based on notions of universalist aims and worldviews. The following paragraph explains what I mean specifically by the term. Chapter 4 provides more examples of its operation.

13 While I acknowledge that other socioeconomic issues have (in the past twenty years) and continue to negatively impact Black communities in the United States—such as gentrification, the school-to-prison pipeline, and so on—I foreground these events to exemplify their publicly articulated or institutionalized white defensiveness.

14 Taylor (2016) charts this culture from the establishment of US nationhood, through slavery, the Civil Rights movement, and on to the era of colorblindness.

15 While we might rightfully acknowledge that extremist Islamic groups do not represent the views of the tenets of the entire religion, such a stipulation was arguably flattened in the national (military) response to the events of 9/11.

16 In 2017, these efforts crystalized in Trump's "Muslim ban."

17 In that game "the body and politics of Barack Obama intersect with the body politics of the nation, reminding rhetorical scholars of the continuing significance of race and (un)marked bodies, as well as of the ease with which anti[B]lack racism can be easily publicly voiced and as easily dismissed as nonracist." (Flores and Sims 2016, 207).

18 See chap. 2, "From Civil Rights to Colorblind" in Taylor (2016).

19 Originally published online on FeministWire.com on October 14, 2014, "A Herstory of the #BlackLivesMatter Movement" is written by Alicia Garza (2014), a Black queer activist and one of the cofounders of the movement. The text can now be found on BlackLivesMatter.com as a kind of manifesto for the movement. It defines the origins and aims of #BlackLivesMatter, explaining how it arose as a response to the vigilante killing of Trayvon Martin. Garza declares "Black Lives Matter is an ideological and political intervention in a world where Black lives are systematically and intentionally targeted for demise. It is an affirmation of Black folks' contributions to this society, our humanity, and our resilience in the face of deadly oppression." The article emphasizes the implications of using Black queer women's work institutionally. It stresses how problematic erasure might occur when such work becomes integrated into discourses and movements that do not acknowledge historically marginalized intersectional positions of Black folk, particularly Black queer women's. But the movement should not only be understood in relation to Black death, as the article highlights a focus on Black life—lives traditionally obscured in media coverage of the Black power struggle, like those of Black queer trans folk, Black undocumented immigrants, and Black disabled folk.

20 Kendrick Lamar (2015a) released "Alright" as part of his album *To Pimp A Butterfly* in 2015. He later published the track as the album's fourth single, released on June 30, 2015. Later in the year, the song's chorus "we gon' be alright" developed into a chant frequently used at #BlackLivesMatter protests across the country. The song's lyrics deal primarily with struggles with materialism that Lamar potentially faces as a gender-conforming straight Black man from an impoverished urban background in the United States, relationships between Black folk and institutional authority, and the role that violence plays vis-à-vis Black masculinity. They also include several Christian references in Lamar's contention with temptation. The audio recording also includes a short poem as a coda, which focuses on the speaker's internal conflict, though it refers to a "you," to whom it is addressed.

21 The track's associated music video (Lamar 2015c) was released on the same day as the audio track. Entirely shot in black and white, the almost seven-minute video begins with shots of inner-city life, significantly including images of mostly Black males in violent interactions with white police. Concurrent images of other Black men drinking and "making it rain" interject, as viewers hear an extended version of the poem attached to the end of the audio track. A short interlude between the poem and the track proper offers images of Lamar and associates in a car actively being carried by four white police officers. Most of the video consists of a rotating series of scenes that show Lamar floating around a West Coast US city, Lamar in a car spewing money, three hoodied black men dancing on a cop car, and shots of urban celebration involving Black youth. Close to the end of the video, Lamar is shot from atop a lamppost by an older white cop gesturing a gunshot with his hands. Lamar's same short poem from the end of the audio track (Lamar 2015a) is again recited; he hits the ground, yet, after a short moment, smiles as though alive in the very last shot of the video.

22 Lamar's Grammy performance (CBS Television Network 2016) of the song uses markedly different kinds of scenes. It begins with a chain gang of Black men entering the stage to the sound of a saxophone, led by Lamar. At the mic, the rapper starts with lyrics from "The Blacker the Berry" that particularly speaks to Black identity—bodily traits traditionally associated with Blackness and particularly sexualized Black masculinity—and rage in relation to oppressive institutional power (Lamar 2015b). Having removed his chains, Lamar moves the performance to an interlude that includes backup dancers clad in neon-colored jumpsuits (CBS Television Network 2016). Lamar moves across the stage to a group of Black men and women dressed in tribal costumes, some with drums, all moving around a large burning fire at the center of the shot. As he moves to this scene, he gets into the lyrics of "Alright" (Lamar 2015a). The women dancing move around Lamar in a circle, as he gets to the first chorus of the song, at which point several other dancers engage with him in a highly choreographed routine (CBS Television Network 2016). Lamar seemingly emphasizes several lyrics in verse two when the backing music stops; he repeats a couple lines that crescendo as the dancers gather closer and hype his escalating volume and intensity. After another break in the backing instrumentation, he moves again to stage right, where, alone, he spits a third (untitled) track that highlights issues related to the material living conditions of impoverished Blacks, along with what might be accounts of his personal confrontations with fame. Toward the end of the performance, his flow escalates almost to an inaudible speed, during which the camera shots of the performance appositely switch focus and range. A flashing light also intensifies images of Lamar's face during this frantic climax. When his rapping stops, all lighting on him is removed. We see his silhouette against a bright image of Africa, with the text "Compton" embedded in it in black, lined with large chains on either side, in frank focus.

23 Blacklivesmattersyllabus.com (Roberts 2016) presents a semester-long multi-modal schedule for an interdisciplinary course on the #BlackLivesMatter movement. The instructor, Frank Leon Roberts—a faculty member at New York University and grassroots political activist, taught the class at New York University in fall 2016. A section of the site explicates Roberts's renown for his "pioneering work as the 'Black Lives Matter Professor,'" which "has been featured in Fader Magazine, NPR, CNN, and an extensive variety of other national media outlets." The syllabus aims to include considerations of the movement in relation to the rise of the prison industrial complex vis-à-vis Black US urban communities, the relationship between (popular/national) media and race, the place of racial activism in the Obama era, and the "increasing populist nature of decentralized protest movements" in the United States. Required films range from the documentary work of Laurens Grant to Ava DuVernay, while required alphabetic texts highlight writing by Michelle Alexander, Angela Davis, the Movement for Black Lives, Audre Lorde, Kimberlé Williams Crenshaw, Cornel West, Alicia Garza, and other figures. The syllabus includes links to videos that feature a range of public figures from #BlackLivesMatter activists, professors, and politicians, to Beyoncé's "Formation." Each weekly class session includes a blurb discussing the ideas to be engaged in for that class, required texts for each respective week, and reflective writing assignments. Notably, the syllabus's title and core logistical information (instructor, date time, etc.) come after a centered graphic of white text on a black background. The text, written in capital letters reads, "WE GON' BE ALRIGHT," while a line runs through the middle of the horizontally oriented phrase. Weekly topics of discussion include the history and historicizing of the #BlackLivesMatter movement, its aims and methods, and its relationships to feminist intersectionality, to the 2016 presidential election, and to popular culture.

24 My reading will in no way attempt to be exhaustive and will potentially offer more questions than solid digestible notions about these texts. Offering fluid interpretations, my rhetorical analysis reflexively seeks to welcome future engagements with its process—my explanations should be means, rather than ends. This method of reading attempts to promote engagement with some deep ecologies that make up and will make up the #BlackLivesMatter movement, motivating afterlives from the relations, intersections, and fractures in my analytical process.

25 I mean to conjure Henry Louis Gates's (1989) theory of "signifyin'" here. Later in the chapter, I discuss specific applications of the theory for inter(con)textual reading in Black texts at hand in the US milieu.

26 Lamar's (2015a) track is used as a frame in Robert's (2016) unit on #BlackLivesMatter in popular culture, however, it is only mentioned as a part of a trend.

27 This question is also signifyin with Beyoncé's (2016) "Formation."

28 Consider in relation to chapter 2's argument about Black hashtags as counter/public commonplaces, as marginalized literacy.

29 Merriam-Webster.com (2020a) defines 'woke' as "a byword of social awareness likely started in 2008, with the release of Erykah Badu's song 'Master Teacher,'" though it dates first used to 1972. The Dictionary explains that "*Stay woke* became a watch word in parts of the [B]lack community for those who were self-aware, questioning the dominant paradigm and striving for something better (Merriam Webster 2020b). But *stay woke* and *woke* became part of a wider discussion in 2014, immediately following the shooting of Michael Brown in Ferguson, Missouri. The word *woke* became entwined with the Black Lives Matter movement; instead of just being a word that signaled awareness of injustice or racial tension, it became a word of action. Activists were *woke* and called on others to *stay woke*" (Merriam Webster 2020b). For more, refer to: *Merriam-Webster.com Dictionary*, 2020a, "woke," accessed June 26, 2020, https://www.merriam-webster.com/dictionary/woke; Merriam-Webster.com Dictionary, 2020b, "woke Meaning Origin," Last Modified September 2017. Accessed June 26, 2020. https://www.merriam-webster.com/words-at-play/woke-meaning-origin.

Compare with Urban Dictionary's top three definitions with the term that speak to notions of liberal intellectual superiority and 'fakeness': Urban Dictionary. 2020 "woke" Accessed June 26, 2020. http://www.urbandictionary.com/define.php?term=woke.

30 I am not interested in making judgments about Lamar's character, or defining what "charismatic" might imply. Here, I engage with the possibility of this phrase referring to Lamar as a cis-het Black man that has gained popularity in relation to #BlackLivesMatter.

31 A video recording of the chanting can be viewed at Piffin (2015).

32 Emphases in both Ahmed (2010) quotations in original.

33 This heading uses this phrase from Assata Shakur's (1973) "To My People."

34 Garza's (2014) article includes a hyperlink to a longer text of Shakur's (1973) from which the quotation is referenced.

35 The video is one of several found embedded in Roberts (2016): http://www.black livesmattersyllabus.com/blmlive/. Accessed April 2, 2017.

36 This heading quotes Garza's (2014) stance on the importance of sharing the histories of Black liberation from which #BlackLivesMatter draws.

37 This section's heading references Garza's (2014) thoughts on the prison industrial complex.

38 This reference could be to Jesus's tough visit to Nazareth after being raised elsewhere. See Luke 4:14–30.

39 We could potentially read this as Lamar (2015a) establishing an ethos in the song based on honesty and truth, but other biblical references suggest otherwise.

40 By "faith" I do not refer to "Faith" as in the church as a whole but belief in a Christian God.

41 This quotation is a part of an italicized statement from Garza's (2014) "Herstory": "When Black people get free, everybody gets free." It echoes the Combahee River Collective's Statement that "if Black women were free, it would mean that everyone else would have to be free since our freedom would necessitate the destruction of all systems of oppression" ([1977] 2017, 23).

Chapter 4: The Politics of Belonging . . .

1 While Rice does admit that feeling actually cannot be divorced from pedagogy or rhetorical publicness, seeking instead an alternate imaginary for the possibilities of inquiry (2012, 168), the material conditions of Black and brown folks in the United States (and the West proper) demand that rhetorical theorists pay attention to the role of affective feeling in these moments and the way that subjectivity co-constitutes pedagogy and rhetorical publicness. Moreover, Wynter (2005) avers that raciality generates our notions of affect and desire that influence even posthumanist imaginaries (which inherently tussle with matter and meaning).

2 Dr. Kynard graciously provided me with an alphabetic text copy of the presentation, from which I cite directly. I thank her for her generosity and for supporting my project.

3 I intentionally begin with the date of the Black Lives Matter in Classrooms Symposium.

4 The act is named after a white female student at Lehigh University who was sexually assaulted and killed by a Black male student in 1987 (Gross and Fine 1990). The document itself, therefore, has historical context that racializes and genders it to play into historical scripts of Black men in relation to white women's safety.

5 Identified as such by visible hijab.

6 Susan Smith is a white South Carolina woman who drowned her two infant sons in 1995 and then accused a Black man of the crime.

7 The British legal principle of *partus sequitur ventrem* stipulated that the mark of slavery was passed on via the enslaved Black mother during Trans-Atlantic slavery. The implication, then, remains that Black motherhood—or, more specifically, the Black womb—physically and culturally functions as means by which Blackness, sociogenically, could be continually produced. See Sharpe (2016) for further implications.

8 Such data refer to "data collected by organizations about how they are perceived by external communities" (Ahmed 2012, 34).

9 The Department of Public Safety's (2017) Crime Report published in 2017 presents 2016 statistics only by the type of crime, rather than by identity markers. A comparison between the total number of individuals involved in crimes reported and those described in detail in alerts to confirm whether suspects were *only* Black individuals in the six-month period could not therefore be performed via publicly provided information.

10 Several web-hosting services denied Anglin their space after *The Daily Stormer's* role in organizing the far-right rally that resulted in the death of a counter-protestor in Charlottesville, Virginia, in August 2017.

11 As unpacked in chapter 3.

12 Section title quoted from Lorde's (1978) "A Litany for Survival."

Conclusion: De Ting about Blackness

1 I learned at some point that this "droiyn room" came from "drawing room," but I'm not sure why we use this terminology. I would guess it was passed along through British colonialism.

2 The entire text of Smith's (2014) poem can be found at *Split this Rock*, an online database of social justice poetry.

3 Singing Sandra, Sandra DesVignes-Millington, became only the second woman (after Calypso Rose) to win the National Calypso Monarch competition in Trinidad and Tobago history. "Voices from De Ghetto" and "Song for Healing" won the 1999 title for Sandra, who routinely focuses on sociopolitical issues affecting African diasporic communities and (Black) women in the Caribbean.

4 See note 6 in the introduction on para/ontological Blackness.

5 I paraphrase here from Sharpe's description of J.M.W. Turner's painting *Slave Ship: Slavers Throwing Aboard Dead and Dying—Typhoon Coming On*. Sharpe describes, "In the roiling, livid orpiment of Turner's painting, the dead are yoked to the dying. That Turner's slave ship lacks a proper name allows it to stand in for *every* slave ship and every slave crew, for every ship and all the murdered" (2016, 36; emphasis in original).

6 Saying something "could salt" in Trini dialect suggests that something or someone is useless for consideration—as in that thing could be left out to dry and wither away. The expression is similar to the Jamaican "dash weh" or "dash dem way," meaning to throw away or throw (something) away.

7 The last two of these can often be found (per)formed in the energy of the "hotep," a stereotype of contemporary toxically "woke" Black masculinity.

References

Adams, Tony E., Stacy Holman Jones, and Carolyn Ellis. 2015. *Autoethnography: Understanding Qualitative Research*. New York: Oxford University Press.

Ahmed, Sara. 2010. *The Promise of Happiness*. Durham, NC: Duke University Press.

Ahmed, Sara. 2012. *On Being Included: Racism and Diversity in Institutional Life*. Durham, NC: Duke University Press.

Alexander, Michelle. 2012. *The New Jim Crow: Mass Incarceration in the Age of Colorblindness*. New York: New Press.

Anderson, Alonzo B., William H. Teale, and Elette Estrada. 1980. "Low-Income children's Preschool Literacy Experiences: Some Naturalistic observations." *Newsletter of the Laboratory of Comparative Human Cognition* 2 (3): 59–65.

Anglin, Andrew. 2016. "[MwSU] Administration Tell Black Lives Protestors to GTFO or Get Arrested and Expelled." *Daily Stormer*. Accessed August 30, 2016. URL removed.

Angulo, Carlos T., and Ronald Harris Weich. 2003. "Wrong Then, Wrong Now: Racial Profiling before and after September 11, 2001." Washington: Leadership Conference Education Fund / Leadership Conference on Civil Rights. Last accessed April 2, 2017. https://civilrights.org/publications/wrong-then/.

Anti-Defamation League. 2018. "Identity Evropa." Accessed January 7, 2018. https://www.adl.org/resources/profiles/identity-evropa.

Appadurai, Arjun. 1996. *Modernity At Large: Cultural Dimensions of Globalization*. Minneapolis: University of Minnesota Press.

Aristotle. (4 BCE) 1932. *The Rhetoric of Aristotle*. Translated by L. Cooper. Englewood Cliffs, NJ: Prentice.

Baker, Houston A. 1995. "Critical Memory and the Black Public Sphere." In *The Black Public Sphere: A Public Culture Book*, edited by Black Public Sphere Collective, 3–33. Chicago: University of Chicago Press.

Banks, Adam. 2006. *Race, Rhetoric, and Technology: Searching for Higher Ground*. Urbana, IL: National Council of Teachers of English.

Banks, Adam J. 2010. *Digital Griots: African American Rhetoric in a Multimedia Age*. Carbondale: Southern Illinois University Press.

Barad, Karen. 1996. "Meeting the Universe Halfway: Realism and Social Constructivism without Contradiction." In *Feminism, Science, and the Philosophy of Science*, edited by Lynn Hankinson Nelson and Jack Nelson, 161–94. Boston: Kluwer Academic Press.

Barad, Karen. 2003. "Posthumanist Performativity: Toward and Understanding of How Matter Comes to Matter." *Signs: Journal of Women in Culture and Society* 28 (3): 801–831.

Barnett, Timothy. 2000. "Reading Whiteness in English Studies." *College English* 63 (1): 9–37.

Bartholomae, David. 1986. "Inventing the University." *Journal of Basic Writing* 5 (1): 4–23.

Bawarshi, Anis. 2003. *Genre and the Invention of the Writer: Reconsidering the Place of Invention in Composition*. Logan: Utah State University Press.

Beech, Jennifer. 2004. "Redneck and Hillbilly Discourse in the Writing Classroom: Classifying Critical Pedagogies of Whiteness." *College English* 67 (2): 172–186.

Bell, Derrick. 1992. "Racial Realism." *Connecticut Law Review* 24 (2): 363–379.

Benbow, Candace. 2016. "Beyoncé's 'Lemonade' and Black Christian Women's Spirituality." *Religion and Politics*. John C. Danforth Center on Religion and Politics, Washington University in St. Louis. https://religionandpolitics.org/2016/06/28/beyonces-lemonade-and-black-christian-womens-spirituality/.

Bennett, Jane. 2010. *Vibrant Matter: A Political Ecology of Things*. Durham, NC: Duke University Press.

Benovitz, M. G. 2010. "'Because There Aren't Enough Spoons': Creating Contextually Organized Argument through Reconstruction." *National Communication Association Annual Conference, Conference Proceedings*, 124–130. Washington, DC: National Communication Association.

Benston, Kimberly W. 2000. *Performing Blackness: Enactments of African-American Modernism*. London: Routledge.

Beyoncé. 2016. "Formation." By Beyoncé Knowles, Asheton Hogan, Aaquil Iben, Shamon Brown, Khalif Malik, Ibin Shaman Brown, and Michael Len Williams. Track 12 on *Lemonade*. Warner Chappell Music, Inc, Sony / ATV Music Publishing LLC, digital audio.

Beyoncé. 2016. *Lemonade*. By Beyoncé Knowles, Kevin Garrett, James Blake, Diplo, Ezra Koenig, Jack White, Diana Gordon, MeLo-X, Weeknd, Dannyboystyles, Kevin Cossom, Alex Delicata, Mike Dean, Ingrid Burley, Vincent Berry II, Malik Yusef, Midian Mathers, Jonny Coffer, Carla Marie Williams, Kendrick Lamar, King Henry, Mike Will Made It, Swae Lee, Asheton Hogan, Warsan Shire, Kahlil Joseph, Onye Anyanwu, Chayse Irvin, Bill Yukich, and Chris Grant. New York: Parkwood Entertainment; Columbia, digital audio.

Beyoncé, and Nicki Minaj. 2014. "Beyoncé-Flawless (Remix) ft. Nicki Minaj." Beyoncé. October 6, 2014. YouTube video, 5:13. https://www.youtube.com/watch?v=56qgOoC82vY.

Biesecker, Barbara A. 1989. "Rethinking the Rhetorical Situation from within the The-matic of 'Différance.'" *Philosophy and Rhetoric* 22 (2): 110–130.

Bigo, Didier. 2008. "Globalized (In)Security: The Field and the Ban-opticon." In *Terror, Insecurity and Liberty: Illegal Practices of Liberal Regimes*, edited by Didier Bigo and Anastassia Tsoukala, 10–48. New York: Routledge.

Bitzer, Lloyd F. 1968. "The Rhetorical Situation." *Philosophy and Rhetoric* 1 (1): 1–14.

Black Study Group (London). 2015. "The Movement of Black Thought—Study Notes," *darkmatter: in the ruins of imperial culture* 10. Accessed July 31, 2019. http://www.darkmatter101.org/site/2015/09/29/the-movement-of-black-thought-study-notes/.

Blum, Adam. 2016. "Rhythm Nation." *Studies in Gender and Sexuality* 17 (3): 141–149.

Bolter, Jay David, and Richard A. Grusin. 2000. *Remediation: Understanding New Media.* Cambridge, MA: MIT Press.

Bonilla, Yarimar, and Jonathan Rosa. 2015. "#Ferguson: Digital Protest, Hashtag Eth-nography, and the Racial Politics of Social Media in the United States." *American Ethnologist* 42 (1): 4–17.

Brand, Dionne. 2001. *A Map to the Door of No Return: Notes to Belonging.* Toronto: Double Day Canada.

Brock, Andre. 2012. "From the Blackhand Side: Twitter as a Cultural Conversation." *Journal of Broadcasting and Electronic Media* 56 (4): 529–549.

Brooms, Derrick R. 2017. *Being Black, Being Male on Campus: Understanding and Con-fronting Black Male Collegiate Experiences.* Albany: State University of New York Press.

Brown, Jayna. 2015. "Being Cellular: Race, the Inhuman, and the Plasticity of Life." *GLQ: A Journal of Lesbian and Gay Studies* 21 (2–3): 321–341.

Browne, Kevin Adonis. 2013. *Tropic Tendencies: Rhetoric, Popular Culture, and the Anglo-phone Caribbean.* Pittsburgh, PA: University of Pittsburgh Press.

Browne, Simone. 2015. *Dark Matters: On the Surveillance of Blackness.* Durham, NC: Duke University Press.

Bruns, Axel, and Jean Burgess. 2015. "Hashtags from Ad Hoc to Calculated Publics." In *Hashtag Publics: The Power and Politics of Discursive Networks*, edited by Nathan Rambukkana, 13–28. New York: Peter Lang.

Cacho, Lisa M. 2012. *Social Death: Racialized Rightlessness and the Criminalization of the Unprotected.* New York: New York University Press.

Calafell, Bernadette Marie. 2013. "(I)dentities: Considering Accountability, Reflexivity, and Intersectionality in the I and the We." *Liminalities: A Journal of Performance Studies* 9 (2): 6–13.

Campbell, Kermit E. 1997. "'Real Niggaz's Don't Die': African American Students Speak-ing Themselves into Their Writing." In *Writing in Multicultural Settings*, edited by Carol Severino, Juan C. Guerra, and Johnnella E. Butler, 67–78. New York: Modern Language Association of America.

Campt, Tina M. 2017. *Listening to Images.* Durham, NC: Duke University Press.

Canagarajah, A. Suresh. 1999. "On EFL Teachers, Awareness, and Agency." *English Lan-guage Teaching Journal* 53 (3): 207–214.

CBS Television Network. 2016. "58th Annual Grammy Awards." Produced by Ken Ehrlich. Aired February 15, 2016. Live broadcast.

Census Bureau, US. 2020. "Race." *Census.gov*. US Department of Commerce. Accessed June 25, 2020. https://www.census.gov/topics/population/race/about.html.

Césaire, Aimé. 1972. *Discourse on Colonialism*. Translated by Joan Pinkhan. New York: Monthly Review Press.

Chandler, Nahum Dimitri. 2017. "Paraontology: A Public Lecture with Nahum Dimitri Chandler." "Sediments and Arrhythmias" Seminar Series at Institute of Advanced Studies, London, June 30.

Chang, Jeff. 2016. *We Gon' Be Alight: Notes on Race and Resegregation*. New York: Picador.

Chen, Mel Y. 2012. *Animacies: Biopolitics, Racial Mattering, and Queer Affect*. Durham, NC: Duke University Press.

Chilisa, Bagele. 2012. *Indigenous Research Methodologies*. Thousand Oaks, CA: SAGE Publications.

Chilisa, Bagele. 2017. "Decolonising Transdisciplinary Research Approaches: an African Perspective for Enhancing Knowledge Integration in Sustainability Science." *Sustainability Science* 12 (5): 813–827.

Chilisa, Bagele, Thenjiwe E. Major, and Kelne Khudu-Petersen. 2017. "Community Engagement with a Postcolonial, African-Based Relational Paradigm." *Qualitative Research* 17 (3): 326–339.

Choi, Franny. 2014. "To the Man Who Shouted 'I Like Pork Fried Rice' at Me on the Street." *Poetry Foundation*. https://www.poetryfoundation.org/poetrymagazine/poems/56850/to-the-man-who-shouted-i-like-pork-fried-rice-at-me-on-the-street.

Christian, Barbara. 1987. "The Race for Theory." *Cultural Critique* 6 (Spring): 335–345.

Cohen, Cathy J. 2004. "Deviance as Resistance: A New Research Agenda for the Study of Black Politics." *Du Bois Review* 1 (1): 27–45.

Cohen, Cathy. 2015. *Whose Black Lives Matter? The Politics of Black Love and Violence*. WGSS [MwSU]. March 6, 2015. YouTube video, 1:30:51. https://www.youtube.com/watch?v=YfO4AViCgZ8&t=306s.

Combahee River Collective. (1977) 2017. "The Combahee River Collective Statement (1977)." In *How We Get Free: Black Feminism and the Combahee River Collective*, edited by Keeanga-Yamahtta Taylor, 15–28. Chicago: Haymarket Books.

Condon, Frankie. 2012. *I Hope I Join the Band: Narrative, Affiliation, and Antiracist Rhetoric*. Logan: Utah State University Press.

Conference on College Composition and Communication. 1974. "Students' Right to their Own Language." *College Composition and Communication* 25 (Fall special issue). https://secure.ncte.org/library/NCTEFiles/Groups/CCCC/NewSRTOL.pdf.

Conley, Tara L. 2017. "Decoding Black Feminist Hashtags as Becoming." *Black Scholar* 47 (3): 22–32.

Coole, Diana H., and Samantha Frost. 2010. *New Materialisms: Ontology, Agency, and Politics*. Durham, NC: Duke University Press.

Cooper, Brittany. 2018. *Eloquent Rage: A Black Feminist Discovers Her Superpower*. New York: St. Martin's Press.

Cooper, Marilyn M. 1986. "The Ecology of Writing." *College English* 48 (4): 364–375.

Cooper, Marilyn M. 2011. "Rhetorical Agency as Emergent and Enacted." *College Composition and Communication* 62 (3): 420–449.

Corrigan, Lisa M. 2016. "Blackness in the Rhetorical Imaginary." *Southern Communication Journal* 81 (4): 189–191.

Coscarelli, Joe. 2015. "Kendrick Lamar on the Grammys, Black Lives Matter and His Big 2015." *New York Times*. Accessed August 9, 2019. https://www.nytimes.com/2016 /01/03/arts/music/kendrick-lamar-on-a-year-of-knowing-what-matters.html.

Cullors, Patrisse. 2018. "Black Lives Matter." Accessed March 26 2018. https://patrisse cullors.com/black-lives-matter/.

Davis, Angela Y. 2004. *Are Prisons Obsolete?* New York: Seven Stories Press.

Department of Public Safety [Midwestern State] University. 2016a "Alert Notices." *Alert Notices*. [Midwestern State] University. Accessed January 07, 2018. https://dps .[mwsu].edu/alert-notices.

Department of Public Safety [Midwestern State] University. 2016b. "Community Police Academy." Safety Classes: Community Police Academy. [Midwestern State] University. Accessed February 25, 2018. https://dps.[mwsu].edu/community-academy.

Department of Public Safety [Midwestern State] University. 2016c. "Daily Crime Log." [Midwestern State] University. Accessed January 07, 2018. https://dps.[mwsu]. edu/daily-crime-log.

Department of Public Safety [Midwestern State] University. 2016d. "Public Safety Notice—[Campus City]." [Midwestern State] University. Accessed January 07, 2018. https://dps.[mwsu].edu/2016-04.

Department of Public Safety [Midwestern State] University. 2016e. "Public Safety Notice—[Campus City]." [Midwestern State] University. Accessed January 07, 2018. https://dps.[mwsu].edu/2016-05.

Department of Public Safety [Midwestern State] University. 2016f. "Public Safety Notice—[Campus City]." [Midwestern State] University. Accessed January 07, 2018. https://dps.[mwsu].edu/2016-06.

Department of Public Safety [Midwestern State] University. 2016g "Public Safety Notice—[Campus City]." [Midwestern State] University. Accessed January 07, 2018. https://dps.[mwsu].edu/2016-07.

Department of Public Safety [Midwestern State] University. 2016h "Public Safety Notice—[Campus City]." [Midwestern State] University. Accessed January 07, 2018. https://dps.[mwsu].edu/2016-08.

Department of Public Safety [Midwestern State] University. 2016i "Public Safety Notice—[Campus City]." [Midwestern State] University. Accessed January 07, 2018. https://dps.[mwsu].edu/2016-09.

Department of Public Safety [Midwestern State] University. 2016j "Public Safety Notice—[Campus City]." [Midwestern State] University. Accessed January 07, 2018. https://dps.[mwsu].edu/2016-10.

Department of Public Safety [Midwestern State] University. 2017. *2017 Annual Security Report and Annual Fire Safety Report.* [Midwestern State] University.

Diamond, Larry. 2010. "Liberation Technology." *Journal of Democracy* 21 (3): 69–83.

DiAngelo, Robin. 2011. "White Fragility." *International Journal of Critical Pedagogy* 3 (3): 54–70.

Drahm-Butler, T. 2016. "Decolonising Identity Stories: Narrative Practice through Aboriginal Eyes." In *Aboriginal Narrative Practice: Honoring Storylines of Pride, Strength, and Creativity,* edited by B. Wingard, C. Johnson and T. Drahm-Butler, 26–46. Adelaide: Dulwich Center Publications.

Drake, Simone C. 2016. *When We Imagine Grace: Black Men and Subject Making.* Chicago: University of Chicago Press.

Du Bois, W.E.B. 1903. *The Souls of Black Folk: Essays and Sketches.* Chicago: A.C. McClurg.

Dyer, Richard. 2005. "The Matter of Whiteness." In *White Privilege: Essential Readings on the Other Side of Racism,* 2nd ed., edited by Paula S. Rothenberg, 9–13. New York: Worth Publishers.

Edbauer, Jenny. 2005. "Unframing Models of Public Distribution: From Rhetorical Situation to Rhetorical Ecologies," *Rhetoric Society Quarterly* 35 (4): 5–24.

Edgar, Amanda Nell, and Andre E. Johnson. 2018. *The Struggle over Black Lives Matter and All Lives Matter.* Lanham, MD: Lexington Books.

Edwards, Mary Morgan. 2016. "Occupation Ends at [Midwestern State] University's [Building Name] Hall after Arrests, Expulsion Threatened." *The [City News].* Accessed January 07, 2018. https://www.[citynews].com/article/20160407/news/304079745.

Erasmus, Desiderius. (1512) 1978. *Collected Works of Erasmus Section 2, 2, Literary and Educational writings.* Translated and edited by Craig Ringwalt Thompson, Brian McGregor, and Betty I. Knott. Toronto: University of Toronto Press.

Ewald, Helen Rothschild, and David L. Wallace. 1994. "Exploring Agency in Classroom Discourse, or, Should David Have Told His Story?" *College Composition and Communication* 45 (3): 342–368.

Fact Magazine. 2015. "Activists Chant Kendrick Lamar's 'Alright' in Protest at Police Harassment." *FACT Magazine: Music News, New Music.* https://www.factmag.com/2015/07/29/activists-chant-kendrick-lamar-alright-police-harassment/.

Faithful, Rachael. 2014. "#BlackLivesMatter Kitchen Talk." *National Lawyers Guild Review* 71 (Winter): 246–256.

Fanon, Frantz. *Black Skin, White Masks* (1952) 2008. Translated by Charles Lam Markmann. London: Pluto Press.

Fanon, Frantz. 1967. *Toward the African Revolution: Political Essays.* Translated by Haakon Chevalier. New York: Grove Press.

feimineach. 2018. "Why Governments Should Introduce Gender Budgeting." Reblog. Feimineach. Tumblr.com. https://tumblr.feimineach.com/post/171557804321/why-governments-should-introduce-gender-budgeting/amp.

Ferreira da Silva, Denise. 2007. *Toward a Global Idea of Race.* Minneapolis: University of Minnesota Press.

Flores, Lisa A., and Christy-Dale L. Sims. 2016. "The Zero-Sum Game of Race and the Familiar Strangeness of President Obama." *Southern Communication Journal* 81 (4): 206–222.

France, Alan W. 2000. "Dialectics of Self: Structure and Agency as the Subject of English." *College English* 63 (2): 145–165.

Frazier, Demita. 2017. "Demita Frazier." In *How We Get Free: Black Feminism and the Combahee River Collective*, edited by Keeanga-Yamahtta Taylor, 111–144. Chicago: Haymarket Books.

Freelon, Deen, Charlton D. McIlwain, and Meredith D. Clark. 2016. *Beyond the Hashtag: #Ferguson, #BlackLivesMatter, and the Online Struggle for Offline Justice*. Washington, DC: Center for Media and Social Impact.

Freire, Paulo. 1970. *Pedagogy of the Oppressed*. New York: Herder and Herder.

Friedman, Joely. 2016. "[Midwestern State] Encourages Students to Participate in Black Lives Matter Movement." *Campus Reform*. The Leadership Institute. https://www.campusreform.org/?ID=7195.

Gaillet, Lynee L. 1996. "Commonplace Books and the Teaching of Style." *Journal of Teaching Writing* 15 (2): 285–294.

Gallon, Kim. 2016. "Making a Case for Black Digital Humanities." In *Debates in Digital Humanities*, edited by Matthew K. Gold and Lauren F. Klein, 42–49. Minneapolis: University of Minnesota Press.

Garza, Alicia. 2014. "A Herstory of the #BlackLivesMatter Movement by Alicia Garza." *Feminist Wire*. https://thefeministwire.com/2014/10/blacklivesmatter-2/.

Garza, Alicia. 2017. "Alicia Garza." In *How We Get Free: Black Feminism and the Combahee River Collective*, edited by Keeanga-Yamahtta Taylor, 145–176. Chicago: Haymarket Books.

Gates, Henry Louis, Jr. 1989. *The Signifying Monkey: A Theory of African-American Literary Criticism*. New York: Oxford University Press.

Gilyard, Keith. 1991. *Voices of the Self: A Study of Language Competence*. Detroit: Wayne State University Press.

Glissant, Édouard. 1997. *Poetics of Relation*. Translated by Betsy Wing. Ann Arbor: University of Michigan Press.

Gordon, Jeremy. 2015. "Kendrick Lamar's 'Alright' Chanted by Protesters during Cleveland Police Altercation." *Pitchfork*. https://pitchfork.com/news/60568-kendrick-lamars-alright-chanted-by-protesters-during-cleveland-police-altercation/.

Gordon, Lewis. 2007. "Through the Hellish Zone of Nonbeing: Thinking through Fanon, Disaster, and the Damned of the Earth." *Human Architecture: Journal of the Sociology of Self-Knowledge* 5 (3): 5–12.

Grabill, Jeffrey T., and Stacey Pigg. 2012. "Messy Rhetoric: Identity Performance as Rhetorical Agency in Online Public Forums." *Rhetoric Society Quarterly* 42 (2): 99–119.

Grant, Laurens, dir. 2016. *Stay Woke: The Black Lives Matter Movement*. Aired May 26, 2016. Black Entertainment Television, Television.

Greene Wade, Ashleigh. 2017. "'New Genres of Being Human': World Making through Viral Blackness." *Black Scholar* 47 (3): 33–44.

Gries, Laurie. 2015. *Still Life with Rhetoric: A New Materialist Approach for Visual Rhetorics*. Logan: Utah State University Press.

Gross, Ken, and Andrea Fine. 1990. "After Their Daughter Is Murdered at College, Her Grieving Parents Mount a Crusade for Campus Safety." *People Magazine* 33 (7). https://people.com/archive/after-their-daughter-is-murdered-at-college-her-grieving-parents-mount-a-crusade-for-campus-safety-vol-33-no-7/.

Guha, Ramachandra. 1989. "Radical Environmentalism and Third World Preservation: A Third World Critique." *Environmental Ethics* 11 (1): 71–83.

Halualani, Rona Tamiko. 2011. "Abstracting and De-racializing Diversity: The Articulation of Diversity in the Post-race Era." In *Critical Rhetorics of Race*, edited by Michael Lacy and Kent Ono, 247–264. New York: New York University Press.

Hammonds, Evelynn. 2004. "Black (W)holes and the Geometry of Black Female Sexuality." In *The Black Studies Reader*, edited by Jacqueline Bobo, Cynthia Hudley, and Claudine Michel, 301–314. Routledge: New York.

Harney, Stefano, and Fred Moten. 2013. *The Undercommons: Fugitive Planning and Black Study*. New York: Minor Compositions.

Hartman, Saidiya. 2008. "Venus in Two Acts." *Small Axe*, Number 26, 12 (2): 1–14.

Heath, Shirley Brice. (1982) 2001. "Protean Shapes in Literacy Events: Ever-Shifting Oral and Literate Traditions." In *Literacy: A Critical Sourcebook*, edited by Ellen Cushman, Eugene R. Kintgen, Barry M. Kroll, and Mike Rose, 443–466. New York: Bedford St. Martin's.

Herndl, Carl G., and Adela C. Licona. 2007. "Shifting Agency: Agency, Kairos, and the Possibilities of Social Action." In *Communicative Practices in Workplaces and the Professions: Cultural Perspectives on the Regulation of Discourse and Organizations*, edited by Mark Zachry and Charlotte Thralls: 133–154. Amityville, NY: Baywood.

Hesford, Wendy S. 1999. *Framing Identities: Autobiography and the Politics of Pedagogy*. Minneapolis: University of Minnesota Press.

Hesford, Wendy S. 2011. *Spectacular Rhetorics: Human Rights Visions, Recognitions, Feminisms*. Durham, NC: Duke University Press.

Hesford, Wendy S. 2015. "Surviving Recognition and Racial In/justice." *Philosophy and Rhetoric* 48 (4): 536–560.

Hill Collins, Patricia. (1990) 2000. *Black Feminist Thought: Knowledge, Consciousness, and the Politics of Empowerment*. 2nd ed. New York: Routledge.

hooks, bell. 1992. *Black Looks: Race and Representation*. Boston: South End.

hooks, bell. 1994. *Teaching to Transgress: Education as the Practice of Freedom*. New York: Routledge.

Howard, Phillip N., and Malcolm R. Parks. 2012. "Social Media and Political Change: Capacity, Constraint, and Consequence." *Journal of Communication* 62 (2): 359–362.

Huckin, Thomas. 2002. "Critical Discourse Analysis and the Discourse of Condescension." In *Discourse Studies in Composition*, edited by Ellen Barton and Gail Stygall, 155–76. Creskill, NJ: Hampton Press.

"infect, verb." 2010. *New Oxford American Dictionary*. 3rd ed. Edited by Angus Stevenson and Christine A. Lindberg. Oxford: Oxford University Press.

Inoue, Asao B. 2015. *Antiracist Writing Assessment Ecologies: Teaching and Assessing Writing for a Socially Just Future*. Fort Collins, CO: WAC Clearinghouse.

i-will-personally-eat-yourhand. 2018. "This Blog Stands for More Asian Representation in the Western Media." i-will-personally-eat-yourhand. Tumblr.com. Accessed March 05, 2018. https://i-will-personally-eat-yourhand.tumblr.com/post/171562 783630/this-blog-stands-for-more-asian-representation-in.

Jackson, Matthew. 2006. "The Enthymematic Hegemony of Whiteness: The Enthymeme as Antiracist Rhetorical Strategy." *JAC: A Journal of Composition Theory*, 26 (3/4): 601–641.

Jackson, Sarah J., Moya Bailey, and Brooke Foucault Welles. 2020. *#HashtagActivism: Networks of Race and Gender Justice*. Cambridge, MA: MIT Press.

Jackson, Zakiyyah Iman. 2020. *Becoming Human: Matter and Meaning in an Antiblack World*. New York: New York University Press.

Jacobs, Alan. 2012. "'Commonplace Books': The Tumblrs of an Earlier Era." *Atlantic*. https://www.theatlantic.com/technology/archive/2012/01/commonplace-books -the-tumblrs-of-an-earlier-era/251811/.

Jacobs-Huey, LaNita. 2002. "The Natives Are Gazing and Talking Back: Reviewing the Problematics of Positionality, Voice, and Accountability among 'Native' Anthropologists." *American Anthropologist* 104 (3): 791–804.

Jaffe, Sarah. 2015. "What a Band of 20th-Century Alabama Communists Can Teach Black Lives Matter and the Offspring of Occupy." *Nation*. https://www.thenation .com/article/archive/what-a-band-of-20th-century-alabama-communists-can -teach-black-lives-matter-and-the-offspring-of-occupy/.

James, Joy. 1996. *Resisting State Violence: Radicalism, Gender, and Race in U.S. Culture*. Minneapolis: University of Minnesota Press.

Jardine, Lisa, and Anthony Grafton. 1990. "'Studied for Action': How Gabriel Harvey Read His Livy." *Past and Present* 129: 30–78.

Jones, Feminista. 2013. "Is Twitter the Underground Railroad of Activism?" Salon.com. https://www.salon.com/2013/07/17/how_twitter_fuels_black_activism/.

Jordan, June. 1985. "Nobody Mean More to Me than You and the Future Life of Willie Jordan." In *On Call: Political Essays*, 122–139. Boston: South End Press.

Judy, R. A. T. 1994. "On the Question of Nigga Authenticity." *boundary 2* 21 (3): 211–230.

Keep[MwSU]Public. 2016. "[MwSU] Administration Threatens Expulsion against Students." April 07, 2016. YouTube video, 5:28. https://www.youtube.com/watch?v= __iQGaoOkIs.

Kelley, Tina. 2006. "New Jersey Tribe Member Dies After Police Shooting at a Back-Roads Party." *New York Times*. Accessed July 10, 2017. https://www.nytimes.com /2006/04/11/nyregion/new-jersey-tribe-member-dies-after-police-shooting-at-a -backroads.html.

Kennedy, Randall. 2003. *Nigger: The Strange Career of a Troublesome Word*. New York: Vintage Books.

Kennedy, Tammie M, Joyce I. Middleton, and Krista Ratcliffe. 2017. *Rhetorics of Whiteness: Postracial Hauntings in Popular Culture, Social Media, and Education.* Carbondale: Southern Illinois University Press.

King, Martin Luther, Jr. 1963. "I Have a Dream." National Archives. Accessed March 8, 2018. https://www.archives.gov/files/press/exhibits/dream-speech.pdf.

King, Shaun. 2016 "Shaun King Solutions for Police Brutality." *New York Daily News.* Accessed April 2, 2017. https://www.nydailynews.com/tags/shaun-king-solutions -for-police-brutality/.

Kline, Malcolm A. 2016. "Black Lives Matter 101." *Accuracy in Academia.* https://www .academia.org/black-lives-matter-101/.

Kozol, Wendy. 1995. "Fracturing Domesticity: Media, Nationalism, and the Question of Feminist Influence." *Signs: Journal of Women in Culture and Society* 20 (3): 646–667.

Kynard, Carmen. 2013. *Vernacular Insurrections: Race, Black Protest, and the New Century in Composition-Literacies Studies.* Albany: State University of New York Press.

Kynard, Carmen. 2015. "Teaching While Black: Witnessing Disciplinary Whiteness, Racial Violence, and Race-Management." *Literacy in Composition Studies* 3 (1): 1–20.

Kynard, Carmen. 2016. "'Ain't New to This': Black Lives Matter and the New Black Campus Movement." Black Lives Matter in Classrooms Symposium, [Lecture City], April 1, 2016.

Kynard, Carmen, and Robert Eddy. 2009. "Toward a New Critical Framework: Color-Conscious Political Morality and Pedagogy at Historically Black and Historically White Colleges and Universities." *College Composition and Communication* 61 (1): W24–44.

Lamar, Kendrick. 2015a. "Alright." By Kendrick Lamar Duckworth, Kawan Prather, Pharrell Williams, and Mark Spears. Track 7 on *To Pimp a Butterfly.* Sony / ATV Music Publishing LLC, Warner Chappell Music Inc., BMG Rights Management, digital audio.

Lamar, Kendrick. 2015b. "The Blacker the Berry." By Kendrick Lamar Duckworth, Jeffrey Campbell, Stephen Noel Kozmeniuk, Matthew Jehu Samuels, Zale Epstein, Alexander Izquierdo, Ken Lewis Kolatalo, and Terrace Martin. Track 13 on *To Pimp a Butterfly.* Sony / ATV Music Publishing LLC, Warner / Chappell Music Inc., BMG Rights Management, digital audio.

Lamar, Kendrick. 2015c. "Alright." Kendrick Lamar. June 30, 2015. YouTube video, 6:54. https://www.youtube.com/watch?v=Z-48u_uWMHY.

Legal Information Institute. 2018. "20 U.S. Code § 1092-Institutional and Financial Assistance Information for Students." *LII / Legal Information Institute.* Cornell Law School. Accessed January 08, 2018. https://www.law.cornell.edu/uscode/text /20/1092.

Leong, Nancy. 2013. "Racial Capitalism." *Harvard Law Review* 126 (8): 2151–2226.

Lester, Neal A. "At the Heart of Shange's Feminism: An Interview." *Black American Literature Forum* 24, no.4 (1990): 751–764.

[Liberal Arts College] Division of Institutional Advancement. 2009. *[Liberal Arts] Magazine.* [City]: [Liberal Arts College] Office of Marketing and Communications.

Lindsay, Robert B. 1975. *Energy: Historical Development of the Concept.* Stroudsburg, PA: Dowden, Hutchinson and Ross.

Lipsitz, George. 1998. *The Possessive Investment in Whiteness: How White People Profit from Identity Politics.* Philadelphia: Temple University Press.

Lorde, Audre. 1974. "Power." *Village Voice,* October 31, 1974.

Lorde, Audre. 1978. "A Litany for Survival." In *The Black Unicorn: Poems,* 32. New York: Norton.

Lorde, Audre. 1984. *Sister Outsider: Essays and Speeches.* Trumansburg, NY: Crossing Press.

Lorde, Audre. 1990. "Foreword." In *Wild Women in the Whirlwind,* edited by Joanne M. Braxton and Andree Nicola McLaughlin, xi–xiii. New Brunswick, NJ: Rutgers University Press.

Lorey, Isabell. 2015. *States of Insecurity: Government of the Precarious.* Translated by Aileen Derieg. New York: Verso Books.

Lundberg, Christian, and Joshua Gunn. 2005. "'Ouija Board, Are There Any Communications?': Agency, Ontotheology, and the Death of the Humanist Subject or Continuing the ARS Conversation." *Rhetoric Society Quarterly* 35 (4): 83–105.

Lyon, Arabella. 2013. *Deliberative Acts: Democracy, Rhetoric, and Rights.* State College: Pennsylvania State University Press.

Maraj, Louis. 2016. "Monkey on Down." *Poets.org.* Academy of American Poets. Accessed September 1, 2016. https://poets.org/academy-american-poets/ohio-state -university-poetry-prize-2016.

May, Vivian M. 2015. *Pursuing Intersectionality, Unsettling Dominant Imaginaries.* Routledge: New York.

Maybin, Janet. 2005. "The New Literacy Studies: Context, Intertextuality, and Discourse." In *Situated Literacies: Theorising Reading and Writing in Context,* edited by David Barton, Mary Hamilton, and Roz Ivanic, 197–209. London: Routledge.

Mbembe, Achille. 2017. *Critique of Black Reason.* Translated by Laurent Dubois. Durham, NC: Duke University Press.

McGuire, Meghan. 2017. "Reblogging as Writing: The Role of Tumblr in the Writing Classroom." In *Engaging 21st Century Writers with Social Media,* edited by Kendra N. Bryant, 116–131. Hershey, PA: IGI Global.

McIntosh, Peggy. 1989. "White Privilege: Unpacking the Invisible Knapsack." *Peace and Freedom Magazine* (July/August 1989): 10–12.

McKittrick, Katherine. 2014. "Mathematics Black Life." *Black Scholar* 44 (2): 16–28.

Micciche, Laura R. 2004. "Making a Case for Rhetorical Grammar." *College Composition and Communication* 55 (4): 716–737.

Merriam-Webster.com Dictionary. 2020a. "Woke." Accessed June 26, 2020. https://www .merriam-webster.com/dictionary/woke; Merriam-Webster.com Dictionary.

Merriam-Webster.com Dictionary. 2020b. "Woke Meaning Origin." Last modified September 2017. Accessed June 26, 2020. https://www.merriam-webster.com/words-at -play/woke-meaning-origin.

[Midwestern State] University. 2018a. "[Midwestern State] University." [Midwestern State] University. Accessed February 25, 2018. https://www.[mwsu].edu/.

[Midwestern State] University. 2018b. "Discover [Midwestern State]." [Midwestern State] University. Accessed February 25, 2018. https://visit.[mwsu].edu/discover.

[Midwestern State] University. 2019. "[MwSU] Statistical Summary." [MwSU] Statistical Summary. Accessed August 01, 2019. https://www.[mwsu].edu/[mwsu]today/stuinfo.php.

Miller, Susan. 1998. *Assuming the Positions: Cultural Pedagogy and the Politics of Commonplace Writing.* Pittsburgh, PA: University of Pittsburgh Press.

Milson-Whyte, Vivette. 2015. *Academic Writing Instruction for Creole-Influenced Students.* Mona, Jamaica: University of West Indies Press.

Minaj, Nicki. 2014. "Lookin' Ass." By Onika Maraj, Noel Fisher, Kemion Cooks, and Maurice Brown. Track 8 on *Young Money: Rise of an Empire.* Kobalt Music Publishing Ltd., Sony / ATV Music Publishing LLC, Universal Music Publishing Group, digital audio.

Mirowski, Philip. 1989. *More Heat than Light: Economics as Social Physics, Physics as Nature's Economics.* New York: Cambridge University Press.

Morrison, Toni. 1987. *Beloved.* New York: Plume Contemporary Fiction.

Moss, Ann. 1996. *Printed Commonplace Books and the Structuring of Renaissance Thought.* Oxford: Clarendon.

Moten, Fred. 2003. *In the Break: The Aesthetics of the Black Radical Tradition.* Minneapolis: University of Minnesota Press.

Moten, Fred. 2013. "Blackness and Nothingness (Mysticism in the Flesh)." *South Atlantic Quarterly* 112 (4): 737–780.

Murakawa, Naomi. 2014. *The First Civil Right: How Liberals Built Prison America.* New York: Oxford University Press.

[MwSU]BLMIC.org, Black Lives Matter in the Classroom. 2016. "#BlackLivesMatter in the Classroom Symposium." January 7, 2018. http://[mwsu]blmic.org.

Nakamura, Lisa, and Peter Chow-White. 2012. "Introduction: Race and Digital Technology: Code, the Color Line, and the Information Society." In *Race after the Internet,* edited by Lisa Nakamura and Peter Chow-White, 1–18. New York: Routledge.

Nash, Jennifer C. 2015. "Teaching about Ferguson: An Introduction." *Feminist Studies* 41 (1): 211–212.

National Council of Teachers of English / CCCC's Black Caucus. 2015. "NCTE Statement Affirming #BlackLivesMatter." https://ncte.org/wp-content/uploads/2020/04/Statement_Affirming_BlackLivesMatter.pdf.

Naylor, Gloria. 1986. "A Word's Meaning Can Often Depend on Who Says It." *New York Times,* February 20, 1986.

Noble, Safiya Umoja. 2018. *Algorithms of Oppression: How Search Engines Reinforce Racism.* New York: New York University Press.

O'Brien, Luke. 2017. "The Making of an American Nazi." *Atlantic,* November 14, 2017. https://www.theatlantic.com/magazine/archive/2017/12/the-making-of-an-american-nazi/544119/.

Olson, Scott. 2014. "Powerful Scenes from Ferguson, Missouri (74 of 76)." ABCNews. com. https://abcnews.go.com/US/photos/powerful-scenes-ferguson-missouri -24953212/image-24953358.

PBS NewsHour. "Why Do You March? Young Protestors Explain What Drives Them." PBS NewsHour. December 8, 2014. YouTube Video, 10:17. https://www.youtube .com/watch?v=JfC_pfsqLqw&feature=youtu.be.

Pew Research Center. 2018. "Social Media Fact Sheet." Pewinternet.org. Accessed March 5, 2018. https://www.pewresearch.org/internet/fact-sheet/social-media/.

Piffin, Blake. 2015. "Police Harassment Leads to Crowd Singing Kendrick Lamar's 'Alright.'" July 28, 2015. YouTube video, 1:21. https://www.youtube.com/watch?v= VUC_DOhfzwQ.

Pliny (the Elder). (77 AD) 1979. Natural History. Edited and translated by H Rackham, W.H.S. Jones, and D.E. Eicholz. Cambridge, MA: Harvard University Press.

Prasad, Pritha. 2016. "Beyond Rights as Recognition: Black Twitter and Posthuman Coalitional Possibilities." Prose Studies 38 (1): 50–73.

Pratt, Mary Louise. 1991 "Arts of the Contact Zone." Profession: 33–40.

Price, Margaret. 2011. Mad at School: Rhetorics of Mental Disability and Academic Life. Ann Arbor: University of Michigan Press.

Pritchard, Eric D. 2017. Fashioning Lives: Black Queers and the Politics of Literacy. Carbondale: Southern Illinois University Press.

Puwar, Nirmal. 2004. Space Invaders: Race, Gender and Bodies Out of Place. Oxford: Berg.

Rambukkana, Nathan. 2015. "From #RaceFail to #Ferguson: The Digital Intimacies of Race-Activist Hashtag Publics." In Hashtag Publics: The Power and Politics of Discursive Networks, edited by Nathan Rambukkana, 29–46. New York: Peter Lang.

Ransby, Barbara. 2017. "Comments by Barbara Ransby." In How We Get Free: Black Feminism and the Combahee River Collective, edited by Keeanga-Yamahtta Taylor, 177–185. Chicago: Haymarket Books.

Ransby, Barbara. 2018. Making All Black Lives Matter: Reimagining Freedom in the 21st Century. Berkeley: University of California Press.

Ratcliffe, Krista. 2005. Rhetorical Listening: Identification, Gender, Whiteness. Carbondale: Southern Illinois University Press.

reginad1984. 2018. "Congrats Daniella This Is a Great Step Forward." Regina DeLovely. Tumblr.com. https://reginad1984.tumblr.com/post/171559850979/congrats -daniela-this-is-a-great-step-forward.

Reynolds, Nedra. 2007. Geographies of Writing: Inhabiting Places and Encountering Difference. Carbondale: Southern Illinois University Press.

Rice, Jenny. 2012. Distant Publics: Development Rhetoric and the Subject of Crisis. Pittsburgh, PA: University of Pittsburgh Press.

"rightful, adj., n., and adv." 2020. OED Online. Oxford University Press. Accessed June 26, 2020.

Roberts, Frank Leon. 2016. "Black Lives Matter: Race, Resistance, and Populist Protest." Black Lives Matter Syllabus. Gallatin School of Individualized Study, New York

University, New York. Accessed April 02, 2017. http://www.blacklivesmatter
syllabus.com/.

Robinson, Cedric J. 1983. *Black Marxism: The Making of the Black Radical Tradition.*
Chapel Hill: University of North Carolina Press.

Rodriguez, Richard. 1983. *Hunger of Memory: The Education of Richard Rodriguez: An
Autobiography.* Toronto: Bantam Books.

Rose, Mike. 1990. *Lives on the Boundary: A Moving Account of the Struggles and Achievements of America's Educationally Unprepared.* New York: Penguin.

Rosinski, Paula. 2017. "Students' Perceptions of the Transfer of Rhetorical Knowledge
between Digital Self-Sponsored Writing and Academic Writing: The Importance of
Authentic Contexts and Reflection." In *Critical Transitions: Writing and the Question
of Transfer,* edited by Chris M. Anson and Jessie L. Moore, 247–271. Logan: Utah
State University Press.

Rothenberg, Paula S., and Soniya Munshi. 2016. *White Privilege: Essential Readings on the
Other Side of Racism.* 5th ed. New York: Worth Publishers.

Royster, Jacqueline J. 1996. "When the First Voice You Hear Is Not Your Own." *College
Composition and Communication* 47 (1): 29–40.

Ruderman, Wendy. 2012. "For Women in Street Stops, Deeper Humiliation." *New York
Times.* https://www.nytimes.com/2012/08/07/nyregion/for-women-in-street
-stops-deeper-humiliation.html.

Ryden, Wendy, and Ian Marshall. 2012. *Reading, Writing, and Rhetorics of Whiteness.* New
York: Routledge.

Safronova, Valeriya. 2014. "Millennials and the Age of Tumblr Activism." *New York
Times: Style.* https://www.nytimes.com/2014/12/21/style/millennials-and-the-age
-of-tumblr-activism.html.

Saunders, Patricia J. 2008. "Fugitive Dreams of Diaspora: Conversations with Saidiya
Hartman." *Anthodium: A Caribbean Studies Journal* 6 (1): 1–16.

Selfe, Cynthia L, and Richard J. J. Selfe. 1994. "The Politics of the Interface: Power and
Its Exercise in Electronic Contact Zones." *College Composition and Communication*
45 (4): 480–504.

Seneca, Lucius Annaeus. (65 AD) 2001. *Seneca. Epistles V.* Translated by Richard M.
Gummere. Cambridge, MA: Harvard University Press.

Shakur, Assata. 1973. "Assata Shakur: To My People July 4, 1973." *The Talking Drum,*
edited by Jacuma Kambui. Accessed April 2, 2017. http://www.thetalkingdrum.com
/tmp.html.

Shange, Ntozake. 1982. *for colored girls who have considered suicide / when the rainbow is
enuf.* New York: Bantam.

Sharma, Sanjay. 2013. "Black Twitter? Racial Hashtags, Networks and Contagion." *New
Formations* 78 (2): 46–64.

Sharpe, Christina. 2016. *In the Wake: On Blackness and Being.* Durham, NC: Duke University Press.

Sikarskie, Amanda Grace. 2015. "Living the #Quilt Life: Talking about Quiltmaking on
Tumblr." In *Hashtag Publics: The Power and Politics of Discursive Networks,* edited by
Nathan Rambukkana, 169–178. New York: Peter Lang.

Silverstein, Michael. 1976. "Hierarchy of Features and Ergativity." In *Grammatical Categories of Australian Languages*, edited by R.M.W. Dixon, 112–171. Canberra: Australian Institute of Aboriginal Studies.

Singing Sandra. (1999) 2001. "Voices from de Ghetto." By Sandra DesVignes-Millington. Track 5 on *Carnival in Trinidad* (various artists). Cooking Vinyl, digital audio.

Smith, Barbara. 2017. "Barbara Smith." In *How We Get Free: Black Feminism and the Combahee River Collective*, edited by Keeanga-Yamahtta Taylor, 29–70. Chicago: Haymarket Books.

Smith, Danez. 2014. "not an elegy for Mike Brown." *Split This Rock.* https://www.split thisrock.org/poetry-database/poem/not-an-elegy-for-mike-brown.

Smith, W. A., W. R. Allen, and L. L. Danley. 2007. "'Assume the Position . . . You Fit the Description': Psychosocial Experiences and Racial Battle Fatigue among African American Male College Students." *American Behavioral Scientist* 51 (4): 551–578.

Smitherman, Geneva. 1977. *Talkin and Testifyin: The Language of Black America.* Detroit: Wayne State University Press.

Spielberg, Steven, dir. 1985. *The Color Purple.* Burbank: Warner Home Video, 2011. DVD.

Spillers, Hortense. 2003. "Mama's Baby, Papa's Maybe: An American Grammar Book." In *Black, White, and in Color: Essays on American Literature and Culture*, edited by Hortense J. Spillers, 203–229. Chicago: University of Chicago Press.

Staff, Writing. 2009. "Tomorrow's Stellar Alumni." *[Liberal Arts College] Magazine.* [City]: [Liberal Arts College] Office of Marketing and Communications (2009): 8–11.

Staples, Brent. (1986) 2001. "Black Men and Public Space (1986)." In *Essays in Context*, edited by Sandra F. Tropp and Ann Pierson-D'Angelo, 564–566. New York: Oxford University Press.

Street, Brian V. 1999. *Literacy in Theory and Practice.* Cambridge: Cambridge University Press.

Street, Brian V. 2000. "Literacy Events and Literacy Practices." In *Multilingual Literacies: Comparative Perspectives on Research and Practice*, edited by M. Martin-Jones and K. Jones John, 17–29. Amsterdam: John Benjamins' Publishing.

Sumara, Dennis J. 1996. "Using Commonplace Books in Curriculum Studies." *JCT: An Interdisciplinary Journal of Curriculum Studies* 12 (1): 45–48.

Taylor, Keeanga-Yamahtta. 2016. *From #BlackLivesMatter to Black Liberation.* Chicago: Haymarket Books.

Tumblr.com. 2020. "Press Information." *Tumblr.com.* Accessed June 28, 2020. https://www.tumblr.com/press.

van Dijk, Teun A. 1986. *Racism in the Press.* London: Arnold.

Vieregge, Quentin D., Kyle D. Stedman, Taylor Joy Mitchell, and Joseph M. Moxley. 2012. *Agency in the Age of Peer Production.* Urbana, IL: National Council of Teachers of English.

Villanueva, Victor. 1993. *Bootstraps: From an American Academic of Color.* Urbana, IL: National Council of Teachers of English.

Wainz, Rachel. 2016. "Reclaim [MwSU] Has Claimed [Building Name] Hall." *The Tab*. Tab Media. https://thetab.com/us/ohio-state/2016/04/07/reclaim-osu-claimed -bricker-hall-3549.

Walker, Alice. 1982. *The Color Purple: A Novel*. New York: Harcourt Brace Jovanovich.

Wallace, Michelle. 1990. *Invisibility Blues: From Pop to Theory*. New York: Verso.

Warren, Calvin L. 2018. *Ontological Terror: Blackness, Nihilism, and Emancipation*. Durham, NC: Duke University Press.

Weheliye, Alexander G. 2014. *Habeas Viscus: Racializing Assemblages, Biopolitics, and Black Feminist Theories of the Human*. Durham, NC: Duke University Press.

West, Cornel. 2004. *Democracy Matters Winning the Fight against Imperialism*. New York: Penguin Press.

Wilderson, Frank B., III. 2015. "Afro-Pessimism and the End of Redemption." Inter-departmental Seminar: Translations at John Hope Franklin Humanities Institute, Duke University, Durham, NC, October 20.

Williams, David R., Harold W. Neighbors, and James S. Jackson. 2008. "Racial/Ethnic Discrimination and Health: Findings from Community Studies." *American Journal of Public Health* 98 (9): 29–37.

Wodak, Ruth. 2001. "What CDA Is About: A Summary of Its History, Important Con-cepts and Its Developments." In *Methods of Critical Discourse Analysis*, edited by Ruth Wodak and Michael Meyer, 1–13. London: Sage.

Woodson, Carter G. 1928. *African Myths: Together with Proverbs*. Washington, DC: Asso-ciated Publishers.

Wynter, Sylvia. 1994a "A Black Studies Manifesto." *Forum N.H.I.: Knowledge for the 21st Century* 1 (1), "Knowledge on Trial": 3–11.

Wynter, Sylvia. 1994b. "'No Humans Involved': An Open Letter to My Colleagues." *Forum N.H.I.: Knowledge for the 21st Century* 1 (1), "Knowledge on Trial": 42–73.

Wynter, Sylvia. 2001. "Towards the Sociogenic Principle: Fanon, Identity, the Puzzle of Conscious Experience, and What It Is Like to Be 'Black.'" In *National Identities and Sociopolitical Changes in Latin America*, edited by Mercedes F. Duran-Cogan and Antonio Gomez-Moriana, 30–67. New York: Routledge.

Wynter, Sylvia. 2003. "Unsettling Coloniality of Being/Power/Truth/Freedom: Towards the Human, After Man, Its Overrepresentation—An Argument." *CR: The New Centennial Review* 3 (3): 257–337.

Wynter, Sylvia. 2005. "Race and Our Biocentric Belief System: An Interview with Sylvia Wynter." In *Black Education: A Transformative Research and Action Agenda for the New Century*, edited by Joyce E. King, 361–366. Mahwah, NJ: American Educa-tional Research Association / Lawrence Erlbaum Associates.

Wynter, Sylvia. 2007. "On How We Mistook the Map for the Territory and Reimpris-oned Ourselves in the Unbearable Wrongness of Being, of *Désêtre*: Black Studies toward the Human Project." In *A Companion to African-American Studies*, edited by Jane Gordon and Lewis Gordon, 107–118. London: Blackwell.

Wynter, Sylvia, and David Scott. 2000. "The Re-enchantment of Humanism: An Inter-view with Sylvia Wynter." *Small Axe* 8 (September 2000): 119–207.

Young, Morris. 2004. *Minor Re/visions: Asian American Literacy Narratives as a Rhetoric of Citizenship.* Carbondale: Southern Illinois University Press.

Young, Vershawn. 2004. "Your Average Nigga." *College Composition and Communication* 55 (4): 693–715.

Young, Vershawn A. 2007. *Your Average Nigga: Performing Race, Literacy, and Masculinity.* Detroit: Wayne State University Press.

Zardar, Ziaudinn. 2008. "Foreword to the 2008 Edition." In *Frantz Fanon, Black Skin, White Masks (1952)*, translated by Charles Lam Markmann, vi–xx. London: Pluto Press.

Zekany, Eva. 2017. "Technical Intimacies and Otherkin Becomings." In *Mediated Intimacies: Connectivities, Relationalities and Proximities*, edited by Rikke Andreassen, Michael N. Petersen, Katherine Harrison, and Tobias Raun, 240–253. London: Taylor and Francis.

A native of Trinidad and Tobago, **Louis M. Maraj** is an assistant professor of English in the Composition Program at the University of Pittsburgh. His scholarship spans rhetorical theory, Black studies, digital media studies, and antiracist pedagogies. Specifically, it engages with anti/racism, anti/Blackness, and expressive form. Maraj's work can be found in *Precarious Rhetorics* (2018), *Prose Studies* (2019), and *Women's Studies in Communication* (2020). Maraj is the cofounder of DBLAC (Digital Black Lit and Composition), a digital and in-person mentorship network of Black graduate students in fields studying language.

Index

academy, academics, 26, 35
activism, 160(n23); Black, 61, 72, 89; political, 119; student, 127; on Twitter, 69–70
affective economy, of white institutions, 36–37
African American, as term, 75, 138
African American Policy Forum, 91
African indigenous relational model, 12, 14, 17; inquiry, 104–5
Africans, 11, 12
Afropessimism, 11, 144
agency, 8–9, 12, 18, 51; student, 129–30
Ahmed, Sara, 3, 7, 9, 16, 42, 56, 89, 120, 150(n5); *On Being Included*, 15, 106
Alexander, Michelle, 97; *The New Jim Crow*, 95
Algorithms of Oppression (Noble), 50
#AliveWhileBlack, 53, 145
All Lives Matter, 73
"Alright" (Lamar), 19, 79, 85, 94, 139, 159(nn20, 21), 160(n22); Black Christianity theme in, 97–98; as #BlackLivesMatter anthem, 88–89, 92; interrogating white supremacy, 86–87
Anderson, Alonzo, 78
anger, 38
Anglin, Andrew, 127, 163(n10)
animacy hierarchies, 143
annotation, Black, 45–46
antiBlackness, 105, 123, 140, 141; objects of, 143–44

antihumanism, Black, 11, 144
antiracism, 20, 42, 57; Blackness used in, 6–7; conservative reaction to, 123–24; hashtags, 54–55, 141; research, 10, 13–14
Antiracist Writing Assessment Ecologies (Inoue), 10
Anzaldúa, Gloria, 26
Arabs, 81
Are Prisons Obsolete? (Davis), 95
Aristotle, 51, 151(n13)
assimilation, and rhetorical reclamation, 138
authenticity, Black, 28–29
autoethnography, 42, 149(n1), 152(n3), 156(n21); Black, 12–13, 17, 20, 24, 25–26, 27, 29–30, 31, 138, 141, 145, 146, 154(n18); methodologies, 32–33

Bailey, Moya, *#HashtagActivism*, 48
Baker, Houston A., 34–35, 100, 144, 158(n8)
Banks, Adam, 10, 50
Barad, Karen, 24, 76, 143
Bartholomae, David, "Inventing the University," 47
Becoming Human, 143
Being Included, On (Ahmed), 15, 106
Bell, Derrick, 131
Bennett, Jane, *Vibrant Matter*, 142
Beyoncé, 65; "Flawless (Remix)," 66; "Formation," 64, 100; *Lemonade*, 98, 99
birther movement, 82